President James Archibald Campbell

CAMPBELL
COLLEGE

Big Miracle at Little Buies Creek
1887-1974

CAMPBELL COLLEGE

Big Miracle at Little Buies Creek

1887-1974

J. Winston Pearce

77-4197

BROADMAN PRESS / NASHVILLE, TENNESSEE

ISBN: 0-8054-6527-8

4265-27

Dewey Decimal Classification: 378.109756
Subject heading: CAMPBELL COLLEGE
Library of Congress Catalog Card No. 76-7092
Printed in the United States of America

DEDICATION

This story is dedicated to the children of James Archibald Campbell and his wife Cornelia Pearson Campbell:

Leslie Hartwell Campbell
Arthur Carlyle Campbell
Elizabeth Campbell Lynch

In these three honor came back to earth in quiet dignity; nobleness walked our ways again. And through them we entered into our heritage.

CONTENTS

Appendixes:

INTRODUCTION

To spend three years or five with a truly great man, reading what he said and wrote, observing him as he errs, stumbles, falls and rises again; to watch his talents grow if he is an artist, his wisdom develop if he is a statesman—this cannot but seize upon a writer, one might almost say transform him. When the book is done the author returns to the outer world, but actually he will not be the same again.

Catherine Drinker Bowen [1]

THE story of Campbell College is a story of people. Carlyle and Emerson affirmed that all history is biography. Possibly. The history of Campbell College is just that.

To talk about ideas, ideals, philosophy, movements, sacrifices, and achievements at the school simply means getting back to persons who had the ideas, cherished the ideals, embodied the philosophy, backed the movements, and endured the sacrifices—and were thus responsible for the success of the school.

> The art of biography
> Is different from geography.
> Geography is about maps,
> Biography is about chaps. [2]

So is history. But to write about "chaps" is both more interesting and more difficult than to write about maps and institutions. People cannot be pegged or pigeon-holed. There is always something you do not know about a human being and that something may be exceedingly important. It does not have to be something that is big and momentous; often a small incident is more revealing than a headline, and an anecdote more trenchant than a documented thesis.

Old Samuel Butler once quipped that while God could not alter the past, historians could and that was probably the reason the

9

Lord tolerated historians! It is easy for the historian to alter the past. It can be done even while the writer is remaining true to the facts. The selection, arranging, emphasizing, not to say slanting and interpreting, are enough to do it.

It is good that writers do not have to take the court oath: "Do you promise to tell the truth?" That should cause only minor difficulty. But to "tell the *whole* truth"—"aye, there's the rub." And the third agreement, "and nothing but the truth," presents real difficulties. Brickman's cartoon, "the small society," has one politician asking another if that is all there is to a certain story? The other replies that he thinks it is for he has already told more than he heard.

I make no case for full objectivity. That would be impossible, even if desired, and I do not so desire. No biographer or historian is completely objective; some try to be. All write from a point of view. Only God could be totally objective; he chooses to slant his words toward his children in love. I write from the perspective of Christian faith, from the standpoint of a grateful alumnus, from the attitude of a close personal friend. This does not mean that my story is thereby less reliable. According to the divine record, the Lord Jesus appeared only to his friends following the resurrection. The story I have told is true. Names are not withheld even "to protect the innocent." The facts have not been deliberately slanted; I have tried to be fair in the selection of data.

It is a story, not a critical study; it is about people, not about theories or institutions. The people are good, sometimes great, frequently weak, but always "aiming at the stars through difficulty." The record here produced is for the "average" reader, not primarily for the research student. It is hoped that the story has the quality of making the reader want to turn the page. Some of the material is being released for the first time. Most of the story will not be new to the Campbell family or to those who have been close to the developing institution. To these the chief value of the account will be the "getting it all together." A boyhood friend of Mark Twain's in Hannibal, Missouri, said to a reporter: "Why, yes, I knowed Mark. Knowed them stories he told, too. Onliest thing is, Mark wrote 'em down." The story of good and illustrious men needs to be "wrote down." In the writing we grasp as much of the spirit and genius of a person as we can comprehend at that point in time. In another time, another place, a writer will understand more fully and tell the story more completely. But at every stage of life's adventure the statement is true: "In darkness dwells a people/ That knows its annals not." We tell it the best we can.

At Founder's Day in 1974 and again on the same occasion in 1975 I was invited to give the formal address. In '74 the subject was James Archibald Campbell, and I chose as the title of the address "Fortunes of the Founder." In 1975 the subject was President Leslie Hartwell Campbell, and the title chosen was "Accession of the Son." These two addresses have been included in the appendix. By admitting these two addresses, materials have been duplicated, but it is felt that their inclusion will serve a purpose. The two chapters will give, in a brief space, some facts, a bit of atmosphere, and a "feeling" that "he who runs may read." Too, there may be those, including young people, who would like to know something about the college and its history but would find reading the entire book placing them in the class with the man who, on reading a book on giraffes, said: "This book told me more about giraffes than I wanted to know."

The greatest growth of the school took place under the leadership of President Leslie H. Campbell. Yet, more space has been given to the administration of his father, President James A. Campbell. We have our proverbs about beginnings: "To begin well is to end well," and "The end is a consequence of the beginning," etc. Too simple? Of course. Yet, to a surprising degree, any understanding of Campbell College in the present requires an understanding of the school in its beginning. It was there that the course of the school was determined; its motivation and goals stamped as with die and hammer. Of course, the administration of President Norman A. Wiggins is too brief to admit of assessment yet too significant to pass over. But it was President Wiggins' suggestion that the book deal only with the administration of the two Campbells. What has been done with the present management is to give facts, figures, and directions only. This is enough to affirm that the school continues in its course "toward the stars" and that difficulties along the way, while very different, are tackled now in much the same way as they were undertaken earlier by the Campbells.

I have sought to unify the spelling of "Buies Creek." There has never been complete uniformity in the spelling. In the earlier days of the school the possessive was most often used, "Buie's." In recent years the possessive has usually, but not always, been left out. By attempting to make the spelling uniform, often the spelling in quotations has been changed.

To President Wiggins and the trustees of Campbell College who invited me to write this history, I extend my sincere thanks. The invitation resulted in one of the rich experiences of my life. The Campbell family, especially Mrs. Leslie H. Campbell, Dr. Carlyle Campbell, and Mrs. Bessie Campbell Lynch have been patient and helpful in furnishing memorabilia, records, and personal knowledge. Professor Edgar Lynch, Dr. J. A. Campbell's son-in-law, has been my constant "encourager" and traveling companion to "far away places with strange sounding names" as we ferreted out the haunts of the young James Archibald Campbell. To Bernadette Hoyle, my deepest thanks. She gave attention to writing a history of Campbell College years ago. Her material was available to me. Ms. Hoyle had an invaluable asset, she did her work during the lifetime of Mrs. James A. Campbell and President Leslie H. Campbell. Hence, she was able to glean facts and insights that could be secured from no other source. To Mrs. Gladys Strickland Satterwhite I do obeisance! She read, read carefully, the manuscript, and when she had turned the last page, the entire composition resembled the terrain at Gettysburg after Grant and Lee had finished with it, bloody but still mine own!

And, to Mrs. Berles Johnson, knowledgeable, faithful, and tireless secretary, my genuine thanks. To my wife, Winnie, an admission: she could have written this story herself had she been married to such a wife as I am!

Notes

1. *Biography: The Craft and the Calling* (New York: Little, Brown and Co., 1969), p. 47.
2. Bentley, Edmund Clerihew, *International Dictionary of Thoughts,* (New York: Doubleday, 1969), p. 83.

1.
THIS IS HOW IT WAS

Large streams from little fountains flow,
Tall oaks from little acorns grow.

David Everett

JAMES Archibald Campbell, the founding father of Campbell College, was born January 13, 1862, just over one hundred years ago. There are people living who are older.

That is a calendar measurement. However, the calendar is not always the best instrument for measuring time; events are often better. And by events, James Archibald Campbell was born a thousand years ago.

Consider how it was. The War for American Independence was only a little over eighty years in the past. The War Between the States was raging. Little Jimmie Campbell would be a year old before Lincoln's Emancipation would be put into effect. The day young Campbell was born the following announcement appeared in the New York Times:

> William Lloyd Garrison,
> The Pioneer of the Anti-slavery Movement
> will deliver a lecture upon
> "The Abolitionists and Their Relationship to the War,"
> At the Cooper Institute
> On Tuesday Evening, January 14.

Every third person in North Carolina was a slave. On January 6, just seven days before Jim Archie's birth, The *Fayetteville Observer* carried the following:

> SALE OF NEGROES—The following sale of Negroes
> took place in this city yesterday. The sale was
> conducted by J. J. Moore, auctioneer, and con-
> sidering the times, the prices realized were very
> good:

13

Bett, 65 years old,	$800
Ida, 60 years old,	400
Caroline, 11 years old,	475
Lemuel, 32 years old,	550
Louisa, 18 years old,	660
Lizzie, 17 years old,	535
Wiley, 80 years old,	1

The dogs of war never raced over the yard and fields where little Jimmie played, but their baying cannons could be heard in the distance. On January 11, 1862, two days before his birth, Burnside's expedition was off the coast of Pamlico Sound. He was four months old when Sherman's forces destroyed the Confederate arsenal at Fayetteville, thirty-five miles away. Just twelve miles from his home, "In the misty light of that rain-driven dawn of March 16, 1865," the Battle of Averasboro began. Within a few hours the North lost 684 men—dead, wounded, and captured. The South lost 600 the same way. Little Jimmie was three years old. Harnett County, his own, sent 1,000 men to that war, it was equal to one man for every family in the county.[1]

North Carolina was deeply involved in the war. It furnished more men than any other Confederate state; and its men suffered the largest number of casualties. About 125,000 of her sons bore arms. This was one-seventh of all men under arms from the South; although North Carolina had only one-ninth of the South's population. Most of the men who fought did so as volunteers. One out of every six soldiers with Lee at Appomattox was from the "Tar Heel" State. Seven hundred men from the state died at the Battle of Gettysburg, the largest casualty list from any southern state by almost two to one. Georgia had 435; Virginia had 399. The remaining Confederate states had many less.[2]

It is understandable, then, that the aftermath of the war was particularly hard on the state. It lay prostrate. Crops were burned; homes and farm buildings were destroyed. Fences were down; livestock had been killed or driven off. Roads, railroads, bridges, and factories were nonexistent or worn-out. Money had about the same status as the proverbial "hen's teeth." The price of bacon was $7 per pound; eggs were $5 per dozen; wheat $50 per bushel; and a barrel of flour sold for $500.[3]

During young Campbell's early and impressionable years unscrupulous politicians and carpetbaggers ruled the state. There were 300,000 freed slaves. Most of these were poor, uneducated, with no experience in making decisions and in projecting plans for their lives. They had lived, they still lived, in log cabins. Their masters had given them food, clothing, medicine, and, usually, a garden, a pig, and a few chickens. The black and white children played together. The black "mammies" raised the white children. The more enlightened slaves usually worked in the house while others went to the fields. The blacks worshiped in the churches of the whites, often sitting in the balconies. They had their church membership in the same church with the whites. There were 30,000 former slaves in the state before the war.

Before the birth of young Campbell and before the war spread over the land, North Carolina had made remarkable progress in business, manufacturing, and education. It stood second among the southern states in the production of oats and rye. It was third in the production of tobacco, rice, and wheat. It was first in the number of cotton mills.[4]

For twenty-five years, at the beginning of the century, North Carolina was known as the "Golden State." During the years 1804-1828 all the domestic gold coined at the mint in Philadelphia came from the gold fields of North Carolina. In 1837 a U. S. mint was opened in Charlotte. It was said that you could hardly get across the fields around Charlotte without falling into a gold mine! In 1848 Gold Hill had no less than fifteen gold mines. These employed a thousand or more men. There were five stores, four doctors, and an adequate number of taverns—the "Queen City" was on its way! The Carolina gold fields yielded more than $50,000,000. Then in 1848 came the "call of the West." Gold was discovered in California. The gold rush was on, and North Carolina was no longer the "Golden State."[5]

Before the war, real progress had been made in education. Some historians say that North Carolina had the best public school system in the South.[6] There were nearly 3,000 schools. These ran an average of four months to the year and enrolled 100,000 children. After the war, the schools, like everything else, lay prostrate. For the next thirty-five years progress in education was painfully slow—so slow and so painful that it has been estimated that as late as 1900, thirteen years after James Archibald Campbell began his little school, North Carolina had the poorest school system in the nation. At that time less than half the children of school age were in school. The total financial outlay for the schools in the year 1900 was $718,000. All the school buildings in the state were valued at less than one million dollars.[7] Teachers were paid an average of $25 per month. In the year 1862, the year J. A. Campbell was born, Harnett County, his own county, had only twelve teachers, and they were paid a total of $555.35 for the entire year.[8]

Soon after the birth of J. A. Campbell small private academies began to appear. These schools were usually operated by preachers. Reason? The preacher was usually the best educated man in the community; he cared more deeply and he needed to supplement his meager salary. These schools were sometimes held in the preachers' homes; sometimes a small building would be erected by the preacher assisted by the neighbors. There were less ambitious schools, even, than these. Often a mother would sweep out a place in the barn or corn-crib and there hold forth in teaching her own and neighbors' children. A member of Campbell's faculty, now retired, remembers that this was how he received his own first schooling.

There was some higher education in the state. The University of North Carolina, the oldest state university in the nation, chartered in 1789, opened its doors in 1795. The Baptists had Wake Forest, the Presbyterians had Davidson, the Methodists had Trinity, and the Quakers had Guilford. There were a few schools for women: Greensboro Female College, St. Mary's, Davenport, Flora, Chowan, Louisburg, Oxford, and Statesville. There were a few others.[9]

When young Campbell saw the light of day there was beginning a stirring in the top of the literary trees. James M. Barrie was two years old; George Bernard Shaw was six; Robert Louis Stevenson was twelve. When little Jimmie was eight months old, O. Henry was born. The inventors were coming; so were the statesmen and educators. Thomas Edison was fifteen at the birth of Campbell; Alexander Graham Bell was fifteen. Four months after the birth of Campbell, Josephus Daniels was born. William Louis Poteat preceded Campbell by six years. The day before young Campbell's birth *The Register*, forerunner of the *Raleigh News and Observer*,

carried an "ad" on a new book by a George Eliot (English), called
The Mill on the Floss and one by a Nathaniel Hawthorne (American)
called *The Marble Fawn*. Aye, the tops of the literary trees were
beginning to shake.

Generally speaking, all too generally, there were six different
and differing groups of people in North Carolina when young
Campbell came on the scene. First, there was the gentry, the
wealthy and the respected. They were the large planters, the leading
lawyers, doctors, and clergymen. Five percent of the whites in the
state belonged to this group. They lived, mainly, along the fertile
rivers and the coastal lowlands. They were the large slaveholders
because this group owned the large plantations.

Second, there was the much larger group termed the "middle
class." In this group were to be found the small slave owners, the
farmers, merchants, manufacturers, public officials, rural doctors,
lawyers, and preachers. As always, much of the stability of the
state was with this group.

The great mass of whites was in the third class—small farmers,
laborers, tenants, slave overseers, carpenters, mill workers, black-
smiths. People in this group had little education. Generally they
lived in log houses. Here were good, solid, honest, and independent
people. They had the right to vote and did. They worked hard,
tried to help themselves and others. About 60 to 65 percent of
the population was in this group.

Next came the "poor whites." This was the lowest white group
on the economic scale. They owned no land; they had no education.
For the most part, they were without pride, ambition, or initiative.
They lived by hunting, fishing, and cultivating small patches of
land and by doing odd jobs. They were often weak and disease-
possessed.

The free Negroes formed the fifth group. As stated, in 1860, before
the war, there were 30,000 of these. Usually they had mixed an-
cestry. They had obtained their freedom with money saved from
hard work and with great frugality. Some had been set free by
masters who did not believe in slavery. In this group were to be
found some respected and valuable citizens. Finally, there were
the slaves. Earlier it was seen that one out of every three of these
was owned by a white man. They worked the large plantations

where cotton, tobacco, and rice were grown.[10]

To conclude this view of "how it was," here is a final incident. It was on November 28-29, 1887, just nine months after Buies Creek Academy was opened. The incident took place in Chickering Hall, New York City. It was a benefit reading on behalf of the American Copyright League. Here appeared the chief representatives of American literature: James Russell Lowell, Oliver Wendell Holmes, John Greenleaf Whittier, James Whitcomb Riley, Samuel Clemens (Mark Twain), Edward Eggleston, author of the popular *Hoosier Schoolmaster,* and George William Curtis, editor of *Harper's Monthly* and *Harper's Weekly.* It was said "No more remarkable gathering of literary men had ever appeared in America." [11] So, if you like Dickens, you may say of those years when James Archibald Campbell was moving toward his destiny that "it was the best of times and the worst of times." If you prefer your Old Testament, you may ask, "Watchman, what of the night?" And he will respond, "The morning cometh, and also the night; return, and inquire again." That is how it was.

Notes

1. Fowler, Malcom, *They Passed This Way* (Harnett County Centennial, Inc., 1955), pp. 96, 74.

2. Newsome and Lefler, *The Growth of North Carolina* (World Book, 1942), pp. 286-7. Mullen, John M., *Facts to Know,* North Carolina History (Mullen Feature Syndicate, 1937), p. 14.

3. Newsome and Lefler, ibid, p. 94.

4. Ibid, pp. 244-5.

5. Roberts, Bruce, and Nancy, *The Golden Land* (New York: Doubleday, 1973), pp. 110ff. Newsome and Lefler, ibid, p. 246.

6. Newsome and Lefler, ibid, p. 241.

7. Mullen, ibid, p. 59.

8. Fowler, ibid, p. 115.

9. Newsome and Lefler, ibid, p. 253.

10. Ibid, p. 246f.

11. Ziff, Larzer, *The American 1990s* (New York: Viking, 1966), p. 15.

2.
BOY: FATHER TO THE MAN

You cannot write about a great man in the cool dispassionate manner of the average scholar. You have got to have a love affair, not just a marriage with the person you are describing. You have got to be with him constantly; you must have him in your thoughts all the time. Without a little passionate, furious, mad relationship with your subject you will not be able to make him live in your writing.

Emil Ludwig

THE weather report for January 13, 1862, was as follows: "The weather is bright today, with a high wind prevailing, that dries the road quickly." [1] Prophetic? That morning little Jim Arch Campbell was born. And, as long as he lived, when he appeared, the sun came out! He invested his life drying roads, giving a firmer foundation for the marching feet of the children of God. "The weather is bright today, with a high wind prevailing, that dries the road quickly."

The place of young Campbell's birth was a small, vertical clapboard house. It still stands on the county road between Angier and Fuquay-Varina, about ten miles from Campbell College. The Campbells were not newcomers to the area. The ancestor of the clan had been a member of what Malcom Fowler called "The Legion of Restless Men," who came over from Scotland in 1739. There was a whole boat load of them. From that group of "restless men," came Alexander Campbell. He had a son, Lauchlin Campbell, who had a son, Archibald, who had a son, John, who had a son by the name of Ransom, 1811-1869. Ransom married Mary Johnson. They had a family of nine children, four boys and five girls. One of these sons was Archibald Neill Campbell; he married Huma Maniza Betts, the daughter of a Baptist preacher, and they were

The old home where I was born and reared. Sold in 1890 with 100 acres of land for $300. Shown from an right is my old sleeping room.

"The little house where I was born."
The writing is Dr. J. A. Campbell's.

the parents of James Archibald Campbell, the founder of Campbell College.[2]

The Cape Fear region where the progenitor of our present Campbells settled was a "goodly land." It was, to quote the historian, "a land of rolling hills and fertile bottoms covered with forests of long leaf pine, interspersed with mighty oaks, poplars, massive elms, beeches and walnut trees. . . . Through these forests ran scores of streams, emptying their waters into a great river, known as the Cape Fear, which snaked its tawny way northwest to the southwest across the country, down to the Atlantic Ocean at Wilmington, North Carolina."

Archibald Neill Campbell, the father of the founder, was born in 1837 and died in 1904. He was known as "Mr. Archie." Small of stature but long on energy, he was peppery, quick moving, and quick speaking. He had little formal education but he possessed a sharp and inquiring mind. He was interested in events and people and was a lifelong student of the Bible. "Mr. Archie" was a tenant-farmer, a part-time blacksmith, and later a full-time country Baptist preacher.

On the farm the Campbells grew corn, wheat, oats, cotton, and vegetables; never tobacco because he hated the "weed" with a vehemence matching that which his son was to have. There were chickens for dinner with their eggs for breakfast. There were hogs for meat and lard. A cow was kept for milk and butter.

Work was hard; the hours were long. There were few educational advantages and no one explained the meaning of culture. But conditions were not resented. The Campbells were not complaining people; besides, their lot was no worse than the lot of friends and neighbors. Honest toil was a badge of honor. A man was weighed in the scales of character for what he was, not for what he did. God did not measure his heroes with a measuring line; men of small stature could have stout hearts. The family was close. Little Jimmie was the only child; an older child, Lonnie, had died at three years of age. The church was influential in the life of the home. The Bible was loved and read daily; prayers were said, and, like the founder of their faith, they always returned thanks before breaking bread. Preachers were welcome and were frequent guests in the home.

The year 1870, possibly 1871, "Mr. Archie" began preaching. The services were held in the Eli Carter schoolhouse, just a few miles from the Campbell home. In October of 1872 "Mr. Archie" led in the organization of Hector's Creek Baptist Church, now Chalybeate Springs Baptist Church. In the same month he was ordained to the gospel ministry at the annual meeting of the Raleigh Baptist Association. The association was meeting with Johnston Liberty Church, later to become the Clayton Baptist Church in Johnston County. "Mr. Archie" was called as pastor of the Hector's Creek Church.

For the next thirty-two years he served as pastor of churches throughout the area. He is credited with leading in the organization of sixteen Baptist churches, and he baptized more than a thousand people. Two thousand people attended his funeral that was held in a big tabernacle at the school his son founded. The following words were spoken at the memorial service: "He was zealous and faithful as a pastor, missionary and evangelist, going out into the highways and hedges, preaching in schoolhouses, under brush-arbors, and in private homes, leading many a soul to Christ." [3]

For many years before his death, he and his wife, "Miss Humy," lived with their son. She took over the running of the Campbell home, making it easier for Mrs. Campbell to join her husband in teaching and administering the school. "Miss Humy's" last years were marred by emotional and mental difficulties.

The son, James Archibald Campbell, had a high and firm allegiance to Jesus Christ as the Lord and Master of his life. It is necessary to keep this in mind or there will be no real understanding of the man or what he did. From the night when a man, who happened to have a black skin, turned the boy's life toward Jesus to the day when he died with his face bathed in sunlight, James Archibald Campbell was a possessed man—possessed by Jesus Christ and his way of life.

He was eleven years old when "Uncle Mac," the black man, spoke to him about his relationship to the Lord. In later years Dr. Campbell often commented on that experience. "I never knew any peace in my heart after that," he would say, "until one night in the little schoolhouse used for a church, down at the 'mourner's bench,' I settled it all and gave my heart and life to Jesus. That night, and every night thereafter, I went to bed in the little shed room all by myself and knew no fear, because I knew that everything was all right between me and God. But," he would add, with a tremor of emotion, "I never did tell 'Uncle Mac' how glad I was he asked me. When I get to heaven, I want to look him up and thank him from the bottom of my heart." [4]

Shortly after this simple but moving spiritual experience the Hector's Creek Baptist Church was organized by his father. There young Jimmie asked for baptism and membership in the church. He was baptized by his father, "Mr. Archie," on the fourth Sunday in October, 1872. Young Jimmie was the first person his father ever baptized. It is interesting to think that of the more than 1,000 persons "Mr. Archie" baptized, the first person he baptized, his own son, would become the best known and the most influential, as well as the most deeply loved of the thousand.

Harnett Chapel, first school attended by J. A. Campbell, 1886.
The building still stands.

The young boy was quiet, obedient, industrious, and in love with life. Although he liked to read, opportunities were limited. The people of the community referred to him as "that little Campbell boy who loves to read books." They would add, "Why, do you know, he even reads the Bible!" His interest in reading had something to do with his lack of interest in other pursuits that normally claim the attention of boys on the farm, such as hunting and fishing. He never cared for guns. He felt it was cruel and unnecessary to kill animals. He was seldom with gangs of boys at the "ole swimming hole." This was partly due to the lack of leisure time in the Campbell home, but more, the boy found other pursuits more interesting. Yet, according to the memory of a few and available records, he was liked by young people of his own age, boys and girls.

While educational opportunities were limited, it was not by the choice of his parents. They earnestly desired that their son have educational advantages. But public schools had failed. When the boy was six years old, he attended a one-room subscription school at Harnett Chapel near his home. The Reverend A. D. Holland was his teacher. We do not know how long he attended this school, probably only a few months.

Four years later, when he was ten, he, along with his father, went to a grammar school in the community with a two-month term. Father and son were in the same class. The school had the old "cut-down" system of recitation. The pupils would stand in a line at the front of the room. A question would be asked by the teacher. If the student could not answer the question, it would be passed to the next person in line. This procedure would continue until a student was able to answer the question correctly. Then the student would "cut-down" or move up the line ahead of all those students who had missed the answer. The son and the father found the experience to be stimulating; sometimes the father would go ahead of the son, or the son would "cut-down" the father. Young Campbell learned two valuable lessons. One, he got his first firm grounding in the use of correct English grammar; it was his ally as long as he lived. Second, he saw that his father placed a high value on education; he even wanted it for himself.

When the boy was seventeen he attended a boarding school in Apex, North Carolina. He lived with Reverend J. M. Holleman, a man who was to play a large and helpful role in Campbell's life. At Apex he studied with Professor John Duckett. His influence on the youth was great; he felt that Professor Duckett was one of the strongest teachers he ever had.

In the fall of that year, when he was seventeen years of age, young Campbell taught his first school. The school was in the area of Hector's Creek, now Chalybeate Springs. His salary was $22.50 per month. Professor Duckett had strongly recommended him for the position.

The following year, 1881, Campbell was a student again, this time at Oakdale Academy in Alamance County, near Graham. The stone steps and the old well beneath a giant white oak tree are the only physical remains of the school. Jim Arch was at Oakdale for two years, and he taught penmanship to assist with his school expenses. He was a good student. The school's records for the spring semester, 1881, reveal the following: On a grading scale of 6 to 4 (6 denotes perfect, 5½ high, 5 good, 4 low) "Young Campbell's grades were Arithmetic 6, Algebra 6, Latin 5½, Dictionary 5¾,

Absences 0." [5]

Meanwhile, back in his home community of Harnett County, some forward-looking men were feeling the need for a good preparatory school in their midst. These men were religiously motivated in their concern for educational advance. Because persons from different denominations were ready to cooperate in the project, they decided to call their school "Union Academy." The names of the men on the board of trustees have been preserved. Reverend P. J. Wray was elected president of the board; Neill A. Betts was secretary; Thomas H. Wray was treasurer. Others on the board were: Reverend Allen Betts, J. H. Morgan, William Guy, J. A. Morgan, Reverend A. N. Campbell (young Campbell's father), S. G. Collins, J. C. Williams, S. N. Betts, E. D. Smith, and R. H. Smith.

Without a dissenting voice, the group elected young Campbell to take charge of the school. He accepted and returned home. As his assistant in the school he had Miss Pattie Reid, a graduate of Louisburg Female College. She also taught instrumental music. Others on the teaching staff were: A. Lonnie Betts, D. E. Matthews, H. Y. Smith, and C. S. Churchill.

The schoolhouse was made of pine boards. Its dimensions were 40 × 18 feet. It was located at Winslow in the northern part of the county, ten miles from Lillington, twenty miles from Raleigh, ten miles from Poe (now Buies Creek), and, as the young schoolmaster would write, "ten miles from the nearest saloon." The old building is still standing. School opened on the morning of January 7, 1884, with sixteen pupils. That number would increase to seventy-eight before the term was over.

It was here that J. A. Campbell was, for the first time, in charge of a school and, therefore, able to put his ideas and philosophy to the test. He wrote, "All our teachers are earnest Christian workers." All students were required to attend religious exercises. The program consisted of Bible reading, recitation of Scripture texts, and prayers. The school read, in concert, from the Psalms every other morning. Every student who could read was required to memorize a verse of Scripture each day and recite it before the group. His proficiency in this determined his grade in Bible. The catalogue announced in bold letters: "STRICTLY NON-

SECTARIAN."

Since the young principal believed that each student should be able to express orally his thoughts, declamations and essays were an important part of the school. The young men declaimed every week and wrote essays on alternate weeks. The young women wrote essays or had recitations every Friday. The young men were required to give extemporary speeches every week. The catalogue stated: "Lectures in morals and ethics, etc , will be given by the principal as thought necessary."

Again, from the catalogue, "Discipline is mild and parental but firm and decisive." The student's person was respected, and his sense of right and wrong was appealed to; but it was made clear that the rules of the school were to be obeyed, and the rules stated clearly that as a last resort corporal punishment and expulsion would be used. Parents were encouraged to visit the school. There was strict grading of the student's speech and these grades were read out before the entire school.

Objectives and aims of the school were set forth in the catalogue:

> The design of this institution is to prepare young men and young ladies for higher institutions, or, if such is not desired, to engage at once in the active duties of an ordinary business life. We intend to put everything so low that anyone who has a desire to raise himself to a higher standard shall not have any excuse. We guarantee perfect satisfaction in every department. The course of instruction will be thorough and practical, training the mind according to the best methods, we make English a specialty, although Latin and French will receive due consideration. The principal and assistants expect to visit the Normal Schools this summer and acquaint themselves with the latest Normal methods.

Expenses for five months of school were as follows:

Primary department	$ 5.00
Primary English with higher mathematics	7.00
Higher English with Latin & French	15.00
Music, with use of instruments	15.00
An incidental fee	.25
Board, including room	6.50 to $7.00

The young principal was never hesitant in stating the advantages of the school. He had a way with words and he marshaled them for promotional purposes:

> The academy is situated in a beautiful grove, within two or three hundred yards of the Post Office, and is convenient to Methodist and Baptist

churches. The community is exceedingly healthful and quiet, and is noted for the kindness of the people, for its devotion to religion, and affords fewer causes for diversion from study, fewer temptations to extravagance, and especially fewer temptations to dissipation and vice than perhaps any other. The nearest point where intoxicating liquors are sold is ten miles. For these reasons, we insist that no school in the state can boast of a better location than ours for the education of the young.[6]

There it is. There J. A. Campbell was and there J. A. Campbell stayed, so far as basic ideas were concerned. He was concerned for the moral, physical, religious, and intellectual health of the student. He was concerned for the welfare of the whole person. He wanted no diversions that would interfere with the student's ability to study. He wanted no temptations to extravagance, vice, and dissipation. The attitude of the people in the community was important. The purpose of the student's presence in the school was that he might learn and that he might be prepared, first, to make a life and, second, to make a living—both, but in that order.

Attention, all who have romantic inclinations! The records show that for the fall term, 1884, Cornelia Pearson was a student! [7]

The work went well at Union Academy. J. A. Campbell enjoyed the school and he had fine cooperation from his students, his teachers, and the people in the community. But his work at Union Academy served to increase his desire for additional schooling for himself. On his twenty-first birthday, January 13, 1885, he resigned as principal of the school and enrolled as a student at Wake Forest College. That was the year Grover Cleveland was elected president, Victor Hugo died, and the North Carolina flag was adopted.

He remained a student at Wake Forest for the spring and fall semesters of 1885 and the spring semester of 1886. Wake Forest had giants on its faculty in those days. Dr. Charles E. Taylor was president and professor of Latin. He had been elected president in October, 1884. The position had first been offered to Matthew T. Yates, an alumnus of the school who was serving as a Baptist missionary to China. Dr. Yates declined, using words that have become a part of the annals of the world missionary cause. In a letter from China on September 15, 1884, he wrote: "I could not come down from the position of Ambassador of Christ to an Empire, to become president of the College or to accept any other position in the gift of the people of the United States."

Serving with President Taylor are the following competent and, in most cases, outstanding members of the faculty: W. G. Simmons, physics and chemistry; W. B. Royall, Greek; L. R. Mills, pure mathematics; W. Royall, modern languages; W. L. Poteat, natural history; L. N. Chappell, tutor in languages and mathematics. Dr. R. T. Vann was pastor of the local Baptist church. Young Campbell's grades at Wake Forest were from good to excellent.

For the school year 1884-85 Wake Forest had 144 students. The next year, 1885-86, the school enrolled 188 students. Young Campbell had some schoolmates during his stay at Wake Forest who would make their mark in business, education, government, journalism, and the Christian ministry: J. B. Carlyle, C. E. Brewer, H. B. Conrad, Oscar Haywood, T. E. Holding, W. W. Holding, Claude Kitchin, E. L. Middleton, M. H. Riggsbee, B. W. Spilman, G. T. Watkins.[8]

Through the years Dr. Campbell cherished his experiences at Wake Forest and the friends he made while there. He served on the college board of trustees long enough to cast his vote for three presidents for the school. He was on the board when Dr. W. L. Poteat was elected in 1909. He was a trustee and chairman of the trustees' committee to nominate a president when Dr. Francis Pendleton Gaines was elected in June, 1927. Again, he was a member of the board of trustees when Dr. Thurman D. Kitchin was elected president, July, 1930.[9]

Young Campbell was unable to return to college after the spring term of 1886. In October of that year he was called as pastor of his first church, Hector's Creek Baptist Church where he had been baptized and licensed to preach, the church that his father had organized and served so effectively.

Jim Arch was now a pastor, but he had never been ordained. So, in November of the same year, at the annual session of the Little River Baptist Association meeting with the Juniper Springs Baptist Church, he was ordained. The minutes of that meeting read: "On motion, this association, in compliance with the request of the Hector's Creek Church appoint a presbytery to examine Brother Campbell, and, if found qualified, ordain him to the ministry. The presbytery to consist of all ordained ministers of this body and such others as may request to act with them." The following ministers constituted the presbytery: Elders J. N. Booth, W. G. King, G. W. Manley, and I. T. Newton. It did not take them long to decide that Campbell was qualified. During the forty-five-minute intermission allowed for dinner, they ate their fill, examined the candidate, and were ready to report at the afternoon session.

The association reassembled to witness the ordination of J. L. Ennis and J. A. Campbell. (Ennis had been examined at the previous associational meeting.) The Reverend Newton offered the ordination prayer. The address of welcome was given by the Reverend Allen Betts; the Reverend J. M. Holleman gave the charge; young Campbell's father, the Reverend A. N. Campbell led the closing prayer, and the Reverend J. L. Ennis pronounced the benediction.[10] It is interesting that the Reverend A. N. Campbell preached the annual association sermon that year.

James Archibald Campbell was now a duly-ordained minister of the gospel. He was pastor of a church, and he looked forward to having his own school, come January, 1887. He was on his way. But, how had he gotten the school?

Notes

1. *New York Times*, January 13, 1862.
2. "Campbell Heritage," in college archives.
3. Minutes, Little River Baptist Association, 1904.
4. From personal memory; Dr. Campbell frequently spoke of the incident in his chapel messages.
5. Record of grades for year in college archives.
6. From catalogue of Union Academy, college archives.
7. Student Roll Book, kept in Dr. Campbell's own hand, is in the college archives.
8. Wake Forest Catalogues, 1884-1885, 1885-1886.
9. Paschal, George Washington, *History of Wake Forest College*, Vol. III, pp. 398-9.
10. Minutes, Little River Baptist Association, 1886.

3.
"IN THE BEGINNING"

Gamaliel Bradford said of James G. Blaine,

"He moved the souls of others because their souls and their welfare and their hopes moved him."

IN the summer of 1886, the writer was canvassing for books and walked into the gate of Mr. William Pearson after sunset, and was kindly permitted to spend the night."

That was when and where and how it started. Dr. Campbell spoke of the incident again and again, returning to it as the apostle Paul returned to his Damascus road experience.

Young Campbell was not a stranger to Squire Pearson. He was clerk of the Little River Baptist Association, having been elected to that position in 1880 when he was eighteen years old. Mr. Pearson regularly attended the meeting of the association. Too, he had sent his daughter, Cornelia, to school at Union Academy for the spring term that had just ended. Young Campbell was principal of the school. It is probable that the older man had been present when the younger was ordained at Juniper Springs Baptist Church the preceding November. It is certain that he knew the young man had been called to be pastor of the Hector's Creek Baptist Church. Then, when young Campbell turned into the Pearsons' gate on that summer evening, it was more than southern hospitality and the absence of motels in the area that was responsible for his being invited to spend the night.

If future events are considered, that was a significant invitation. Young Campbell had decided that he could not return to Wake Forest College for the fall term. He would have to assist the family with a mortgage that was on the home. With a small legacy from a grandmother, Mrs. Mary Johnson Campbell, a down payment had been made on the small farm, but the family was unable to meet the recurring payments. The son had undertaken a job as salesman; his total line of goods consisted of two books, *The Story of the Bible* and *The Story of the Baptists*. He was, and always would be, interested in those two subjects, but he discovered that it took more than an interest to make an effective salesman. Before he entered the Pearson gate he had come to the conclusion that he would not be a success as a book salesman.

Squire Pearson asked the young man what he was going to do during the coming year. The salesman was not sure. He would not be able to return to college. He frankly admitted that he had come to the conclusion that he could not continue selling books. He had been offered a field of four churches and a school in the eastern part of the state. The churches and the teaching would pay eight hundred dollars a year, a handsome salary in those days. But he preferred to remain in his own area and among his own people if possible.

Squire Pearson said that there was need for a school in the immediate area. Would the young man be interested in teaching there if something could be arranged? Yes, young Campbell thought he would be interested. He was asked what salary he would require. Well, what about forty dollars per month? Squire Pearson did not believe the community could pay that much. Finally, it was suggested that the community build the schoolhouse and young Campbell teach without salary, getting his income entirely from tuition paid by the students. Very frankly, Squire Pearson thought the remuneration would be small at the beginning, but eventually the school might pay a living income. Campbell thought about it, and before leaving the next morning, he told his host that he would be willing to try such a plan.[1]

So, young Campbell was to have a school; he was to have his *own* school. Both facts are significant. It was important, of course, that he have definite work ahead. It was important that the work be that of teaching, and it was especially important that it be his own school. For since the community was unable to pay him a salary and since he would have to depend entirely upon tuition from his students, he would be able to operate the school without benefit or hindrance from school boards or supervisory committees. From the first day the school would be under his sole directorship.

He would be able to instill his own philosophy, curriculum, and methods. The school's success or failure would rest upon his own shoulders in a way that it would not under other plans. It was a situation that would quickly "separate the men from the boys." Soon, young Campbell would know, and the community would know, if he could successfully operate a school on his own.

Something else was significant about young Campbell's night in the Pearson home. Cupid was pleased, but the god of love and romance would have to be patient. At present the salesman's affections were centered elsewhere. But Cupid could wait, and so could Cornelia Pearson, the young daughter of the home. And, given time, young Campbell and Miss Pearson, with Cupid's help, would "get it all together!"

Late in the evening a tired and discouraged young man turns in at a gate. He is given a welcome and invited to spend the night. Before he leaves the next morning, his vocation finds direction and influences are set in motion that will lead to the woman with whom he will spend his life, mother his children, and make possible the great good that he will do and the lives he will influence. What if J. A. Campbell had turned in at another gate that night? Would there have been a Buies Creek Academy and a Campbell College? Would the same two lives have been joined?

Squire Pearson immediately began canvassing the community to secure funds and pledges toward constructing the school building. "He went to see every citizen in the district and secured a promise from all, except perhaps one, to give something toward the house. Plans were drawn to build a house 40 x 22 feet." [2] Three hundred and fifty dollars were secured for the project and the work began.

Mr. and Mrs. James H. Gregory gave an acre of land for the school site. The property joined that which the Gregorys had earlier given for the Baptist church. From the beginning the school and the church were side by side. The first school classes would be held in the church. The land for each was given by the same man. Much of the leadership in each institution would be the same. The same man would head the two for nearly half a century. The student body of one would form a large portion of the congregation for the other. The anxiety felt in the school would be carried over into, and often solved, by the church. The strength and consolation

Mr. and Mrs. William Pearson, parents of Mrs. J. A. Campbell

found in the church were drawn on in the school. The life and fortunes of one was so closely intertwined with those of the other that at times it would be impossible to tell where one would leave off and the other begin. Like Saul and Jonathan who were "lovely and pleasant in their lives," not until after J. A. Campbell's death would they be separated.

Who was this man Squire William Pearson in whose home young Campbell spent the night, the man who interested Campbell in coming to teach school in the community? He was a leading citizen in the area, educated above most of his neighbors and having the ability to see further into the future. Some day he would be his county's representative in the North Carolina Legislature.

Mr. Pearson was a big man physically as well as large in mind and vision and character. He was over six feet tall, with broad shoulders, brown eyes, and big ears. At times he wore a beard. He accumulated large land acreage, as old deeds in the Campbell College archives attest. He was a stalwart Christian in his home and public life. Mrs. Pearson was small, reserved, and quiet. The daughter, Cornelia, remembered her as a skilled and efficient homemaker, easily the equal of her husband, keeping to her own domain, the home and family.

Mr. Pearson was eager to have a good academy in the community because he wanted his own children to have the advantages that such a school would give. His two older children, Elizabeth and William, now married, had been sent to a boarding school in Lillington. He had sent his younger daughter, Cornelia, to Union Academy where she had studied with young Campbell. Mr. Pearson liked what Cornelia had gotten from the young schoolmaster; he wanted her to have more. Then, there was John, a younger brother of Cornelia; he must have his chance with education. Lucy, a daughter next to Cornelia in age, had died when she was five years of age.

The minutes of the annual session of the Little River Association in the fall of 1886, before the school was to open in January, reveal the following: "On motion of Reverend J. M. Holleman this association endorses the school at Buies Creek, under the management of Bro. J. A. Campbell, and allows him the privilege of advertising his school on the flyleaf of our minutes." The motion was carried; on the flyleaf of the associational minutes for the year 1886 appears a full-page advertisement of the school.

There was no schoolhouse; there were no students. But there was a young man by the name of J. A. Campbell. They knew him and they trusted him. So, they trusted the school that he proposed to establish.

The year J. A. Campbell began teaching in Buies Creek, 1887, the community had been without a school for three years. The small schoolhouse that had been used was rotting down. The com-

Original Building (1887)

**J. A. Campbell's first school building
at Buies Creek, 1887**

munity had only seven families and received mail only once each week. The nearest railroad was thirty miles away, and the largest incorporated town in the county had less than fifty people. There was no industry in the county. Farming was the occupation, and cotton was the crop; it had to be hauled thirty miles to the nearest market, either Raleigh or Fayetteville. There was no telephone in the county, and it would be eleven years before the first rural delivery service came to the state—that would be in Rowan County in 1896. The War Between the States had ended at Appomattox less than twenty-five years before.

But to meet a great need there was a red-haired Scotsman by the name of James Archibald Campbell; within one week he would be twenty-five years old. The two got together on the morning of January 5, 1887. It was a bitterly cold day, and the new schoolhouse was not finished; so the school was given permission to meet in the church. The sixteen students who answered to that first roll call ranged in age from six to twenty-one. Actually, twenty-one students had come, but five of the older boys had agreed to work on the unfinished building instead of attending classes. The records preserve the names of all twenty-one. The sixteen who were in class for the first day were: J. M. Byrd, Flossie A. Byrd, Mamie A. Byrd, Frank W. Ennis, J. A. Hamilton, J. H. Hamilton, Harvey M. Holleman, E. B. Johnson, Willis R. Johnson, W. M. McNeill, E. F. McNeill, Clarence McNeill, U. H. Parker, Cornelia F. Pearson, John S. Pearson, and Jimmie Patterson. The five older boys who had agreed to work on the school building were: H. S. Byrd, D. M. Hamilton, J. F. Hamilton, J. H. McNeill, and Lonnie Stewart.

The religious note was evident on the first morning, as it would be on the last morning that J. A. Campbell opened school and all the mornings in between. On that first morning they sang a hymn. It was Charles Wesley's, "Jesus, Saviour, Pilot Me." It would become a tradition. The hymn was sung at the first session of each school year as long as J. A. Campbell lived. He led in the singing. The first Psalm was read. It would become a tradition to read this passage of Scripture at the beginning of every school year. After he led in prayer, J. A. Campbell spoke briefly; this, too, became a tradition.

The young Scotsman's frugal nature showed when he began to call the roll. The students' names were listed in the roll book that he had used at Union Academy. Why not? The book still had some unused pages left! That roll book is before me as I write. The sixteen names listed above are shown as present on January 5, 1887. The additional five students' names appear later. Of course, in that list of sixteen students, the name of Cornelia Pearson, like the name of Abou Ben Adhem, leads all the rest—if not alphabetically, certainly in interest. It was fitting and proper that she be with the young schoolmaster on the first day of school. It is also significant that she shared in the responsibilities of the school on that first day. She was asked to take charge of the youngest of the children. Taking them to the end of the one-room church meeting house, she told them stories and led them in quiet activities while the older students were being instructed by the principal. From that day until the day he died, March 18, 1934, she would be by his side. Together they would pray, plan, direct, teach, and administer.

Harvey Holleman's name was one of the sixteen original students. He had come from Apex and was the first boarding student. He was the son of the Reverend J. M. Holleman, pastor of the church in which the school met the first day. Young Holleman would become an outstanding businessman and would always remain a loyal friend to the founder of the school and to the son who would one day succeed his father as head of the institution.

E. B. Johnson's name was also on that original list; he should be remembered. His father was sheriff of the county. When the boy arrived that first morning, he handed to the young principal a small purse and a note and said, "Papa sent these to you, Mr. Campbell." The young teacher opened the note and read:

> Dear Bro.—Somehow I got it into my old head that
> you might need a little money to pay
> your running expenses. Take the purse
> and the money and credit me with the
> ten dollars on the tuition, and the Lord
> bless you in your work. Yours truly,
> Jas. A. Johnson.

The young teacher's eyes moistened, as I saw them do on a number of occasions when he told the story. He said, "I put my arm about the boy and said, 'God bless you and your father, son.'" Then he would continue, "I had neither purse nor money and here were both with the assurance that somebody was praying for me. I shall never forget the help that it gave me. There are few greater blessings to a young man just starting out in the world than to know that he has the friendship of some good man." Now, he was able to pay the printer for the leaflets he had sent out advertising the new school.

Aware of his own background and experience Professor Campbell sensed that poverty and pride were, and would continue to be, enemies of his school. He sought to deal with both. He set the tuition rates so low that anyone who had a desire to attend would not be prevented from doing so for financial reasons. Following is a list of his charges per month; they are similar to the charges made at Union Academy when he headed that school:

Tuition,	Primary	$1.00
	Intermediate	1.50
	Academic	2.00
	Classical	3.00
	Music: instrumental	3.00
	(Organ and Piano)	
	Board in private families	$6.50-$7.00

He adopted a slogan for his school: "As good as the best, cheaper than the cheapest." As for the enemy, pride, he stated, "No one will fail to be respected here on account of plain dress, honest poverty, or because he is not advanced in class. If you have the character of the true lady or gentleman and know your letters, do not let your ignorance keep you out of school. Come and we will gladly help you."

A close reading of those sentences will show that J. A. Campbell knew pride would spring not only from lack of funds along with inappropriate dress, but also from advanced age. From the first day, the school had grown men and women in the same classes with small children. He knew about this; he had gone to school with his own father by his side. He never forgot the experience, referred to it again and again. Now he would see that the older person who wanted an education was given a chance. "No one will fail to be respected here because he is not in advanced classes."

With so little time, with so small a faculty, with so little space, and with so wide a range of age and ability, how would he bring order and get the most from every opportunity? For one thing he adopted a schedule for classes and activities that would cause any average teacher, even in those days, to be amazed. But, then, J. A. Campbell was no "average" teacher and principal. Nor did he plan to operate an "average" school. Here is the school's schedule: [3]

Daily Program

A.M.

School opens	8:30		
Religious Exercises	8:30	to	8:45
First Spelling Class	8:45	to	9:00
High English Grammar	9:00	to	9:25
Graded Less Grammar	9:25	to	9:50
Third Latin	9:50	to	10:10
Recess	10:10	to	10:20
Composition & Rhetoric	10:20	to	10:40
Elementary Geography	10:40	to	11:00
Manual of Geography	11:00	to	11:20
Second Latin	11:20	to	11:40
First Latin, Penmanship	11:40	to	12:00
Noon Recess	12:00	to	1:00

P.M.

Fifth Reader	1:00	to	1:25
Fourth Reader	1:25	to	1:50
First Reader	1:50	to	2:00
Spelling Class	2:00	to	2:10
Higher Arithmetic	2:10	to	2:20
Common School Arithmetic	2:20	to	2:55
Recess	2:55	to	3:05
Intermediate Arithmetic	3:05	to	3:30
Algebra	3:30	to	3:50
Primary Arithmetic	3:50	to	4:00
Vocal Music	4:00	to	4:30

Just to read that schedule is exhausting! But J. A. Campbell followed it; ran his school by it. His students approved and came back for more. Does one need further proof that young Campbell was a master teacher who brought charisma to the classroom before the word ever came into common use! As his assistants in the school he had: Miss Nola Benson, music; E. B. Johnson, penmanship; and Miss Cornelia Pearson, who assisted with the children.

By the end of the term the enrollment had increased from that, now famous, sixteen to ninety-two pupils, and the little one-room school building, 40 x 22 feet, was overcrowded. Something would have to be done about that. Success brings problems no less than failure. But first there was commencement.

It was held on May 20, 1887; there was no building in the area large enough to accommodate the event. So, they built a brush arbor. Poles were set in the ground; from one to another and across, other poles were laid. Upon these, freshly cut small trees and branches were spread, forming a comfortable shelter from the early summer sun. Underneath, large hewn logs were placed for benches. Along the narrow road leading to and past the school the local citizens built crude stands where cool water was dipped from tubs. Fried chicken, country-ham biscuits, pies, and cakes were sold to those who did not bring lunch. At dinner time the food was spread beneath the trees. It was estimated that no less than a thousand people attended that first commencement.

They were given an ambitious program for their effort. Every student had a part on the program, all ninety-two of them! There were poems, recitations, declamations, vocal and piano numbers, choral groups—fifty-three numbers in all. To climax the day the principal had brought a brilliant young editor all the way from Raleigh to give the main address. It had taken all day for him to get there by train from Raleigh through Benson and on to Dunn, then from Dunn by buggy to Buies Creek. The young editor's name was Josephus Daniels. Although he inspired his audience, no one realized that he would become Secretary of the U.S. Navy under President Woodrow Wilson and that he would serve his country as Ambassador to Mexico. Young Daniels was impressed by what he saw and heard at Buies Creek. Two days later he wrote in his paper:

> Among my pleasant memories of a trip to Harnett, none are more cherished by me with more fondness than the enjoyment of the excellent commencement exercise at Buies Creek Academy. It was a rare feast. The scholars are not prodigies—they do not surpass other boys and girls in the state, but they recite with ease, enunciate with distinctiveness, and gave choice sections of music and evidenced the good training they had received. There was an absence of straining after effect, which was refreshing. There was a simplicity and a regard for the fitness of things that are charming. There was an order and arrangement that showed a thoughtful and sensible management. I congratulate the people of Harnett on the excellent advantages Buies Creek Academy offers for the education of the children of the rising generation.

In his article Daniels commented on the county of Harnett, "Thirty-two acres of tobacco was tried in the county two years ago. It did not pay, and I think those who tried it are about ready to abandon its cultivation." In 1973 Harnett County had 11,996 acres of tobacco under cultivation. Young Daniels wrote his article

from Dunn on his way back to Raleigh. Of Dunn, he wrote, "This place, Dunn, is twenty-five miles from Fayetteville and twenty-five miles from Smithfield—on the Wilson and Fayetteville railroad. The first lots were sold last October. Now there are twelve stores here, a hotel, carriage factory, residences, offices and contracts have been made for building others. I saw the plans for a fine Baptist church which is to be erected at once." [4]

Editor Daniels came back, thirteen years later, 1900, for another address at the academy. He said this concerning his first commencement:

> There were no less than a thousand people present, gathered to cheer the young teacher in his noble undertaking. The parents, seeing the eagerness with which their children learned their lessons, felt that it was no ordinary man who had the training of their offspring. The older men, seeing the practical methods, sublime faith, and marvelous industry, said, "He is made of the right stuff," and they held up his hands. [5]

At the spring commencement in 1935, forty-eight years after that first commencement address, Daniels was back again. This is what he said on that occasion:

> If you should ask me what the greatest revolution in North Carolina has been during the last half century and in what county, I should not hesitate to say it has been the building of this educational institution in Harnett County by Jim Arch Campbell. What he has done gives me faith in mankind. [6]

Professor Campbell believed that a satisfied customer was good advertisement. Acting on this belief he secured an endorsement for his school from its patrons. He used this during the summer as he was preparing for his next term, the fall of 1887. Here is the endorsement and the individuals who signed their names to it: [7]

> We, the undersigned citizens of the community of Buies Creek, are personally acquainted with James A. Campbell, Principal of Buies Creek Academy, and have been patrons of the school under his management during the past session. We gladly bear testimony to his faithful and efficient work in the schoolroom, and heartily endorse the school under his management.

William Pearson	W. P. Johnson	A. J. Byrd
A. D. Byrd	B. F. Hamilton	W. R. Spence
Redding Byrd	William Johnson	G. D. Stewart
James Reardon	W. T. Morgan	N. R. Gregory
W. A. Stewart	A. L. Johnson	Jas. A. Johnson

A. W. Stewart	L. H. Marks	J. H. Gregory
H. Barnes	H. H. Poe	Mrs. Penelope Briggs
J. W. Stewart	David Stewart	William A. Turlington
W. M. McNeill	R. B. Crowder	A. J. Ennis
J. A. McKay	W. B. Boyles	Lorenzo Gaskin

Professor Campbell had secured the endorsement of the Little River Baptist Association for his school before he had taught a day. The people believed in him; they knew his school would be worthy. Now he had the endorsement of his school from those who had observed and whose children had attended. These said it was a good school. He could look forward to another school year.

Notes

1. *Little River Record*, January, 1900, "How Buies Creek Began."
2. Ibid.
3. "A Short History of Buies Creek School," college archives.
4. *State Chronicle* (forerunner of the *Raleigh News and Observer*), May 21, 1887.
5. *Little River Record*, March, 1900.
6. *News and Observer*, May 30, 1900.
7. Copies on file in college archives.

4.
HIS SECOND WIND

The first virtue in a soldier is endurance of fatigue; courage is only the second virtue.

Napoleon

THE fall term of school opened on August 1, 1887. It was announced that Miss Cornelia Pearson was the newly appointed assistant to the principal. There was an increase in enrollment. During the summer the community, inspired by the fine work being done and seeing that the small one-room building was severely crowded, added an east wing to the original structure. This new addition was for the primary grades and was 18 x 24 feet in size.

To promote the spring term of 1888, which began, December 31, 1887, young Campbell produced an attractive leaflet. It gave information as to the location of the academy:

> The academy is situated a little east of the center of Harnett County, six miles from Lillington, ten miles from Dunn, the nearest station on the Wilson and Fayetteville Railroad, and six miles from the nearest bar-room.

Information was given as to the work proposed:

> It is the purpose of the principal that no school of similar grade shall offer better advantages or do better work than is done here.

> We give thorough drills in arithmetic, mental and written, and give special attention to English grammar, pronunciation, letter writing, elocution, etc. We give thorough preparation for college, for teaching in the public schools or for business.

He knew that finances would be a problem for many students:

> Our rates are lower than any other similar institution, and we give special inducement to worthy young men who are unable to pay their tuition. Don't fail to come because you are ignorant or poor. We have classes that will suit you and will rejoice to help you prepare yourself for usefulness.

43

He listed the low tuition rates given earlier and he stated that those students who were preparing for the Christian ministry, whatever the denomination, would pay only half tuition.

The folder included letters from leading citizens approving his work and recommending his school: Professor J. A. W. Thompson, superintendent of Oakdale Academy, where the young principal had studied; J. D. Pegram, Harnett County public school superintendent; Reverend J. M. Holleman of Apex, in whose home he had boarded while at Apex; James A. Johnson of Barclasville, sheriff of Harnett County; William Pearson of Poe's, who had encouraged the young man to begin the school and had just been elected as Harnett's Representative to the North Carolina General Assembly, and other well-known persons from surrounding towns and communities.

The Little River Baptist Association met with the Piney Grove Church that fall, November 3-6, 1887. The committee appointed to bring a report on education was James A. Campbell, E. B. Johnson, and James A. Senter. Young Campbell read the report:

> To secure an education requires time, money and labor. God has called many young men to preach the gospel who have not the means to obtain an education necessary to be of greatest use to God and the church. It is the sense of this body that it is the duty of all our churches and individuals to give some part of what God has given to aid these young men to prepare themselves to preach the gospel in our country and in foreign lands. We note with peculiar pride the increased interest in religious education within the bounds of our association. Several academies and high schools have sprung up in our bounds within the last two or three years, and are now in successful operation.

The spring and fall terms were uneventful for the school. The teachers who had been present at the beginning were continuing. The principal's work was a joy. Patrons were pleased and encouraging. There was only one difficulty: his finances were inadequate to support him. He had undertaken the school with the understanding that his only remuneration would be what he received by way of tuition from the students. The enrollment had been good, so good that a wing had to be added to the original building. Still, the tuition rates were so low that he simply was not receiving enough money to continue. He was pastor of Hector's Creek Baptist Church, but the income there was negligible. He was trying to assist his parents financially. He saw no way that he could continue the school.

Then came another blow, a blow that brought mixed reactions. The state began to allocate a small amount of money to the community for a public school. The young principal was glad. He believed in the public school system, promoted it in every way that he could, would eventually serve as county superintendent of public schools on two different occasions. Still, it made his financial problem more severe. If the hard-pressed farmers could send their children to the same place, have them taught by competent teachers, and have it done free of charge, certainly they would not want to pay the tuition that he was charging, even though that tuition was small.

About this time a new opportunity opened. He was invited to become pastor of the Baptist Church at Dunn. The church had been organized in 1884 and its original name had been Greenwood. The church met in the local schoolhouse in Dunn, but in 1888 a new and, for that time, commodious building was erected. The first pastor, the Reverend I. T. Newton, had resigned to accept other work, and the church invited young Campbell to come as pastor.

Although he still felt responsible for the little school at Buies Creek, he was able to persuade his capable assistant, Miss Cornelia Pearson, to head the school, with McKoy Byrd assisting. There were no boarding students. With this arrangement he accepted the pastorate of the Dunn church as of January, 1890.

As a preacher and as a pastor he was highly successful. In 1898 J. C. Clifford, leading citizen and valued member of the church, wrote:

> Brethren I. T. Newton and J. A. Campbell had charge at a most difficult period. The incoming population of Dunn was a curious admixture of religious odds and ends, who had come together for commercial and business purposes, bringing with them every shade of religious creed, from the most orthodox adherence to truth, to the wildest heterodoxy. To these two pastors, having oversight of the church during the first years of its existence in town, was the difficult task of laying sure the foundation, of awakening interest in the lethargic and placing the church upon a plane from which she could command respect even of those who would oppose her progress.[1]

Then 1890 was a significant year in the life of young Campbell. He gave up his school, accepted the pastorate of a church, was elected and accepted the office of superintendent of public schools in Harnett County, was married in November, and in December returned to the school at Buies Creek.

By this time the citizens of the Buies Creek community realized that they had suffered a severe loss in letting this young man leave their midst. They urged him to return and conditions were beginning to look a little brighter for the school. There was need for the private academy, even if there were limited funds for public education. The public school made no provision for the boarding student nor did it prepare students for advanced work in other institutions and for the professions and trades. It needs to be said, too, that while he loved his preaching and would always be devoted to it, he was beginning to realize that for his life to be satisfying and purposeful he would have to include teaching. So, finally, like his proverbial Scotsman ancestor who when asked which of the Bible characters he would rather have for his wife, Mary or Martha, replied, "Faith, I'll take both; Martha before dinner and Mary after," J. A. Campbell decided that he would take both preaching and teaching; he would be a pastor *and* he would be a schoolman.

This decision to go back to the schoolroom, seen in retrospect, was one of the momentous decisions of J. A. Campbell's life. When he left the school to become the Dunn pastor, his career was uncertain. He had tried preaching and teaching. He was at the point of choosing to give his life to preaching. That might have remained his decision, but it did not. What brought him back to the school? The people in the Buies Creek community who appreciated his worth only after he had left them? Yes. His growing romantic attachment to Miss Cornelia Pearson with whom he would be associated, again, in the schoolroom? Probably. Special talents and gifts that he began to realize could be given full expression only in and through educational channels? No doubt. The guiding hand of divine Providence that is loving and conserving, not wanting to see any good gift wasted? I verily believe it to be true. And, there may have been other motives. What is very clear is that it was a decision of great importance in his life, the life of Miss Pearson, my own life, and the life of thousands who would come within the light of the school that he would build and lead, and come under the beneficent shadow of his powerful influence. Robert

Young "Preacher Campbell," 1888

Frost would say that he came to a place where two roads diverged, and he, J. A. Campbell, took the road less traveled and that made all the difference. Yes, it did.

The little school at Buies Creek did well while under Miss Pearson's guidance. But in the spring, 1890, it had to close because of a measles epidemic in the community. Miss Pearson went to

Bunnlevel, a nearby community, to teach for the rest of the term.

Another evidence of the esteem in which J. A. Campbell was held came in July of that year, 1890, when he was elected to serve as superintendent of Harnett County public schools. He accepted and served in that capacity until 1894 when he resigned. He would be elected again in 1897 and serve for two additional years.

In anticipation of his school's reopening on December 2, 1890, he sent out announcements. The school would run for a period of five months. He said that by beginning early the children would be out in time to assist with the crops. He urged the parents to see that every child was present on the first day of school.

He explained:

> At the earnest solicitation of many people of the Buies Creek and adjoining sections, the Principal has been induced to enter the schoolroom again for awhile; hoping thereby to add whatever he can to the upbuilding of the educational and religious interests of his native county and adjoining sections. In this undertaking, he hopes to have the aid, sympathy and hearty cooperation which the people have been pleased to give him in every effort he has made to sustain a school in their midst. We return our sincere thanks for the support we have heretofore received, and hope to merit a continuance of the same. . . .
>
> Miss Cornelia Pearson, who has been very successful as a teacher, will assist in the school, and such other competent assistance will be secured as the patronage of the school demands.

He gave the location of the school, saying:

> The community is exceedingly healthful and quiet, its citizens kind and obliging, it would be hard to find a better place for pupils away from home than is found here.[2]

He described the facilities saying that the buildings consisted of one room 43 × 22 feet and another 24 × 18 feet. He said the buildings were new and commodious, that they had been recently painted and were furnished with desks, blackboards, etc. He gave the expenses, the same as formerly stated, no increase. Then this revealing sentence, "Indulgence given worthy parties who are not able to pay tuition." The school was always known for this characteristic. It was a well-known principle that the school never turned away any student for lack of funds. If the student was worthy and willing to work, giving his best effort, that student could always find a place in Professor Campbell's school.

So, he was back; he had "crossed his Rubicon." He would never leave the "halls of learning" until his death. He had started it in 1887. He had left it for a few months in 1890. Now he was back, and his fortunes would henceforth be so intertwined with those of the school that narrators and historians would find it impossible to speak or write of one without considering the other.

At this point another important decision was made in the life of the school, important from the standpoint of the academy and important from the standpoint of the public school in the community. It was decided that the public school and academy classes would be taught in the same building and the students of each would be taught by the same teachers. This plan would continue for many years, not without some opposition. Frequently the argument for "separation of church and state" would be advanced. But it would be many, many years before the public school would build its own separate building. For a time the county would pay the Academy for teaching the public school children. Later the county would lease the space from the Academy and pay the salary of the teachers, but it would continue to be a joint enterprise.

Professor Campbell returned and began his teaching on December 2, 1890. From that date the direction of the school was onward and upward. From 1890 to 1900 there was scarcely a pause in the upward march. The motto of the school became the experience of the school: *Ad astra per aspera*, "to the stars through difficulties." He wrote in the *Little River Record*, January, 1900:

> The growth of Buies Creek Academy is a marvel to all who have been acquainted with its history. Through the fourteen years of its work it has sent out hundreds of young men and young women and has influenced for good thousands of lives. . . . Many of those who prepared here have gone out to form other institutions, to preach Christ, to fill places of honor and trust in every work of life. Through influences set in motion here thousands will come at last to glory. . . . Now there are enrolled more than three hundred students this year and we are rejoicing in the great things that are being done for the people.

He proudly pointed out that twenty-one young men and women who attended Buies Creek Academy in 1890 were then engaged in teaching. He said that the Academy and her students together were every day instructing over a thousand pupils. He felt that if you added to that number those Buies Creek students who had gone out before 1890, the number taught would exceed two thousand. "Thus," he wrote, "the waves of education, set in motion here, are enlightening and uplifting—widening areas of our loved State."

By the spring term in 1894 the enrollment of the Academy had reached 175. There was a faculty of seven. The school was described as "An English, Classical, Mathematical and Music School, with Telegraphy, Business Course and Normal Department. Both sexes are admitted." The principal taught English, Latin, Greek, and the Normal Department; his wife, "Miss Neelie," taught mathematics, natural science, French, history, and penmanship; W. M. Montgomery's field was bookkeeping, commercial law, and typewriting; P. H. Rogers, vocal music; Miss Nolia Benson, instrumental music; and D. G. Wilson taught telegraphy.

Increased enrollment necessitated further enlargement of facilities. In 1893 a wing was added to the west side of the main building, 18 × 28 feet. It was possible, by sliding doors, to turn all three sections into one large hall. A small separate building was constructed for the music classes.

The school was attracting the attention of persons in places of influence. The Reverend Samuel Judson Porter, outstanding clergyman, pastor of the First Baptist Church of Durham and later of the First Baptist Church in Washington, D. C., wrote:

> I had heard of this school and for a long time had cherished a desire to visit it. But when I saw it I felt that the half had not been told. Beginning in the woods, Professor J. A. Campbell has built up an institution second to none in the state. . . . He is doing a work whose influence permeates almost the entire state and reaches over into some of the neighboring states. He has gathered about him as assistants a fine core of instructors. . . . It was a genuine pleasure to talk to the aspiring young people in the school, from whose ranks we confidently look for some strong and active advocates of education and religion. We strongly recommend Buies Creek Academy to young men and women desiring to attend school, and especially to those desiring to prepare for college.[3]

Josephus Daniels, distinguished citizen, first commencement speaker, wrote:

> As I looked into the faces of three hundred bright-eyed boys and girls who attended this academy . . . my mind went back thirteen years, and dwelt upon them then and now . . . I felt impelled to say, "What hath man, blessed by God, wrought!" . . . About fifteen years ago, Reverend J. A. Campbell, who had made sacrifices to secure an education, went

out from Wake Forest College. He was in debt. He had no rich and influential friends, and as he returned to the humble home of his preacher-father in Harnett County, I doubt if anybody looked to see him accomplish a great work that would lift up a whole county and bless a large section of the state. . . . It is an inspiration to see what this man, endowed with energy and ambition, has accomplished in this remote country neighborhood. Is it any wonder that Buies Creek Academy is the pride of Harnett County? [4]

Endorsement came from the governor of the state. Governor Charles B. Aycock wrote on June 8, 1901:

Dear Sir: I enjoyed my trip to Buies Creek very much, and your school has been a source of comment by me ever since. You are doing a great work—little short of wonderful. I do not know of any school that has given me more joy than yours. I see in it the possibility of educating all our people. . . . To see a school twelve miles away from railroads in a thinly settled community grow through such proportions as yours is an inspiration and hope. . . . Thanking you for your kindness and courtesy to me and Mrs. Aycock, I am, with best wishes.

> Very sincerely your friend,
>
> C. B. Aycock,
> (Governor of North Carolina)[5]

An interesting, insightful and, at times, tongue-in-cheek view of the school and area was written by Dr. B. W. Spilman in 1898:

I reached Dunn, a town on the main line of the ACL Railroad, in the afternoon about four. I took supper at Buies Creek, twelve miles west of Dunn. A long way off the railroad you say; too inaccessible. If you could only see that crowd of young men, who have found the way there from Brunswick County, on the south to Rockingham, on the north and from Washington, on the east to Burke, on the west, together with a host of others from sixteen other counties in North Carolina, you would be convinced that they could at least find Buies Creek if they tried. . . .

The parent knows when sending a child to Buies Creek, that the body will not be liable to injury. The school is in the country, a beautiful, rolling hill country, with green fields, pine trees and flowing streams. The drainage is perfect; the water is pure. . . .

With an abundance of exercise, fresh air, pure water and wholesome food, one could hardly be sick if he wanted to be. It is hard on physicians. I saw one during my stay, but he was twelve miles away and so far as I could find out he did not know the road to Buies Creek. . . . But if a physician should ever be needed it is easy to secure one, there being a telephone in the library and one in the residence of Brother Campbell connected with Dunn on one side and Lillington five miles distant on the other. . . .

There are no loafing places, no places of public amusement. The danger from vicious associates is reduced to the minimum. There are few temptations to vice as possible. Not a bar-room in the county. The students board in the homes of the people or eat in small clubs. The school is opened every morning with a service of song and prayer-meeting and preaching monthly in the church a hundred yards in front of the academy. . . .

It is positively cheaper to go to school at Buies Creek than it is to stay at home—at least many of the homes that I know. Just think of it! A young man can go to Buies Creek Academy, take a course for ten months, taking the language and higher mathematics, and the cost of tuition, boarding, lodging, lights, fuel and washing need not cost over $70. Wonderful, isn't it? If you want to know how it is done drop a note to the Reverend J. A. Campbell, Poe's, N. C.[6]

Professor Campbell was always grateful, especially grateful, for the endorsement that friends in colleges and universities gave to the work being done in Buies Creek Academy. President Edward A. Alderman of the state university wrote, "It is doing a high quality of work and is a credit to its principal and the section which maintains it." President Kilgo of Trinity College, later to become Duke University, wrote, "Worthy of confidence and esteem; methods up to the best." Dr. Charles E. Taylor, president of Wake Forest College, wrote, "The young men who have come from it to Wake Forest College have all made good records as men and as students." (Difficult to get a better recommendation.) Editor J. W. Bailey, later to become U.S. Senator, wrote, "One of the greatest—we use the word with all weight—educational institutions in the South." Such words of commendation, from such sources, spoke of the progress the school had made, of the work that the school was doing, and it forecast greater days ahead.

In 1900 the school found a new friend and benefactor. It was the first time the school had found help and encouragement from a wealthy individual. M. C. Treat was a Baptist layman and businessman in Washington, Pennsylvania, and California. Mr. Treat learned of Buies Creek Academy through the efforts of Secretary John E. White, head of the mission board for Baptists in North Carolina. Dr. White made the first contact with Mr. Treat and suggested to Professor Campbell that he follow up. Professor Campbell did so and Mr. Treat began to give assistance. The help was given through loans made to boys and girls of "good habits who are preparing for the ministry to the Baptist Church." The loans were made with the expectation that they would be repaid within four years, or whenever the repayment could be made. When the money was returned it went to help other similar students. Mr. Treat urged the students not to accept pastorates until they had seminary education. He strongly believed in an educated ministry.

Help came from other sources. General Julian S. Carr of Durham, prominent in business and in politics, established a scholarship fund to aid two worthy girls wishing to study at Buies Creek. L. D. Gore, a Wilmington merchant, became interested in the school and established a scholarship for the best all-round student for the fall term and the same for the spring. In announcing this gift President Campbell told the audience that the same mail that brought him news of Mr. Gore's gift also brought a letter with a plea from a girl asking for help. He said, "While I wept to think of her needy and helpless condition and wept the more because I could not help her, I also wept tears of joy that in ways we cannot see God is always answering the prayer of the needy and helpless."

The school needed additional space. In 1896 a two-and-a-half story Academy building was added. Its dimensions were 34 x 50 feet. It had two large recitation rooms on the first floor and a small entrance room across the front, 14 x 16 feet. This provided for cloakrooms and the stairway. The second floor had two society halls, library, and reading room. The third floor, a half-story, was occupied by the business department.

This new building was joined to the old building consisting of the original structure, 48 x 22 feet, built in 1887, the east wing that was added the same year, 24 x 18 feet, and the west wing added in 1893, 20 x 18 feet. The old and the new buildings were connected by a room that served as the principal's office. It was 18 x 10 feet. Combined, the two buildings were impressive, an overall length of 136 feet. The buildings were painted and the ceiling was of native pine. The classrooms were equipped with desks, globes, maps, charts, blackboards, etc. The halls for the literary societies were carpeted and well furnished.

During the spring of 1896 a large open tabernacle was built. It was 80 x 90 feet, large enough to seat 2,000. It was a barn-type building and sawdust formed its floor. A large stage reached across one entire end of the building. Its chief purpose was to accommodate the great crowds that came for the commencement programs, but during the summer it was used, also, for the Sunday School chautauqua programs.

In 1898 a new feature was added to the school, a museum. Dr. William Louis Poteat of Wake Forest College gave the Academy a large collection of fossils, native ore, and other geological specimens. The students and the faculty added to this original collection. By 1900 it had become a valuable collection.

Recreation and play at the school was student-do-it-yourself program, but there was no equipment. The principal believed in recreation and in order to magnify the physical exercise phase of his program he introduced, in 1895, the military drill program. He announced that this activity would improve the posture and appearance of the students, cultivate their attention and give valuable exercise. Although uniforms were not required, the students were encouraged to secure them if they could at $10 each. No guns were used; Professor Campbell had never liked guns. Parents were assured that the drills would take no time from actual study; all the exercise and training would take place at the noon hour and after school. The best student performer would be given a prize. This phase of the school program added much color and interest to school life.

The school made a place for vocal expression. The principal believed that every student should be able to stand and express his own ideas. As stated earlier, this had always been a part of Professor Campbell's program for his students. It had been started at Union Academy; it was continued at Buies Creek. It was difficult to give this phase of the program adequate emphasis in the classroom during class hours. So, in 1893, a literary society for young men was organized. It met each week for debates, declamations, essays, readings, and transaction of business. The young men learned to preside and conduct business according to accepted parliamentary rules. Fast friendships based on skilled debates, social forays, humorous experiences, and salty horseplay were developed.

By 1896 the enrollment of the Academy had reached 226. The *North Carolina Baptist* declared, "Buies Creek is the greatest single factor for Christian education in the Third Congressional District." The principal, never modest where his school was concerned, proclaimed in a promotional leaflet:

AS GOOD AS THE BEST! CHEAPER THAN THE CHEAPEST!

1. Highly endorsed by all its patrons and the public generally.
2. Grows steadily in numbers, areas of patronage and public favor.
3. Specialists in charge of vocal music, penmanship and teacher's course. Instruction in these departments free. Thorough preparation for college and business.
4. Thorough course in business, typewriting and telegraphy. Diplomas awarded to graduates in business course. A practical business education at small cost to everybody.
5. Lower rates of tuition than other schools of similar grades in the state, with fifty percent discount to ministers, their children, orphans and the children of widows.
6. There has never been a death nor serious case of sickness in the school. The buildings are new and well furnished with desks, blackboards, charts, globes, etc. Good literary society.
7. Why has the school steadily grown in patronage?
    (a). Thorough, honest, and practical work done—merit.
    (b). Cheapness. Board, including washing, lights, etc. in private families, $7.00 per month; in 'clubs' $4.00. Tuition, $1 to $3.00.
    (c). Unexcelled moral advantages, churches convenient. Sunday School and young men's Prayer Meeting every Sunday. Being in a quiet country place, we avoid many temptations to vice, idleness, immorality and extravagance in dress, incident to towns and cities. It is six miles to a bar-room.
    (d). We are trying to help the people and are looking to God for guidance and success.
8. Students coming by railroad will be met at Dunn and carried to their boarding places free of charge, by notifying the Principal.[7]

Professor Campbell believed in co-education. He also believed in strict rules that structured the relationship between the sexes. There was a long list of "Rules of Government," to which each student was required to subscribe before he became a part of the school's life. These rules were stated negatively and seem narrow and arbitrary. But the restrictions were in keeping with the climate and social codes of the day and were no more restrictive than the rules at similar institutions of the day. It should be remembered, too, that this was an academy, not a college or university. Still, the rules are interesting:

1. We will not play cards or any games of chance.
2. We will not carry concealed weapons.
3. We do not use profanity.
4. We will not drink wine, whiskey, or any other intoxicants, except it be in cases of dangerous sickness or prescribed by a physician.

5. We will not accompany the opposite sex to or from school.
6. We will refrain from all whispering and talking during school hours, except by permission, and then will not disturb those around us.
7. We will neither write nor pass notes.
8. We will not use tobacco in the schoolroom nor smoke in and around the building.
9. We will not mark, cut, in any way deface the school furniture or buildings and will pay for all damage done to property by us.
10. During school hours we will not be away from our study rooms, except for recitation by permission, and then will promptly return.
11. At night we will not be away from our boarding places after dark, except by permission of the Principal or his representative.
12. We will endeavor to refrain from any conduct, either in or out of school, known to us to be damaging to ourselves or the interests of the school.[8]

Once several of the boys "with malice aforethought" violated the school's rule against passing notes to the girls. The principal hitched up his horse and plow and plowed a deep furrow along the dividing line between the boys' and the girls' activity areas. Later the girls—perish their daring!—walked along the edge of the furrow, held out their hands, and touched fingertips with the boys. When the principal learned of this "outrageous" conduct, he sent the girls to their boarding places with a stiff reprimand.

But all records indicate that there was very little resentment on the part of the students to these rules and regulations. He was warm, human, and available. His discipline was seasoned with common sense and humor. With due apology, his students were saying at lecture time and quiz, the kind of a man I mean to be is the kind of man "Jim Archie" is.

Commencements played an increasingly important role in the life of the school and the community. Attendance reached thousands. It was one of the main educational, social, entertainment events of the year. They came by horse and buggy, carriage, wagons, and horseback. The woods were filled with the stomping, kicking, and neighing of the animals. The whole production took on an air of festivity, becoming a sort of Passover feast where the people went up to rejoice in their deliverance from the bondage of ignorance, isolation, and a hard life generally. The programs began with a sermon on Sunday and ended with speeches the following Thursday. Those who lived near would return to their homes at night, but others would be guests in the homes of the people of the community and nearby areas. Some would campout.

Miss Neelie remembered a time when the people were stranded when heavy rains washed out the bridges. One morning, during that time, she served eighty people at her home for breakfast. She said that her husband was so big-hearted that he just kept inviting the people to come over to his house for breakfast. She and Professor Campbell's mother "pitched in" and cooked. There were not enough seats, the older people were placed at the tables, all others stood. There was not enough silver; she just gave them something to eat on—anything that would hold food. She said that Professor Campbell was delighted. It was like a picnic for him. He had his friends in his home; it brought them all closer together. And, he was able to know the students' parents, through the experience, in a unique way. And, the interesting thing is, she still loved him!

Professor Campbell was always aware of the rumble of Time's chariot wheels. He was especially aware during the fall session of 1899. The spring session would bring them into a new century. Writing in the *Little River Record,* he reminded his readers that the new century would bring new opportunities and new responsibilities. He urged his readers to make it the best century in all the world's history. All should fit themselves for the great demands that the new age would bring. He wrote, "Prepare to be a great part of the greatest century." He bade his students good-by. They went home for Christmas. When he saw them again it would be the 20th century. His wildest imagination could not even hint at the changes the world would see! Yet, he sensed that something great was out beyond the ranges and he was ready to go and look for it.

Notes

1. *Little River Record,* May, 1898.
2. Copy of the leaflet in College Archives.
3. Ibid.
4. Ibid.
5. Ibid.
6. *Little River Record,* May, 1898.
7. College Archives.
8. List repeated in catalogues for years.

5.
"THE COURSE OF TRUE LOVE"

Be noble! and the nobleness that lies
In other men, sleeping, but never dead,
Will rise in majesty to meet thine own.

Emerson

A SMALL diary 2½ x 3½ inches is before me. It is written in the careful script of J. A. Campbell and covers most of the year 1888. It is almost the only thing in existence that resembles a personal diary. He did not keep records of his private thoughts and soul's musings. Why not? I do not know. Was it because he did not care to bring his inmost thoughts to light, even the light of his own eyes? Was it because he believed his own private thoughts of little significance? Or, as I believe is more likely, was the bent of his personality and life toward active and practical considerations? Whatever the cause, the little diary, being almost the only thing of its kind in existence, becomes very important.

At the outset you would be impressed, as the short, terse sentences are read, by the mood and spirit that possessed the young Scotsman at the time. Remember, he was twenty-six years old. His college education had been terminated. He was pastor of a small rural church and principal of a little one-room school. He was often lonely and discouraged, not quite sure of his life's work. He was in love and did not expect other eyes to read what he put in the little book. What he wrote throws light on an important period in his life.

On January 15, 1888, he wrote: "Rec'd a pleasant happy message from my dearest. . . . Pleased after absence and hard work and loneliness." Then this: "Sun shines sometimes." Important words: "loneliness," "hard work," discouragement," "love." Add to that

58

this quotation written a little later, "Feel somewhat like I failed. Maybe the sunshine will come sometime." (Again that longing for the sunshine.)

Brief, pointed, aching camera shots of a young man's soul. Thomas Wolfe wrote that loneliness was, always had been, the central and inevitable experience of every man. Possibly. But that does not alter the fact that when you observe it in a young man who is basically a bright, hopeful, dynamic individual, your sympathy is aroused. During 1888 the only difference in J. A. Campbell and the description that William Sharp, also a Scotsman, gave of himself is geographical. Said Sharp, "My heart is a lonely hunter that hunts on a lonely hill." Young Campbell was a hunter, hunting for his life's work, for a place in the sun, for approval, usefulness, affection, love. And he was finding the hills hard and the hunt lonely.

He was deeply in love. Nowhere does he give the name of the young woman. We know it was not Cornelia Pearson, the future Mrs. Campbell. There are elderly people living who, when they were children, heard their parents talk about the romance. But that was long ago; they cannot be sure. We can affirm that his love, like young men before and since, was a delicious agony. We know that he rejoiced when love smiled; he flinched when love frowned. He was happy when he received the longed-for letter; he was disturbed when the missive did not arrive.

On Saturday, January 21, 1888, this: "Spent the night with my *own loved one* (underscoring his own). 'Twas pleasant after long separation." The next day he wrote, "My school numbers 70 up to the present. 'Twas hard to part." January 28: "Miss C. came to meeting Saturday, was so glad to see her. Spent the night at Bro. J. A. Johnson's. We came to choir meeting at the church. Much enjoyed the pleasant trip. Rode in our new buggy." February 19: "Rec'd the nicest, best message from my dear one on my return. She gets better and better!" March 18: "Was so glad to receive a pleasant message from *you*, dear one, after returning to Sheriff's. God bless *you*." Again, March 24: "Spent the night with my dear one and *Mr. J. E. Ballentine*. But she did not ride on the cart on Sunday." On April 1 there is a longer note, I quote in part; "Went to Raleigh on Saturday. My dearest one went with me. Did so much enjoy my short stay with her. She was so kind to me. Will not soon forget this trip."

Shakespeare affirmed that the course of true love never runs smooth. It did not for young Jim Arch Campbell. He does not comment on this directly, but the little diary reveals it clearly. There are fewer and fewer references to "my dearest," "my dear one," "my future." And the name of "Miss Neelie," short for Miss Cornelia Pearson, appears more and more frequently. Their relationship began on a teacher-student basis when she became a boarding student at Union Academy for the fall term in 1884. Remembering those days, Mrs. Campbell would recall how he, the young principal, would come back to her desk and hear her read Caesar. This teacher-student relationship developed into a warm friendship. And, it seems, to the young principal's surprise, and possibly to Miss Neelie's surprise also, they awoke one day to the realization that they were in love.

It is difficult to tell from available records, including diary and letters, whether the relationship between the teacher and his student fostered and forwarded the break-up between him and his earlier love, or this firm friendship was simply waiting to be built upon when his former relationship deteriorated.

We can know that Miss Neelie was his trusted confidante during the days when the alienation was taking place. The diary—but more specifically, available letters written by Miss Neelie—causes one to wonder whether she was not aware of the "situation" before young Jim Arch was. By her kindness, understanding, reserve, patience, as well as status, she may well have hastened the break.

The following quotations throw light on that possibility. The excerpts are taken from Miss Neelie's letters to her "teacher." Incidentally, she signed her letters, "Your little sister." "I feel unworthy of your entire confidence and the great interest you seem to feel in me." . . . "I assure you that I think of you as one who would scorn even the thought of doing wrong or anything that might cause trouble." . . . "You have given all the explanation necessary or that you could have given, and have told me a great deal more about your affairs than I could have asked or expected you to have told me." . . . "I pray for you much and sympathize with you in your troubles . . . I prize your confidence highly, and hope I may never act as to cause it to be less." . . . "I know you must be anxious for the mail that will probably bring you the long-wished-for decision, or at least enough encouragement to afford you some relief and satisfaction. I do not know what more or what better plan you could have tried than you did. Her duty as to how she should act may not be as plain to her as she would wish it to be in making such a decision." . . . . "I guess she was somewhat surprised at your proposition in reply to her kind and affectionate letter." . . . . "May you both do no wrong but discharge your whole duty toward each other and toward God and may the decision be in accordance with His will. I'll write more tomorrow."

In those citations do you recognize the tactical skill that Eve and her daughters have used with, for, against each other from time's beginning as they fought to win the men of their choice? Possibly. Does it seem unfair, if not downright disloyal on the part of the young teacher to share with another woman the trials and agonies that he was having with his beloved? It seems so. Was it less than "cricket" for Miss Neelie to accept, even encourage, such confidences? Probably. But, "In case of love and war . . ."

One frustrating thing about the whole episode is that we do not have a single letter to Miss Neelie from the hand of James Archibald Campbell. He preserved the letters she wrote to him. She destroyed the ones he wrote to her, or if she did not, the letters have never been found. Therefore, we do not know what encouragement Miss Neelie had from her young red-haired teacher, "brother," friend, and, soon to be, much more. Knowing his warm, affectionate, and reaching nature, we may assume that the encouragement that he gave was strong. And the complete break with his former love did come.

Who finally initiated the break and gave it the "kiss-of-death" the records do not reveal. I once heard him refer to the incident in a chapel talk. He gave it the light and smiling touch, saying that he once asked a young woman to marry him and she refused his offer. He responded, "Well, I'll make you wish you had accepted!" Whether he was merely being gallant or stating facts we had no way of knowing. There were rumors then, and they still persist, to the effect that it was Jim Arch who did the breaking-off, and that when he indicated differently, he was simply being generous and true to his noble nature.

Mrs. J. A. Campbell, Cornelia Pearson, in wedding gown

What the records do show is that on November 18, 1890, in the bride's home, Cornelia Frances Pearson and James Archibald Campbell were married. It was the day before the bride's twenty-fifth birthday and the groom was twenty-eight. The bride wore a high-necked taffeta dress, trimmed in braid and beadwork, her own handiwork. Her black hair, piled high on her head, reached the lobes of her handsome red-haired husband's ears.

It was a "good marriage." She was quiet, sturdy, wise, undemonstrative, with great business ability. Her husband called her "the backbone of the family." She came close to the poet's ideal woman: "A perfect woman, nobly planned, to warn, to comfort and command." She was never "too good for human nature's daily food." Except when the children were very small, she taught and, for many years, served as business manager of the school. Through the years, the school came into possession of farm after farm. Most of the acreage was bought by the Campbells from the Pearson estate. The price and terms for paying were of such a nature that the obligations could be met.

Professor Campbell's admiration of "Miss Neelie" as a person, and his evaluation of her in home, school, and business office was all but boundless. She once said, "He thought I could do anything." To give a case in point, she told the following experience. Once when she was going to Dunn for groceries, he came to the buggy just as she was ready to leave and asked that she buy a new buggy and a horse-collar. She protested that she did not know how to select such things. He only laughed and said that she knew as much about it as anyone he knew. All the way to Dunn she worried over having to buy that buggy and horse-collar. But where her knowledge was limited, her wisdom was adequate. When she arrived in Dunn, she went to see Mr. George Pope, friend and church member. When she told him her problem, he laughed and said, "Just like that red-headed husband of yours! I'll go with you and select the buggy and horse-collar." The purchases were made. The horse-collar was placed in the new buggy and the new buggy tied behind the one she had come in, then she made her way home. Her husband was delighted; she had selected just what he wanted.

A few years before her death Mrs. Campbell said, "He was tender-hearted, high strung, and restless. He was hard working, never idle—he loved to see things hum. At times the load he carried was almost crushing." Continuing, she said, speaking the words gently but with pride, "Many women think their husbands are great men, I knew mine was."

At first the Campbells made their home with the Pearsons, Mrs. Campbell's parents. But early in the year following their marriage, he contracted to buy a few acres of land near the Pearson home. There they built their own house. In November of the same year, 1891, they moved into the new home. They would live in that house until Dr. Campbell's death in 1934. The house was large, larger than their immediate needs but they wanted room to accommodate boarding students. In years to come the original structure would be added to again and again. Dr. Campbell liked gables, and as often as an addition would permit, a gable would be added. This continued until it became, literally, a house of "seven gables." And the porch! That porch grew and grew and grew from year to year! The structure was painted white. The students called it "The White House."

In the fall of 1891, shortly after the Campbells moved into their new home, "Mr. Archie" and "Miss Humy" came to make it their home, remaining until their death. Later, after the death of Dr. Campbell's parents, the parents of Mrs. Campbell, the Pearsons, came to live with them and remained until they died.

During the decade following their marriage the family grew. Three children were born. They came at two-year intervals. The first was Leslie Hartwell, born on April 3, 1892. Arthur Carlyle was born on November 28, 1894. And, on September 26, 1896, a daughter, Elizabeth Pearson, the "light of her father's eye," was born. The children were whole, healthy, endearing, exasperating, intelligent, mischievous, devoted, independent. They were greatly loved, carefully taught, and strictly disciplined.

The father was a devoted, wise, and generous parent. Mrs. Campbell said, "He loved to romp and play with the children. He never slapped them around and whipped them, but reasoned with them about right and wrong." A few years before his own death Leslie said, "Our father controlled us with kindness. He was tender-hearted and would often weep when he would talk to us, because he would be hurt if we disobeyed. This, of course, hurt us when he would call us in and lecture us; we would much rather have had a whipping. In his kind way he controlled us. Both our parents were strict in granting privileges—they always knew where we were. I think we spent only one night away from home without our parents before we went away to college." Then a moment of quiet thoughtfulness: "Papa had definite ideas about correct behavior and his belief was consistent throughout his life."

Whatever the ingredients of the recipe used, it worked successfully. The J. A. Campbells and their three children never became an educational dynasty in North Carolina, but it would be difficult to overestimate their influence upon education in general and on

This house surrounds the original structure built by
Dr. Campbell in 1891. It was his home until he died.

North Carolina in particular. With the exception of a few brief years of business at Buies Creek, Leslie's life was spent with the school that his father founded. He served as teacher, dean, and president, giving altogether almost a half century to the school that his father founded. Carlyle returned to Buies Creek and taught in the Academy when he graduated from Wake Forest College. Later, after his military service, he was president of Coker College in South Carolina, professor of English at State College in Raleigh, North Carolina, and then had a distinguished career as president of Meredith College, also located in Raleigh. Elizabeth Pearson, "Bessie," Mrs. A. E. Lynch, was closely connected with the school her father founded as a teacher and head of the department of music until her retirement.

From childhood, the relationship between parents and children was close. For example, following their graduation from Wake Forest College, Leslie and Carlyle taught at Buies Creek Academy without salary. When they needed money, their father advanced it just as he had done when they were children. I have heard Carlyle speak of how generous he felt his father was in such matters. The father was more concerned than the sons were that they have adequate funds. He often urged money upon them when the boys felt there was no need for it.

Childhood pictures of two distinguished college
presidents, Leslie H. Campbell and Carlyle
Campbell; Leslie is the older.

As indicated, Bessie held a very special place in her father's heart. Being a girl, and the only girl, this seemed to be expected. It certainly was not resented by the boys in the home. Mrs. Lynch has told me how devoted and solicitous her father was of her welfare when she was a student at Meredith College. She said that it seemed he came to Raleigh on an average of once each week and would take her and her friends out to dinner. She admitted that this sometimes interfered with her social life! On numerous occasions she had to hurriedly cancel a date that she had with some boy at State College because her father had called saying that he would come at a certain hour.

The Bible declares that the Lord God saw it was not good for man to be alone. The written record, a fine educational institution, a useful family, and multiplied thousands of lives attest that it was good for James Archibald Campbell and Cornelia Frances Pearson to be together.

6.
A MAN FOR HIS SEASON

You are doing a great work—little short of being wonderful. I do not know of any school that has given me more joy than yours. To see a school four miles away from railroads and in a thinly settled community grow into such proportions as yours is an inspiration and hope.

Charles B. Aycock
Governor, North Carolina

J. A. CAMPBELL was six feet tall. He had sandy-red hair and mustache, both carefully trimmed. His eyes were blue, sharp but gentle. They mirrored his emotions, quickly changing from one mood to another from smiles to tears, from deep conviction to light-hearted banter, from compassion to righteous indignation.

He blushed like a modest maiden. His coloring would forecast his own speech, radioing ahead to announce what was coming. In this way we were able to anticipate his humor before it was put into words. The blush would begin at his shirt collar, move up across his cheeks, emphasize the light crow's feet at the corners of his eyes, mount into his temples, and invade his tawny hair. By this time he would be speaking the words, whose anticipation had brought the glow to his countenance. He once reminded us of the freshman who wrote to her parents: "I love college," she declared, "I feel good! I have made lots of friends; I have added weight. In fact," she continued, "I weigh 118 pounds stripped for gym." Her father wrote back, "Your mother and I were glad to receive your letter and to know that you are well and enjoying college. But we are concerned. Just who is this Jim you are stripping for?" From his shirt collar to the top of his head there was a ruddy glow as he anticipated the punch-line of the story.

He told us about an experience at his home. He kept a large

500-gallon gasoline tank from which he serviced his own car. On one occasion as he was ready to pay the man who had filled the tank, looking at the statement, Dr. Campbell exclaimed, "Ah, man, you have ruined my tank!" "Why, how is that, Professor Campbell?" "Well," said Dr. Campbell, that glow beginning to rise from his shirt collar, "that tank will hold only 500 gallons and I see you have gone and forced 505 gallons in it." The man began to stutter and sputter, "Ah, uh, well, maybe, Professor Campbell, I must have just miscounted. I guess it was only 500 gallons I put in your tank."

Dr. Campbell walked with a firm and steady stride. His gait and carriage announced that he knew where he was going, why, and what he intended doing when he got there. He believed that a person's walk revealed much about his character. Often when asked about a student with whom he had been talking he would say, "I have not had occasion to see much of him since he came— that is a good sign," he would add with a smile. "But let me take a look at the way he walks." He would go to the door and observe the student walking across the campus and give his estimate.

The man had a high and firm allegiance to Jesus Christ as the Lord and Master of his life. If that fact is not kept in mind, it will be impossible to understand the man or the work that he did. From the night when as a small boy living with his parents in the little clapboard house that rested on the sandy loam of Harnett County, a black man turned his life toward Jesus, to the day when he died with the sunlight full upon his face, he was a possessed man, possessed by Jesus Christ.

His deep, gallant, masculine, religious commitment pervaded his teaching in the classroom no less than it controlled his preaching in chapel and church. Miss Mabel Powell, teacher of English and Latin for more than forty years, recalled the first faculty meeting that she attended when she came to Campbell in 1925. Dr. Campbell began his words to them as follows: "You have not been asked to come to this faculty because of your degrees. Yes, we want capable teachers, for we are concerned that the young people who come here secure a good education. But that is not why you have been asked to join us. You have been invited to teach here because you know Jesus Christ as Savior and Lord and because you love boys and girls." In the last conversation that Miss Powell had with

J. A. Campbell (during his final illness) he said to her: "I want you to promise me that, insofar as it is within your power, if the time ever comes when Christ is not honored in this school, the name 'Campbell' will come off the buildings." He was a committed man.

He felt deep, sometimes excruciating, responsibility for the spiritual welfare of the students who came to his school. He yearned and prayed for them as would a good pastor or a concerned parent. Every worthy influence at his command was brought to bear, every known opportunity was given, that the student might come to know and to accept Jesus Christ as the Lord of his life. He spoke to these students in chapel; he preached to them in church; he often talked and prayed with them individually. He invited outside preachers and laymen to the school and church that new and fresh voices might present the claims of Christ.

Such passionate concern for the spiritual welfare of students is rare, if not unique. It matches the concern that General Robert E. Lee had for his students at what later became Washington and Lee University. A biographer tells of General Lee talking with a well-known minister. The general's feelings were so intense and moving that tears coursed down his cheeks; finally he said, "Oh, Doctor, if I could only know that all the young men in the college were good Christians, I should have nothing more to desire." Commenting on that incident the biographer adds, "You will remember that this man surrendered a great army and saw a nation sink to the dust without a tear." That is how J. A. Campbell cared.

He had rich emotions. His red hair announced that he was not afraid of a fight. He never sought one, never ran away from one, and seldom lost one that was forced upon him. I once heard him say, "There are those of you who talk about controlling temper. Some of us control more temper in an hour than others of you know in a year!"

His promotional ability was legendary. He did not give his support lightly, but once it was given, every stubborn ounce of his energy and resources were at the call of that person or cause. A citizen of the community, one who had often crossed swords with him, said, "J. A. Campbell is the greatest salesman I have ever seen. Had he been a patent medicine salesman he would have become a millionaire!"

Dr. Campbell was a life-long opponent of intoxicating beverages. Along with a concerned group of citizens he appeared before a legislative committee in Raleigh when an important bill on alcohol was before the North Carolina Legislature. He was asked to act as spokesman for the group. One who was present says that the presence and the words of J. A. Campbell at that time have remained a vivid memory. He says that day Dr. Campbell was a cross between Amos and Hosea. His eyes flashed and his righteous indignation rolled like Amos, but then there would come a melting, a sympathetic passion, and tears like those of Hosea would flow down his cheeks. Across the long slanting years the man who reports the incident, remembers the structure of Dr. Campbell's talk: "I like my cause; I like my companions; and I like my Captain."

Knowledge, maturity, and character combined to make him a leader of men and women. Charisma glowed from J. A. Campbell's very presence. Once Dr. Charles B. Howard brought a friend, Charlie Moore, to meet Dr. Campbell. They visited. On the trip back to Franklin County, Mr. Moore was strangely quiet. Finally, Dr. Howard asked, "Well, what do you think of Dr. Campbell?" After a moment of reflection Charlie Moore said, "What do I think of Dr. Campbell? I think this, whatever group he is in he will be the tallest man present." It was a good assessment. Wherever J. A. Campbell sat, that was the head of the table. Coming into a group of people, you would see heads turn toward him, eyes focus upon him. The group would become quiet and attentive, waiting for J. A. Campbell's comments, observations, questions. This was without effort or any suggestion of pushiness. It was not so much what the man said or did. It was something about, within, the man himself. Justice Oliver Wendell Holmes said, "The ferment of genius is quickly imparted, when a man is great he makes others believe in greatness."

Reference has been made to Dr. Campbell's accessibility. True. A student of those early days said, "We knew we could go to him, and he would listen sympathetically and then advise us as wisely as he could. He was never too busy to listen to us, never in a hurry when we wanted to talk to him." Yet, he wore a mantle of natural reserve, an innate dignity that forbade undue familiarity.

There were lines beyond which we did not venture in chummy intimacy.

There was an ancient belief that by alchemy base metals might be changed to precious metals. To a rare and unique extent J. A. Campbell had the ability to change, to transform hardship and privation into benefit and gain. He knew from experience that it could be done; he had proven it in his own life. Since it was true in his own life he knew it could be true in the life of his students. This was one of the major themes of his chapel talks. One of his students said, "He was the most eloquent man I ever met. He knew just how to inspire, just how to make one ashamed for not living up to the highest standards, and just how to make one work harder. I think he had the quality of bringing out the best in everybody. . . . We were poor but when Professor Campbell would quote what some great man had said about being poor, we'd almost be glad of our poverty. I remember he said, 'Poverty and hardship have ever been the great schoolmasters of the race. . . . Prosperity reveals our weakness, adversity our strength. Let us not despise that which shows us our better selves.' "

The following little poem he often quoted in chapel. The verse sets forth what the student referred to above meant:

> It matters little where I was born,
>   Or if my parents were rich or poor;
> Whether they shrank at the cold world's scorn,
>   Or walked in the pride of wealth secure;
> But whether I live an honest man,
>   And hold my integrity firm in my clutch,
> I tell, brother, plain as I can,
>   It matters much.

Another poem that he loved is the following; it give with clarity his philosophy. Once after he had quoted it, I asked if it would be possible for me to get a copy. A few days later I received a copy of the poem, copied in his own careful hand. I framed it and hung it above my desk.

MY CHUM

> He stood at the crossroads all alone,
> With the sunrise in his face,
> He had no fears for the path unknown,
> He was set for a manly race.
> But the road stretched east,

And the road stretched west,
There was no one to show him the best.
So my chum turned wrong
And went down, down, down,
Till he lost in life's race and the victor's crown
And fell, at last, in an ugly snare
Because no one stood at the crossroads there.

Another chum, on another day,
At the self-same crossroads stood,
He paused a moment
To see which led to the greater good,
And the road stretched east
And the road stretched west,
But I was there to show him the best.
So my chum turned right,
And went on and on,
Till he won life's race and the victor's crown
And stood at last in the mansions fair
Because I stood at the crossroads there.

Since then I've had one daily prayer,
That God keep me faithful standing there
To show the runners as they come
And save my own and another's chum.

The man seemed to have a special gift for hard work, tight discipline, sane frugality, and disturbing sacrifice. His days were long, often fifteen, sixteen hours. His wife said, "Mr. Campbell was raised to work and he believed in work. He had little time for leisure." For many years he carried a full load of teaching, in addition to administering the school. At times he was superintendent of county schools; at times he sold insurance. At one time he was a bank president. Always he was pastor of churches; always he was a farmer. In the evenings at home, by the fire, he graded papers, wrote and edited a paper, prepared sermons and chapel talks. He answered letters—always by hand, sometimes fifteen to twenty in an evening. Letters were answered the day they arrived. He read papers, magazines, and books. Clippers and paper knife were always handy; he ran a clipping-service before the term was invented. He culled poems, proverbs, folk sayings, jokes, ideas. These were grist for his lectures, teaching, sermons, and editorials.

Like Lincoln, he believed in what is sometimes referred to, not always kindly, as the Protestant ethic. In his writings and speaking he made his position clear. He did *not* believe that prosperity could be achieved by discouraging thrift, that you could strengthen the weak by weakening the strong, that you could help the wage-earner by destroying the wage-payer, that the poor were helped through destroying the rich, that you could build character by taking away initiative and independence, or that you could help persons permanently by doing for them what they could do for themselves.

He said that one reason so many people did not recognize opportunity when they met it in the road was that opportunity frequently went around dressed in overalls and looking like hard work. He affirmed that the undisciplined life was a life not worth living, that the only difference in a powerful, life-giving river and a useless, disease-infested swamp was banks that disciplined the water of the river.

Another ability was possessed by J. A. Campbell, possessed in abundance by him, without which it is doubtful that any man achieves real greatness. He had the ability to *know the moment*. The words were once used by Charles Coburn, the actor. Stewart Kinzie interviewed Coburn. Kinzie immediately asked what Coburn considered the necessary qualities for success: brains, energy, education? Coburn said that these helped, of course, but there was something more important; it was "knowing the moment." The actor explained; he said that it meant the moment to act or not to act, the moment to speak or to keep silent. He said that on the stage, timing was the all important factor. He thought it was the key in life, as well. If one mastered the art of "knowing the moment" in marriage, in work, in relationship with others, one did not have to pursue success and happiness. These would walk right in the front door.

The founder of Campbell College knew the moment. As C. P. Snow, the British novelist said, "The future was in his bones." He watched for the open door, and, was not averse to giving the door a firm shove! Paul Green, distinguished playwright and alumnus of the school as well as personal friend of Dr. Campbell, said, "Campbell College came into existence because the soul of a community needed it and because there was a man who had a vision of how to fill that soul's need." Yes, he did. And, for the life of me, I do not see how J. A. Campbell could have done what he did at another time in history. With all due reverence, it was in the fullness of time that God sent forth his son, James Archibald Campbell. As long as he lived, that son was able to discern the tidal quality of time, to project plans, to float ideas, to undertake movements, to change educational gears—all on the crest of time's tide.

For him education had a two-fold purpose; it was to promote goodness and prepare for usefulness. To quote Paul Green again, "He believed that education should lead to ethical behavior. It was be good, be smart, and work hard." Paul Green continued, "That may leave out beauty." Sharp insight. To a certain extent beauty was neglected. The heritage, character, the experience, the teaching, and the concerns of J. A. Campbell were moral, religious, and practical. He did not object to beauty, to esthetics, provided the end goal and result were moral, religious, and practical.

As far as personal knowledge and research goes, no one ever caught the spirit and tone of J. A. Campbell, his school and what he did for those who came to it better than Josiah William Bailey, editor of the *Biblical Recorder,* later U. S. Senator. In his paper for May 24, 1905, Mr. Bailey wrote, having just attended commencement at Buies Creek:

> Commencement at this man's school begins in the morning, early and, on the last day, ends at 2 o'clock in the night! The final two hours are not long enough for their contents. It was a scene so unique that one could not wish for sleep. The contests, the songs, and the speeches were done before midnight. But there the pupils stayed—tears in their eyes, every boy and girl of them over and over again bidding sorrowful farewells to their teachers and to one another, but centrally to him—the teacher—and the loved spot, the school. They stood together there and prayed. Great big country boys and town boys wept and would not be comforted. One was heard to say over and over—with sobs, "It is the hardest thing I have ever had to do—to tell him good-by"; and it did seem that his heart would break. That boy came there lost. About him somehow the teacher got his arms. These several months he has lived in the joy of the Christian. Heaven began for him here. Much has been learned. He has a prize in his pocket. But there is That besides which no learning is worthy to be compared with. And though all the prizes were his, he would press on to the mark of the prize of the high calling in Jesus Christ.
>
> The teacher stands among them saying little, showing little, wonderfully quiet and surpassingly gentle, with a word for everyone and that a word of life. They love him because he loves them. That is the big reason. That has made his school. No nicknames for him, no disobeying him: it is the rule of love. If a boy comes there bad, he goes away good. And could

you hear the teacher pray and see him live his prayer, you would understand how it is.

They learn, too. There is here the very finest school enthusiasm that we have ever seen—devotion to books, ambition to excel, the development of talent in singing and speaking and thinking and working; but best of all, in this work is character. The young men and women have in their utterances three constantly recurring themes—right living, Christ and service.

He is one teacher who has the gift of imparting his personality, and yet his pupils are not imitators of him. That he would not tolerate. They have received his ways. They know great draughts of his spirit. And, so, poor though most of them are in this world's goods, they seem to have just one consuming aim, and that to enrich all the race of needy-fellow men.

It is this gift that makes the teacher great—the gift of imparting his instructions, also his spirit. It was that that made Arnold of Rugby, that that made Mark Hopkins greater than a university; the want of that is blasting many noble piles of stone, many magnificent endowments, making education a scornful mockery in many a high place . . .

We know many teachers, but we do not know one whom we would not desire to have more of J. A. Campbell's spirit and power at any cost. Buies Creek would do well to decline to exchange him for the endowment of Chicago University.

So came our captain, teacher, with his mighty heart. "Like a bridge over troubled waters," he laid his life down. Over his great heart, his sympathetic mind, his courageous will, we students crossed over to a better and a more useful life. And if the past is to retain the franchise in the present, if voting rights are to be given to heritage, then whatever else may be said about rising costs, inflated fees, and escalating tuition, this must be said: no student can really pay for his education at Campbell College. The hard discipline, the sacrificial work, the lonely vigils, the agonizing prayer and all but actual blood that was mixed with the brick and mortar of the early buildings, buildings that are still standing, place the present student generation under heavy mortgage. That mortgage is held by J. A. Campbell and those noble souls who stood by his side. They laid them down "like a bridge over troubled waters" no less than did their gallant leader, that all those who followed might cross over to a fuller life and a more perfect day.

7.
LIKE THE PHOENIX BIRD

No great man lives in vain. The history of the world is but the biography of great men.

Carlyle

There is properly no history, only biography.

Emerson

It IS doubtful that any other single event so influenced the spirit and character of the school as did the fire of 1900. Like the legendary phoenix bird that every 500 years arose from its flame and ashes to a new and vigorous life, so came resurrection to Buies Creek Academy. When the arsonist (assumed but never proven) lit the torch, the school was accepted and generally approved. But from the flames there arose an institution that was engraved with a pen of love upon the hearts of the people. Small ideas and provincial thinking gave way to lifted horizons and wide vistas of usefulness.

It was the night of Wednesday, December 20, 1900. The fall term was over. The next day, Thursday, the students would leave for the Christmas holidays. Bernadette Hoyle sets the tone in poetic language:

> It was a cold, frosty night and the village, settled down after a busy day, had a Christmas card quality. Smoke curled lazily from the chimneys, lamp lights flickered through the windows and cast shadows on the hard, frozen ground, and one by one disappeared. The academy, dark and empty, stood like a silent and benevolent sentinel guarding its charges in the pale winter moonlight.[1]

Like an athletic contest there were two events that preceded the main attraction. About 8:30 a fire destroyed a tenant house owned by J. McKoy Byrd. The tenant had moved out that day; in fact, had been gone only about twenty minutes when the fire was discovered. The community gathered, but there was no fire department, voluntary or otherwise. The house burned to the ground and water was poured on the embers. That was the first event of the fateful night.

The second round of excitement came at 12:30 in the morning of December 21. This time the fire destroyed the newly built two-story home of Professor Ogburn. Because the fire was well underway when discovered, the professor was forced to escape through a window. Again, many of the people in the community gathered at the scene. Because Professor Campbell's house was on the opposite side of the village, across the creek, he did not awake. The people who came together were now alarmed. It seemed certain that an arsonist was on the prowl, and later events would confirm the suspicion.

The *Harnett County Banner* reported, "The fire originated in this building," the academy building, "in the part most obscure from the outside and could not be discovered until it had gained considerable headway. When it was discovered the odor of kerosene was strong and it was burning rapidly."

"It was," the *Banner* report continued, "undoubtedly the work of enemies and we trust the facts may be brought to light for their punishment. Parties out hunting passed near the Academy an hour before the burning of Ogburn's house and saw a light in the building and heard two men talking, but thought it was some of the boys in the building for books."

In assessing the force of this drama of conflagration, it is necessary to give special attention to two men and to two groups of men and women. Of course, J. A. Campbell, the principal of the school, calls for major attention. He had started the school in 1887. For thirteen years he had nursed and tended it, pouring his youthful energies, ideals, and hopes into it. He had seen it grow in those thirteen brief years from the sixteen students who had been present on that cold morning, January 5, until it was recognized as a major force in the educational field not only in the community and county but throughout the state. The school had adequate buildings and equipment, a capable and responsive faculty, a hardworking, aspiring student body, loyal patrons, and devoted friends in places of influence. He, himself, had, a few months earlier, married a wonder-

Before the fire

After the fire, December 21, 1900

ful young woman from an outstanding family. He had, that year, built and entered into his own home. He was twenty-seven years old. Now this! His school enclosing his cluster of dreams, portraying his very life for thirteen years, had gone up in smoke and down in ashes.

He wrote, "When I looked out from my home toward the Academy about 3:30 A.M. and saw the flames, the terrible flames, that were sweeping away the efforts of a life and the means God was using to save poor boys and girls, I felt I could not bear it." He dressed quickly and rushed toward the fire with several students who had come to awake and give him the tragic news. He arrived just in time to see the roaring flames consume the remaining timbers and bring the building's collapse. He stumbled and fell to the ground; tears coursed down his face.

He felt strong youthful hands slipping beneath his arms, lifting him from the cold ground. It was one of his students, Herman T. Stevens, a youth who was living in the Campbell home and working his way through school. Together they moved toward the group of students, faculty, and friends gathered near the burning building, awed by the tragedy, too limited in vision to grasp the scope and influence of the event. Later the principal wrote: "While I stood there, sinking under my load, one poor boy who had not enough money to buy a ticket home for the holidays, threw his arms around me and said, 'Professor, cheer up. We students are going to build you a brick school.' " [2]

Those words, spoken by the same student who had lifted him from the ground where he had fallen, would live in the memory of J. A. Campbell and become a part of the rich heritage of the school. They would be recalled and quoted again and again at critical times in the school's history. They would be partially responsible for the strong ties that would bind student and teacher together in years to come.

Remembering the events, the young principal would say,

> When I ran up to the fire, the terrible fire, that was burning down chances for poor boys and girls, and I knew that I could not build again . . . the flames that destroyed the labor of years . . . the only hope for hundreds of boys and girls was being swept away, I could not bear up longer. . . . When they asked me my plans, I said, "Well, there's no chance to go on." [3]

The angry flames were hushed for lack of more materials to consume, the glowing coals were slowly turning gray, the friends and neighbors were winding their anxious way to their homes, wondering where and whom the arsonist would next strike. Professor Campbell turned from the tragic scene and headed his weary way back to his home on the hill. There he fell across his bed, exhausted in body and mind, and sick at heart and will. A few hours later, at his accustomed time to rise, he remained in bed. No words could describe his discouragement and sense of utter loss. It was time for a strong friend to appear.

He appeared. His name was Z. T. Kivett, a contractor and builder whose home was across the Cape Fear River, about six miles away. By sunrise he was crossing the river in the boat that his children used in crossing for school. He tied up the boat at McNeill's ferry and walked the four miles to the Campbell home. Strong, tall, brusque, with deep and penetrating eyes, he strode into the young schoolmaster's bedroom and grasped his hand in sympathy and friendship. Campbell was unable to speak; he wept without embarrassment. Kivett understood. But Z. T. Kivett was not only a man of sympathy, he had courage and ability to act.

He said, "Jim Archie, get out of that bed! Time's wastin'. Your name's Campbell; then get a hump on you! We've got work to do." Years later, remembering the grim experience, Mrs. Campbell said, "It was Mr. Kivett who buoyed him up, and from then on, all Mr. Campbell had in mind was to get back to school."

Z. T. Kivett was a competent contractor and builder. A little over two years before he had constructed the big tabernacle on the campus, the one building left standing after the fire, the building that would become the home of Buies Creek Academy for the next three years. Professor Campbell asked for and received Mr. Kivett's pledge that a new brick building would rise from the ashes of the old wooden structures. Writing of that pledge in 1923, Mr. Kivett said, "To this day, twenty-four years afterward, do I remember the time and place, that I put my hand in his, and promised my family and all my plantation if it required them, to rebuild in brick a more suitable building."

Z. T. Kivett was as good as his word. In one half day he built a little "shanty" on the school grounds. He, his twin sons, Herndon and Hendricks, his oldest daughter, Virginia, moved into the shack. They slept on boards; Virginia did the cooking and attended school. By living on the grounds Mr. Kivett was able to have constant oversight of every part of the building project. A brickkiln was constructed and a sawmill was set up. The man was a steam engine in britches! He supervised and sparked everything: drawing the

Mr. Z. T. Kivett, "The Grand Old Man!"

plans, making the brick, sawing the lumber, mixing the sand and lime, the hod-carrying work, everything.

I have before me now, as I write, a detailed financial record of the cost of that construction. The larger portion of the bill was never presented to J. A. Campbell and to Buies Creek Academy. The account reveals that Mr. Kivett, himself, put in 478¾ days on the project at 50¢ per day—the contract called for $2.50 per day. On being asked for a statement of his contribution, the "grand old man" said, "To give this service we neglected our own farm and sold 100 acres of our land to fill the deficit."

Professor Campbell never forgot nor failed to give due credit to Z. T. Kivett for the invaluable assistance rendered as friend, counselor, builder—builder of morale no less than of school structures. Kivett's portrait hangs in the college. His son serves on the board of trustees. His daughters continue to make their contribution to the college. "A friend is your need realized."

And there were the students. When the young principal told the students that he would be compelled to suspend the school, they said, "No, sir, we are coming back here in two weeks time to enter school. We are going to fit up the tabernacle and go on with the work." Professor Campbell continued:

> They passed resolutions and subscribed, this year's students alone, $150 for the work, and more than $125 of that was given by poor boys who are either using borrowed money or spending money they made in cotton mills or on the farm. . . . One boy sold his gun presented by his father . . . and gave the seven dollars to the Academy. Some have stayed here and are spending the Christmas working. Several more are coming back to give a week's work. . . . I have never seen such an example of sacrifice.[4]

The students subscribed the cutting of 325 cords of wood. The girls led in this, subscribing 35 cords. This wood was to be used for making and firing the bricks for the new building. On Saturdays the ring of the axes that the boys were wielding in the forests could be heard.

His old friend Josephus Daniels of the Raleigh *News and Observer* came to his aid and gave liberal coverage to the tragedy. The paper carried the resolutions adopted by the students.

> Pupils of Buies Creek Academy appeal for aid in worthy cause

> To the Editor: Buies Creek Academy, the largest preparatory school in North Carolina, was consumed by flames at 4 o'clock on the morning of

"Shanty" erected on school grounds by Mr. Kivett and his sons. Shown with Mr. Kivett and daughter, Virginia.

Sawmill owned by Mr. Kivett and used to cut the lumber for the new building.

December 20, 1900. No clue to the cause, as yet, can be obtained. The following resolutions were adopted by the student body, and we trust that all will heed the needs of the principal, and the cause of the institution:

Resolved, 1. That we, the students of Buies Creek Academy, do hereby extend our deepest sympathies to the principal and faculty of our much loved and excellent institution. We pray that God may visit them by his spirit, and teach them to be resigned amid tragedy.

2. That we will ever stand by, and uphold the excellent Christian faculty for their kindness, and for the many helps extended to the poor boys and girls of our state, by our principal.

3. That we feel that the trouble and loss is not only upon the students, faculty and community in this Christian work but upon the entire state, and, therefore, we appeal to every generous-hearted educator and Christian worker to support the institution, and see that it is rebuilt; for nothing could do more for the glory of God and the cause of education.

4. That we, the students, will use every effort to raise by contribution, in our respective communities, funds to rebuild, and extend the work of the institution. We pledge our loyal support in the effort to extend its patronage. May God put it into the hearts of the people of our respective communities, and state, to rally to the support of this most excellent institution, and its able faculty, Signed:

> E. B. Poe
> H. A. Rives
> J. D. Howell
> J. B. Tugwell
> Lillie Matthews
> Pennie Daniels
> Norma Burt
> R. T. Upchurch
> J. A. Clark, Com.

Editorially, the *News and Observer* gave its endorsement loud and clear:

The burning of the school building at Buies's Creek Academy is a severe loss to the educational world in North Carolina. Fifteen years ago, in a small cheap building, Prof. J. A. Campbell opened a small school there. It has grown to be one of the leading academies in the state. No man living in North Carolina has wrought more nobly and unselfishly to educate the people than Prof. Campbell. Public-spirited men ought to rally to his assistance in rebuilding.

The paper also began a subscription list for those who wanted to contribute to the rebuilding. The first to respond were T. B. Parker and H. E. Murphy. Others followed: Peel's Business College, B. W. Spilman, J. W. Bailey, Josephus Daniels, Carey J. Hunter, F. M. Simmons, to name a few.

Prophet or teacher, J. A. Campbell was not without honor in his own area. The *Harnett County Banner* wrote that the fire had swept away the gem and pride of the county. It said the school's three-story building had been equipped with all the latest and most modern equipment. The financial loss was great, great to the principal, but the loss to the people of the area was equally great. For, "it was there that the priceless gem of thought and culture was moulded, intellects were expanded, men and women were prepared to meet the obligations of life, the moral status elevated, upon which no financial value can be placed."

The *Banner* also offered its paper and facilities for a subscription fund. It stated that any amount would be appreciated and would be acknowledged through the paper and forwarded to Mr. Campbell. The welfare of the children of the country demanded, the paper affirmed, that the school be rebuilt.

Other papers spoke out. Archibald Johnson, editor of *Charity and Children*, the paper printed by the North Carolina Baptist Orphanage, wrote encouraging words. He told the principal that he was not to be downhearted or discouraged, that God was in the situation. He said that no incendiary could stop the progress of a school like Buies Creek Academy. He was sure that the people would help him rebuild the school and, in addition to that, there would come a tide of love and sympathy whose streams would flow through the years. He affirmed that BCA could not be spared. Let Professor Campbell go right on with his plans to rebuild. He pledged, along with others, to keep the funds coming. He promised that as he went about over the state he would keep the matter before the people.

Josiah W. Bailey, editor of the *Biblical Recorder*, future U. S. Senator, wrote, "Write an appeal to the *Recorder* and I will start a subscription. May God bless you, fear not He is with you."

John A. Oates, editor of the *North Carolina Baptist*, wrote that he had just learned of the tragedy. He counseled that the ashes of the school should become the principal's inspiration. This must be the case, he affirmed, because the future of unborn children was in his hands. He said that BCA would be greater than ever before. He would help in anyway he could. If Professor Campbell would write, the editor would see that his first issue in the new century spoke to the people for Buies Creek Academy. "God will help. God will put it into the hearts of men to carry out his will toward your great work."

These were a few of the papers that came to his aid through editorial and news columns. The principal's files of personal letters grew and grew. These letters were read over and over when the lamp of courage and hope burned low. The letters never failed to warm his heart and strengthen his will to get on with the work of the school, including a letter from the Governor Charles B. Aycock.

One of these rare and unique letters came from his friend, B. W. Spilman. The letter said:

> I was glad to hear of the burning of Buies Creek Academy. The devil set fire to the buildings, but God is going to overrule it, and it will be better in the future than ever. Don't be discouraged, cheer up. You will find friends that you do not know of. While it is so dark, you have my sincere sympathy; when it is brighter, I will rejoice with you. You will have a Christmas present from Raleigh in a few days. I want to be at the dedication of the building.[5]

President Charles E. Taylor of Wake Forest College wrote saying that when he read of the tragedy, read it aloud at home to his family, he was so deeply moved, "I could not command my voice to get through it. Perhaps it may prove a blessing in disguise, and you may yet live to be thankful for the conflagration, at any rate it has served to show how much your people love you. I enclose my check . . ."

In the weeks and months ahead two emotions seemed to control Professor Campbell: at times one was in charge, at times the other prevailed. One was deep gratitude and great joy. The other was an all-but-overwhelming sense of responsibility and an inability to see how what was being undertaken could ever come to fruition. In the Harnett *Banner* he wrote that he did not grieve at the personal loss, which represented most of his earthly possessions, but the chance, the only chance, for many poor boys and girls. That thought made him sick for Buies Creek Academy was a holy place for him.

In his own paper, *The Little River Record*, Professor Campbell wrote of the days that followed the tragic fire:

The citizens gathered and said, "Here are our wagons and teams and our services until you are on your feet again." The telephone line seemed to have been built on purpose to convey sympathy and love and assurances of help in this dark hour. The U. S. Mails seemed to have been ordained of God to inspire courage and keep his work going. Horses and buggies became God's agents to help along his work. They brought brethren from Dunn and other points to tell us not to give up. Close friends drew closer, indifferent ones became red-hot enthusiasts for Buie's Creek and enemies were made friends. December 20th plans were made to fit up the large open tabernacle, 80 x 90 feet, for temporary use. On the 22nd wagons were putting lumber on the ground and on the 24th the carpenters were busy at their work . . . the tabernacle was fitted up and opened January 8th. When it is remembered that the principal had no money and that this disaster came during the Christmas time, one can plainly see that unless God had moved upon the hearts of the people this great amount of work could never have been done in so short a time.[6]

He continued, trying to express his appreciation to individuals and groups:

To Mr. Z. T. Kivett, who came and took charge of the matter of planning and pushing the work, to the students who spent their holidays in helping, to the citizens of the community, to the newspapers, and to friends one and all who in any way helped make it possible for the work to be done, we desire to return our sincere and heartfelt thanks.[7]

In the *Biblical Recorder* Professor Campbell detailed what was saved from the fire. It consisted of the chapel organ and about fifteen desks, a few chairs from the society halls, and a few other items of little value. He said that the property was worth at least $4,000 with only $1,500 insurance. He said that $400 of that would go to the public school fund. The amount owed on the building was almost $500. It would cost $600 to get the tabernacle in shape for use. They would use the church for music classes.

People were, of course, wanting to know about the future of the school. He frankly confessed that he did not know about the future. The way was dark for him. He said that he would give up, quite frankly, except that assurances were coming from everywhere that help was on the way and greater things were in store for the school. He confided that if the school was to be rebuilt, it would be done in brick. If that was done, the people would have to stand by with their help.

He revealed through the *Little River Record* that offers had come from other places:

I have had assurance that if I would go to another place, they would give me five thousand to ten thousand dollars in grounds and buildings. I have also been urged to go to yet another place. . . . At least three locations offered to put up such buildings as would be necessary and make a gift of them, if we would move. . . . But I cannot see duty that way. Plenty of people with wealth and brains will look after those places. If I leave here the people are ruined. I cannot go. I would, I think, be happier over yonder in a log building, with these people who love me so well and to whom I have given my life, than in a brick building elsewhere. Pray for us.

He gave other reasons for staying in Buies Creek. People had invested in Buies Creek because of the school. God had richly blessed the work in Buies Creek. The people of the community were united. He said that there were fewer temptations in Buies Creek than in most communities; so it was a safer place for boys and girls. Because living was cheaper there than in most places, the school could reach a class of boys and girls who, otherwise, would not be helped. Finally he felt that the very difficulty of the task at Buies Creek gave an unparalleled opportunity, a powerful argument for education. So, he would stay.

But he was aware of time. Remember, he is thirty-eight years old. This is what he said: "I cannot at this age in life carry many years the work I have done for the past ten. I fear I shall not live to see the work accomplished." Again, he wrote: "If, however, our friends fail us, there is no chance for us. Those who know me know something of how hard I have worked. I cannot carry for the next ten years what I have borne for the last ten. I am willing to give my life for this cause, but do not think I ought to kill myself." These lines are written beyond the midnight hour and sent out with the prayer that God may use them in arousing friends to save the institution. Whatever is done must be done quickly: "To all lovers of B.C.A., to our personal friends and to all friends of education, we appeal for help."

Such words, such appeals, might be made by a high-powered advertising firm or a driving PR executive and not produce a great reaction. But the people to whom J. A. Campbell appealed did not know about such matters or such people. They did know J. A. Campbell. They knew that he told it like it was, that he had laid his life along beside his words, and that he would continue to do so. They responded—but not with large gifts. The school had few friends who could make large gifts, but it had many friends who could make small gifts, often "gifts in kind." This they did. Mrs. M. A. Byrd wrote to Professor Campbell:

> I have been trying ever since the Academy burned to plan some way to help you. I was poor and had had, what I felt, a ruining misfortune but finally the plan of self-denial suggested itself to me and I decided to raise $5.00 in that way by the first of November. Then it occurred to me that I might get other ladies to join me in this effort. I wrote out my petition and am having wonderful success. I am not asking any lady, only those I know will do just what they say and have not yet an amount less than $5.00. I am sure I will get $100.00 and possibly more. I first thought I would not let you know anything about it, and then concluded it might be best to tell you that you might know that this amount is on the way. I think you may safely add another $100.00 to your amount.[8]

At Lillington the ladies gave an oyster supper, and the net proceeds were $21.16. The young men of the two literary societies in the school at Buies Creek followed the Lillington group's example. They netted $50.00. With this they proposed to buy the bell for the new Academy building. The girls from the Athenian Society gave an "Easter Reception." They advertised the event in the *Little River Record*. There was to be music, pantomimes, recitations, and tableaux "of such a nature as to please the most artistic." The entertainment was to be free. After the entertainment, "the entire proceeds from the sale of ice cream, flowers and confectionaries will be given to the furnishing of the Athenian Hall. Come one, come all; we welcome you to our Festal Hall." It was signed, "Mattie Bain, Minnie Barington, Sarah Stancil, Committee."

At Wake Forest College a former student of B.C.A. wrote that he was starting a club to raise $100.00. Harvey Holleman, the first boarding student, now living in Boston, sent $100.00. Professor Campbell grasped at any idea that he felt would increase income. He had a 1,000 "Brick Envelopes" printed, each envelope having fifty bricks and each brick worth ten cents. He wrote, "Each envelope, therefore, is valued at $5.00. Now if 100 friends will each take an envelope and sell the fifty bricks we shall have raised $500.00 on the brick plan. One thousand friends would secure $5,000.00. Where is the boy or girl who cannot by trying secure fifty ten-cent pieces by October 1st?"

Professor Campbell thought of the idea of memorial doors and windows as a means for securing funds. He wrote that the building,

Brickkiln, built and operated by Mr. Kivett, used
to make brick for the new building

Kivett Building partially finished.

when completed, would be the most magnificent building in the county, one of the most beautiful school buildings in the state. He said that when those who were now living had passed to their reward, it would be a beautiful tribute to their memory for coming generations to read of their sacrifices in saving the school. It was a possibility through purchasing a door or window. He wrote:

> There are 47 double windows and doors that are estimated to cost $10 each; five at $8 each; two at $6 each; fourteen at $3.50 each; twenty-eight at $2.50 each. Appropriate inscriptions will be placed on windows or doors in memory of the giver or of whomever desired. . . . Who will be next? Speak quickly.[9]

On April 8, 1901, Professor Campbell received a letter from M. C. Treat that caused him to "wake the town and tell the people!" Mr. Treat wrote:

> Dear Mr. Campbell: I want to make an offer for your consideration. If you can raise $10,000 for building during 1901, I will pay one-tenth of it, or you will have but $9,000 to raise.
>
> Tell your people this comes from the North, from one you never met, from a businessman who is a large borrower of money himself, and yet interested in your work.[10]

The principal told about the reception of that letter. In the *Little River Record* he said:

> My class had come to recitation, but boys and girls were asked to stop and listen while the answer to our prayers was announced and all paused in our work to silently thank the Great Giver. The letter was sent to other rooms and read. Teachers and students wept for joy, and God did seem so near.

But he would not let joy, gratitude, and exuberance take away realism. He continued:

> But can we meet the conditions? Can we raise $9,000? I cannot, and I do not know of anyone who can. But there are at least 1,000 men and women, boys and girls to whom this institution is dear—to many because of what it has done for them. Hundreds of parents love this institution because of what it has been to their children, many love it because of what it shall be to their children if it is saved in this hour of calamity. . . . Now if a thousand such . . . shall plead with their Father, who is neither poor nor stingy, to give us this institution for the glory of His name and the helping of our fellowmen it will be sure to come. For while we are asking Him, if our ears are open, we shall certainly hear His voice telling us what to do. God will do His work through us if we will permit Him.[11]

The call was heard. God and the people responded. On May 23, 1901, the cornerstone of the new brick building, 70 × 92 feet, three stories high, with a wing 50 × 35 feet, one story, was laid. And through "blood, sweat and tears" on November 2, 1903, the new academy was ready for occupancy. Professor Campbell wrote, again in the *Little River Record,*

> This is the glad day which comes in such beautiful contrast to December 20, 1900. . . . Upon the rostrum sits Mr. William Pearson, who was the man the Lord chose to begin this work; here are the teachers, the workmen and a number of our citizens, who without notice, have come in at the first opening. "Praise God from whom all blessings flow" is sung and then all join in singing the same words. Rev. A. N. Campbell leads the dedicatory prayer. A few words from the principal, a prayer from Rev. J. A. Clark, one of the students at the time of the fire; a few words from Mr. Pearson, prayer by the principal, a few words from Rev. H. T. Stevens, also a student when the fire came; prayer by Prof. Baggett and a few words from Mr. Clark. Without a moment's notice these simple, soul-stirring exercises are held, followed by a raising of hands by everybody, thereby saying that we desire here and now to consecrate the building, students, teachers and all knowledge here obtained to the glory of our God and the salvation of the lost.[12]

Professor Campbell described, with emotion, what was involved in the building. He said that it was one of the most imposing and best arranged school buildings in the state. He said it was built of bricks, bricks made on the very grounds. He affirmed that the building was an "everlasting monument to the love, loyalty and sacrifices of our students and friends." He said it was an inspiration just to look upon the building. Then he described the physical plan of the building:

> On the first floor of the main building are four recitation rooms, 35 × 40 feet each, furnished with new patent desks, blackboards, globes, charts, etc. The second story has four rooms, 35 × 40 each, three of which are Society Halls. The other will be used for recitation. The first floor of the wing is used for Primary Department and piano music. The second story has a large Commercial Hall, with offices and rooms for typewriting, etc. On the front of the main building is a tower 20 × 20 feet, four stories high, with stairways, rooms for telegraphy, band music, etc. On the rear is a similar tower, with basement for heating plant, library on second floor and Art Hall on the third. The rooms are all well lighted with large double windows, having no cross lights; the furniture is new and well adapted and one could hardly wish for conditions more favorable for study.[13]

The work had been done. The building was proof. Within the

brief span of time, just a little more than three years, the building had risen from the ashes formed by the arsonist's torch. It was stated earlier that this event in the life of the school went far toward shaping and influencing its character and its spirit. It is true. The school's motto, "To the Stars Through Difficulties," was more than a slogan now; it was a clear statement of fact. There were stars, there were difficulties; it was possible to pass through one to get to the other. Gerald Johnson, editor of *Charity and Children* had been a true prophet: the people had helped rebuild the school. Through that effort the school, in a way that it had never been before, was now their school. The tides of their love and sympathy would find channels to the school through all years to come. Shakespeare talked about men being a band of brothers and about "gentlemen in England now abed will count themselves accursed they were not here and rouse them at the name of Chryspian." Aye, the phoenix was on the wing.

Notes

1. Hoyle, Bernadette, *The Story of Campbell College*, p. 107.
2. *Little River Record*, January-February, 1901.
3. Ibid.
4. Ibid.
5. Ibid.
6. Ibid.
7. Ibid.
8. Ibid.
9. Ibid, March-April, 1901.
10. Ibid.
11. Ibid.
12. Ibid, November, 1903.
13. Ibid.

8.
"GLADLY LEARN AND GLADLY TEACH"

There are some men who lift the age they inherit until all men walk on higher ground during their lifetime.

Maxwell Anderson
Valley Forge

JAMES Archibald Campbell gave great thought and care to the selection of his teachers. He knew that the teacher makes the difference between a school and a school that is different.

He sought three qualities in his teachers. First, he wanted committed Christians. He made no apology for it; he affirmed it and advertised the fact. Second, he sought teachers who were committed to boys and girls, believed in them and their possibilities. Third, and I think the order is as he would have put it, he wanted teachers who were committed to and competent in the area of subjects taught.

Academic proficiency was of great importance to J. A. Campbell. He put it last because he believed that was where it belonged, not because he discounted its importance. He did believe that there were things in life more important than academic knowledge. For he knew it was possible for an individual to be a useful member of society, a valuable citizen of the state and a participating member of the kingdom of God. But no one should be misled as to Dr. Campbell's evaluation of solid learning. He was a teacher and an educator. In his own life subject matter was never slighted; he was an "A" student. His own children were honor students.

One who knew Dr. Campbell well was present when a committee, sent to investigate the school in view of its accreditation as a junior college, said to the president: "Dr. Campbell, we shall write our report and you will, of course, be notified. We are kindly disposed to what you are trying to do here. We wish you well. But, frankly,

95

the members of your faculty have very poor academic preparation. Only one of your teachers has the Ph.D. degree; many do not even have a master's degree."

Quickly Dr. Campbell said, "You mean you do not think my teachers know enough?" The committee chairman smiled and said, "Well, I would not have put it in those terms but I guess it is about what I mean."

The response was instantaneous, "Well, sir, there may be a lot that my teachers do not know, but most of what they know is so!" The committee was impressed and with the understanding that the school would follow certain recommendations, accreditation was recommended.

I have looked carefully at the name of every person who has taught in the school from that cold January morning in 1887 to the present faculty. I have interviewed persons who knew teachers who are now dead. It would call for a courage and a wisdom that I do not possess to list the "best" or the "most influential" teachers. And yet, it seems only fair and proper, to comment briefly upon a few who made unusual contributions to the school and are, to a large degree, representative of that group of teachers who gave their time and abilities so gladly and so devotedly.

I have studied the long list of teachers in view of selecting two from each decade of the school's existence. An arbitrary decision? Granted. There are two decades when at least three names must be included. In several cases the names of individuals will be included whose chief contribution to the school was not in the realm of teaching, though no person's name will be included who did not teach. In a few cases names will be omitted because of contributions in other categories.

1880's

The first bracket is brief, a three-year span. Teachers were few. But, had there been many teachers, the selection would be the same. The names of James Archibald Campbell and Cornelia Pearson would probably lead the list regardless of how large the list might be. History will list J. A. Campbell in the role of administrator. He was head of the school that came to bear his name. But most of that time he taught; also, he knew that schools were for teaching; that was the reason for their existence. And the larger percentage of his students would contend that his greatest role was that of teacher. John Allen McLeod, distinguished attorney, once told me, "He was the greatest teacher I ever knew. He was an inspired and inspiring instructor. He knew and was comfortable with his subject matter. He knew and cared for the individual student. He believed that whatever God wanted the student to do could best be accomplished if the student were educated. His methods of teaching were sound and creative. He was a master teacher."

From the first day of school Cornelia Pearson taught. She came as a student; she assumed the role of teacher. True, she also studied as a student. But from the first day she taught. A thorough knowledge of her subject, a quiet, poised assurance, a firm but tender patience, particularly with small children, her specialty, and a boundless admiration for the principal! These were some of her characteristics. Along with her role as teacher, she with her husband, was an administrator. She served as business manager of the school long before the title was assigned.

1890-1900

Professor J. R. Baggett came to Buies Creek Academy from Salem where he had been principal of Salem High School. He was a University of North Carolina man and came to Buies Creek to teach "mathematics, science, and history." For almost twenty years he was identified with the school. His diligence in effort, competence in his fields of teaching, sense of humor, and identification with his students made him a favorite with young and old. He was a large man with a high forehead, receding hair, and something of a prune-projecting mouth and retreating chin.

The catalogue stated of Professor J. W. Portis that he was "for twelve years director of music in one of the leading schools in this state and is perhaps the best instructor in band and orchestra music in the state. He will teach violin, guitar, mandolin, cornet, clarinet and harp and is director of band and orchestra." What did he do in his spare time? Why, he taught telegraphy, photography, and watch repair. As for telegraphy, the catalogue stated, "The instructor in this department has had 25 years experience both in practical railroad and commercial telegraphy. He has the reputation of being a good and rapid instructor." He was a short, stumpy man. He wore a handlebar mustache, had dark eyes, heavy eyebrows, and a bald head. He was always busy, a colorful character. Professor Campbell was fond of music, loved to sing and direct singing. He had looked forward to the time when music could have an honored place in the life of his school. The coming of Professor Portis made this possible.

Along with his other achievements, Professor Portis was an inventor. For years he spent time and energy perfecting an electric clock. The catalogue of 1909-1910 states:

> This clock is the invention of Professor Portis and has three automatic circuit switches to one of which is connected by suitable wires a large electric bell in the belfry to ring calls for students to come in at various study hours. No other bell rings when this does. From another switch runs a line to which bells are attached in various recitation rooms. The bells ring at the opening and closing of the recitation period and no other bells ring when these do. Another switch runs a line to the dormitory. These bells announce study-hours, hours of retiring, rising, etc. The clock is provided with a wheel, with various moving parts, giving as much or as little time to each period as may be desired. No one of the bells rings on Saturday or Sunday. The bells in the school building do not ring at night nor do the dormitory bells ring in the day. The whole thing is automatic and nothing need be done except to wind the clock, which also announces the day of the week. For several years we have been using this clock and it is a perfect success, every recitation beginning and closing with perfect accuracy.

1900-1910

The catalogue for 1902-1903 lists the name of Hubbard Fulton Page. He is recorded as teaching Latin, Greek, and Bible. It was one of the school's better days when this man came on its faculty. This is Paul Green's description of his appearance:

> He was an untidy man and in every way looked the part of one touched by the divine afflatus, a local William Barnes—with his mop of flaring reddish hair, his rumpled and awkward necktie, his wrinkled trousers that had never felt the pressing iron, and his equally and single neglected coat. And there he would sit with one of his britches' legs sliding up higher and higher as he read and talked and recited his beloved poets to us, and now and then he would with a quick upward jerk of his head shoot his spectacles up to rest on his upper forehead as he beamed out at us with happy eyes. And then with an opposite jerk he would shoot his glasses back to fit precisely on his nose and continue reading and talking away.

. . . And often he would continue reading right on by class-changing bell, oblivious to all outward sounds, and the students would slip out quietly one by one and leave him there.

Paul Green goes on to say, in the same article, that it was the same Hubbard Page who, more than any other person, caused him to forego the plow and turn to the typewriter. The dramatist affirms that he never knew a man who loved Shakespeare's plays and the British Romantic poets more than this man Page did. Robert Burns and John Charles McNeill were also favorites of "Fesser Page."

The poet-teacher was born near Buies Creek, in Averasboro Township, on the ground that ran red with, and soaked thirstily at, the blood flowing from a thousand men who died in the Battle of Averasboro, referred to earlier. He graduated from Buies Creek Academy, Wake Forest College, and took his master's degree from Harvard in 1911. He then taught in Texas Christian University, Texas A. & M., and Mississippi College. He returned to Buies Creek when it became a junior college and remained until his retirement in 1947. He published *Lyrics and Legends of the Cape Fear County. The Threshold and Other Poems* was published posthumously.

The beginning of the fall term for 1909 saw Burgess Pinckney Marshbanks in the classroom at Buies Creek Academy for the first time. He taught senior mathematics, senior English, and history. He was officially connected with the college until 1953, as teacher from 1909 to 1934 and business manager from 1934 to 1952.

He was a mountaineer from Mars Hill, North Carolina. Dr. Campbell wrote of him in the *Little River Record* for June 1909:

He is 27 years old, 6 feet 2 inches tall, received his M.A. and LL.B. degrees from Wake Forest at the recent commencement, he is an active Christian. He was reared on the farm and is this summer making a crop for his father, who is sick. Before going to college he taught two years in the public schools. He took the M.A. degree in three and one half years, usually requiring five, managed a club for two years, thereby paying his board, and was this year assistant in physics. President R. L. Moore, who prepared him for college, says of him, "I do not know a young man of cleaner life and morals. He is one of the brightest young men going out from us. He is capable of hard work and holds up well under it. He will grip your young men and make an excellent teacher." Dr. W. R. Cullom, of Wake Forest, says: "Of all the men I know there is no one whom I could recommend more heartily and unreservedly. This applies to him as a man in general and also to his special fitness for the place you are trying to fill." We have other letters but these are enough.

During the forty-four years Professor Marshbanks was connected with the school his responsibilities included teaching math, Bible, law, and history. Administratively he was business manager, dean, and vice-president. He first impressed his students as austere and unbending. But those who came to know him, those who had special needs, found that he was generous with his time, outgoing with his help, and genuinely interested in the students' total welfare.

And he was not blind to the "student life-style," though "life-style," as a word, was not in vogue. Dr. B. P. Marshbanks, Jr., recalls one incident when he was a small boy walking across the campus with his father in the early evening. As they passed some tall shrubs along one of the walks, there was a rustling of the branches. Professor Marshbanks stopped to investigate. Behind the shrubs he found two students, a young man and a young woman. The students were embarrassed but the young man was ready with his story. He explained that he and his girl friend had sought a place of quiet retreat where they could pray and have their evening devotions together. Professor Marshbanks informed the students that he was sending them to their respective dorms and counselors. The young man was disturbed, "Why, Professor Marshbanks, you wouldn't send us up for having our evening devotions together, would you?" "No, young man," said the wise older man, "I am sending you up for what I would have been doing had I been in your place!"

He was conservative in outlook and in practice. He was careful and cautious in business and in educational innovations. There was little of the dreamer and none of the gambler spirit in him, and he gave no quarter to "lady-luck." His conservative caution was invaluable in the early days of the school and through the depression years. In a time when it becomes necessary to launch a school and its program on the tidal spirit and movement of the times, the cautious and conservative spirit seems out of step. This explained some of the tension that developed in the administration of the school in the later years of his connection with it.

In that first news release by Dr. Campbell it was said of Professor Marshbanks, "He is an active Christian." He continued to be. For fifty years he was a deacon in the local Baptist church. He gave his support through leadership, finances, presence, and strong influence to his church. He taught; he served on important committees. There were those who felt that his leadership and influence were too strong, but this did not deter him from giving both to the hilt of his ability.

1910-1920

The years 1910 to 1920 saw an influx of Campbells to the faculty. Leslie and Carlyle graduated from Wake Forest and returned to Buies Creek to teach in the fall of 1911. Leslie taught English and mathematics; Carlyle taught Greek and Latin. In the fall of 1916 the third of the Campbell children joined the faculty. This was Bessie who graduated from Meredith that spring. She came home in 1916 to teach piano. She would later study at the New York School of Music and Arts with a world famous teacher; she would also study at Westminster Choir College.

Leslie remained with the school, save for a brief excursion in the business world. Carlyle left in 1917 to enter military service. He then returned to the school for a year and a half. Bessie, Mrs. A. E. Lynch, taught from 1916 to 1928, was away from the school for six years, returning in 1934. She was with the school from that date to her retirement in 1965. Each of the Campbell children had real ability as a teacher. How could they have escaped the ability!

In the fall of 1914 the young man who was to marry the Campbell daughter joined the faculty of the school. He was Archibald Edgar Lynch, instructor in voice. He had graduated from Buies Creek Academy and would study at the New York School of Music and Arts, at the Shenandoah Music College, and at Westminster Choir College. He also had a useful term of service with the Home Mission Board of the Southern Baptist Convention. He was on the faculty at Campbell for twenty-nine years.

For loyal devotion to the school, for high admiration of the founder, for genuine interest in his students, he has probably not been excelled in the life of the school. Through lean and tight budgets he worked faithfully with the music program of the school. His glee clubs sang at crossroads and rural churches, as well as to many town and city groups. He and his glee clubs were one of the chief recruiting agencies for the school for many years. What

Carlyle, Elizabeth, and Leslie Campbell

his group lacked in musical expertise may have been considerable; that had to be the case, for I was a member of several of those groups, but our enthusiasm and love for the school went far to compensate for our lack of musical ability. Too, there were always a few individuals, faculty members and students, who had musical ability. Always at the helm with enthusiasm and undiscourageable goodwill was Professor Lynch.

In 1915 Professor I. M. Wallace came to the school. For the next thirty-five years he gave his love and talents to the institution as few men ever did. He was a Kentuckian by birth, a graduate of Kentucky Normal State College and of Bowling Green Business University. He was an experienced and successful teacher when he came to Buies Creek Academy and there were those who could not understand his willingness to take the "demotion" that seemed involved in his decision to cast his lot with the little school in Buies Creek. But he and his charming, devoted, gifted wife became an inseparable part of the life of the community, school, and church.

The eulogy delivered at Professor Wallace's funeral on December 10, 1952, by President Leslie Campbell is so fitting, accurate in detail, and sensitive in spirit that it needs to be quoted:

> It was indeed a momentous decision in 1915 that caused a comparatively young teacher to pull up stakes, deep-rooted in his beloved bluegrass country, and with his family move far across the Blue Ridge to this small school village. What voice was it, from within or above, that led one who had held such important positions as teacher in the Oklahoma City Schools, Principal of the Commercial Departments of Clinton College and of Ohio Valley College, to take over at his own financial risk the business class of this small academy? Impossible of realization was the fact that the best years of his life were to be spent here in helping to mold the Campbell College we know. Nor could he foresee that here he was to rear his family and identify himself for all time to come with this distant community. It was a momentous decision, the consequences of which no human eye could foresee; but as we his neighbors and friends contemplate today Mr. Wallace's benign influence and constructive labors among us, we are constrained to give thanks to a kind Providence that led him to us.
>
> The wisdom of the decision of the principal of Buies Creek Academy to invite one from such a distance to accept such a responsible position might seem to be fraught with equal uncertainty. How could he know that this prospective teacher would possess, up to the last day of his life a degree of open-mindedness that would enable him to readily accept new truth and to adopt for himself new life patterns, whether in religion or in the field of specialization? How could the principal foresee that he was choosing a man that would demonstrate unwavering loyalty to the

institution through every vicissitude, as during the national panic of the early 1930's when salaries were reduced almost to nothing and payments deferred? Who could discern that here was a teacher, who though efficient in his field, loved his students more than subject matter; and one who, while explaining the science of business, taught boys and girls to fear God and keep his commandments?

He did not teach in vain, for his students saw in him genuineness and dedication. Some of them have become highly successful in business, but wherever you meet them, without exception they refer to their venerable teacher in terms of highest affection.

Speaking more personally I would pay tribute to my departed friend most of all for the many little things in his daily life that reveal the true stature of the man. He was as prompt and reliable in the performance of his duty as the second hand on his watch. During his 20 years as superintendent of this Sunday School, I doubt he was ever late. He never paraded his goodness nor boasted of his efficiency, but like Abou Ben Adhem, he best proved his love for God by simple acts of love for his fellow man. He visited the sick, wept with those in distress, and left with the unfortunate little evidences of his generosity. Often when times were out of joint has he slipped into my office all alone to offer words of encouragement and pledge anew his friendship.

As we reflect upon his 35 years of service to Campbell, we may well conclude, as it was said of another, "The steps of a good man are ordered of the Lord."

Creek Pebbles, December 13, 1952

1920-1930

The twenties saw three persons join the faculty whose work and influence were so great that thousands of students would find it forever impossible to think of the school without thinking of these persons being a part of it. Their names were Mabel Powell, Gladys Strickland, and John Edward Ayscue. Miss Powell came in 1924 and remained until her retirement in 1967, a total of forty-three years. Miss Strickland came in 1925 and stayed until her marriage, resigning in 1953. "Uncle Johnnie," as Professor Ayscue was lovingly called by generations of students, came to the school in 1926 and remained until his retirement in 1950, a total of twenty-four years. Total the years that the three served and you get ninety-five years; in round numbers, a century of competent, committed, Christian teaching.

There are those who say that Mabel Powell is herself a walking miracle. When she was five years old she had a serious spinal illness that left her an invalid. Her doctor was brutally frank with the family. He thought it was doubtful that the child would live. If she lived it was problematical that she would ever walk again. She wore heavy braces and for twenty years she slept on steel. She would seem to get better and then there would be a relapse. Finally, in 1918, when she was twenty-four, her doctor announced that he had done all that he could do for her. Mabel Powell was bedridden.

There is a proverb which says, "Man's extremity is God's opportunity." Mabel Powell believed it. The family continued to pray; they enlisted the prayers of others. Shortly thereafter, the invalid announced, "I want to get up." Six months later she was walking. She continued to improve, and later graduated from Georgetown College, Kentucky; she graduated from the University of North Carolina. She was thirty-four years old, weighed eighty-four pounds, wore no braces, owed $1,200, and wanted to teach. But every school, in spite of her academic excellence and high recommendations from school administrators and teachers, replied to her applications, "Unfit for rigors of classroom teaching."

Finally, J. A. Campbell heard of her. He took a chance and offered her a job in the fields of Latin and English, the very disciplines that she was most interested in teaching. At that the angel who watched over Campbell was content to rejoice and sing for the rest of the livelong day! For from that time in 1924 until her retirement in 1967, the school was her life; her life was the school. President Leslie Campbell said of her, "Who can doubt that this great teacher of queenly character was divinely directed to Campbell College in our time?"

She came to the school at a salary of $100 per month. At times during the years of the depression she received $30 per month. There were stretches when there was no salary; she, along with others, went to the head of the school for a few dollars when they had to buy groceries. But through dark and fair days, with boundless love, amazing energy, steel determination, rare skill, and understanding, she gave herself to Christ through the lives of young men and young women who came to Campbell College. There is a girls' dormitory on the campus that bears her name and the name of her sister Nell, another devoted and gifted teacher at the school. But Mabel Powell's greatest monument is in the hearts and lives of her students who rise up, and lie down, to call her blessed! The writer claims membership in that alumni group.

Gladys Strickland joined the faculty at Campbell in 1925. Her home was the Spring Branch Community, about twenty miles away. Dr. J. A. Campbell had baptized her as a young girl and as pastor had watched over her during her years of adolescence and college. As pastor of the Spring Branch Church he was often in her home. So she came to the school as no stranger. She taught French, English, and journalism. One of her major responsibilities, and areas of greatest service, was faculty sponsor for *Creek Pebbles,* the school paper. When she retired in 1953, President Leslie Campbell wrote in *Creek Pebbles:*

THANK YOU, MRS. SATTERWHITE

For these years the administration at Campbell College has entrusted to you as faculty editor the policies of our college newspaper, with implicit confidence in your journalistic ability and sound judgment. As you terminate your active connection with the college and its paper, our sense of loss is painfully acute. Now, more keenly than heretofore, we are conscious of our good fortune for these years in having an important school activity like 'Creek Pebbles' operate so smoothly that we have hardly been aware of the vast amount of work involved. For this monumental service, as well as for your faithful, scholarly ministry in the classroom, we shall always be grateful. We refuse to believe that in spirit we shall not always have you with us.

She was one of two persons to whom the college annual was dedicated in 1953. The students wrote:

WE PAY TRIBUTE . . .

Mrs. M. C. Satterwhite   1953

During these twenty-six years of faithful service here nothing, save the sacred vows recently taken at the marriage altar, has had priority over Mrs. Satterwhite's self-dedication to the work and welfare of Campbell College. In faculty councils, in the classroom, and in extra-curricular activities, she has made a very potent contribution to genuine Christian Education. By nature and training a perfectionist, she has always demanded of herself and others promptness, accuracy, and superior excellence. For your loyalty, devotion, and genuineness of character, we pay our deepest tribute.

In the classroom she was a hard taskmaster. But she brought to her teaching a charm, personal attractiveness, great enthusiasm, and a deep belief in the value of what she did. She knew her students as individuals, knew their strength and their weakness and their potential. The *Creek Pebbles* "dedicated" the May 19, 1934, issue of the paper to Miss Strickland. In the dedication they said that she was kind, considerate, busy, and helpful. They said that sacrifice was her hobby. Often she was in her classroom by six o'clock in the morning. She would forego her love of tennis, swimming, and reading for her greater love of students. They had often, they said, wanted to write words of their appreciation but she would not allow it. They quoted her as saying, "My greatest purpose is to bring the best out of students and I think I can best do that by remaining in the background." They wrote that what was being affirmed was not flattery, they would not dare risk that! But they said, ". . . the height of flattery would not satisfy our feeling toward her."

The third member of this trio, Professor John Edward Ayscue, "Uncle Johnnie," came to the school from a rich and varied background as minister, teacher, and administrator of public schools. He had built his home in Carthage, North Carolina. He was fifty-three years old and thinking of retirement. Buies Creek Academy had just become Campbell College. Dr. J. A. Campbell invited him to cast his lot with the school. "Uncle Johnnie" accepted, after he had recommended several other men for the position.

He brought with him, as stated, years of experience in pulpit and classroom. He had good formal training, two degrees from Wake Forest College plus a third from the University of Chicago. He had an inquisitive mind; he was a constant student. He had a tub-full of common sense and enough courage to fight his weight in wildcats! His stock of jokes was proverbial and if they were not always new they were always pointed. His patience with a student who did his best was a thing of beauty, and with me, a joy forever. Not only in his own classroom but over and beyond he gave himself to the needs of his students.

He volunteered to coach me in public speech, declamations, oratory, and debate. He worked with me as much as an hour on one sentence. "Never mind about the rest of the speech," he would say, "Get this sentence. If you can speak it correctly, you can speak the rest of the sentences effectively." So, over and over and over and over that one sentence he would have me go.

His faith in his students and their ability was legendary, yet realistic. A few days before I was leaving the state for a teaching assignment in a graduate school on the West Coast, I visited "Uncle Johnnie," then long since retired. He was warm and gracious in his welcome. On leaving I said, "Professor, as you know, I am leaving the pastorate and beginning a teaching career. I have never taught before and I am a little nervous about the whole thing. Tell me, what is the most important quality for a teacher to have in the classroom?" Immediately he responded, as if he had been waiting for me to ask that particular question, "Imagination, Winston. You must not only see the student as he is; you must see the student as he may become."

Professor Ayscue's love for the school was a stream that ran deep. He believed in the dreams and purposes of the school. He loved its founder and had great appreciation for the son who succeeded his father. I have before me a letter that he wrote to President Leslie Campbell. The letter is dated May 4, 1956. It reads, in part:

> You will never know how much I appreciate your many kindnesses to me. . . . It has been a joy to live with the many students through these thirty years. . . . I have rejoiced to see Campbell grow and prosper. You know that I loved your father and understood some of the dreams he had for the school. You have fitted perfectly into the pattern, and you have grown with the institution. In fact, the college today is largely *Leslie* personified. All I have given to the college in prayers and service have come out of sincere devotion to the ideal upon which the college was founded. I am glad that I can add in a material way a little gift to the construction of the library with the feeling that someone may get a little stronger grip on life because of added information from a good book or magazine absorbed in quiet, wholesome environment. You know that I am always your friend and a friend of the college. And what I say for myself is more than true for Mrs. Ayscue.

1930-1940

In 1935 a young man came to the college by the impressive name of Alexander Roman Burkot. "Alexander Roman!" Did his parents have premonitions? Alexander is Greek; Roman is Roman; Burkot is Polish. He teaches five languages, speaks six, and reads no less than twelve. In his forty years of service to the college, in addition to his teaching, he has served as dean of men, registrar, director of admissions, academic dean, vice-president, and provost. He is the only man, with the exception of President Leslie H. Campbell, to be honored twice in having *Pine Burr*, the college annual, dedicated to him. President Leslie was so honored on three different occasions.

Two of Dr. Burkot's major contributions to the college reside in the school's securing accreditation: junior college in 1941, senior college in 1964. His careful, efficient, and tireless work contributed greatly to these two milestones. The Raleigh *News and Observer* listed him as "Tar Heel of the Week" in 1959. Elon College bestowed upon him the honorary Doctor of Humanities degree in 1967.

He now, 1974, has the distinction of having the longest continuous service with the college of anyone connected with it. Probably no person alive remembers more students and is able to recall their names and episodes connected with their student days, including embarrassing, humorous, and tender incidents!

The college annual says of him in its dedication for 1973: "Outside the academic sphere, Dr. Burkot is appreciated as an inspiring Sunday School teacher, a compassionate friend, an ardent athletic fan, a seasoned fisherman and a sometimes golfer." But first, last, and always A. R. Burkot is a teacher, and thousands of Campbell students so remember him. It was a good day for the college when Alexander Roman Burkot came to the school.

In 1934 Dr. Charles B. Howard became pastor of the Buies Creek Baptist Church. He was warm-hearted, evangelistic, dynamic in his preaching and in his living. He had been sought by large city churches but by choice had remained as pastor of small-town and rural churches. Along with his preaching he had taught and served as principal of high schools. He had inspired hundreds of young people to seek further education, and many of these to enter church-related vocations.

On coming to the pastorate of the college church, Dr. Howard became popular with students, faculty, and community. He had a brilliant mind, great oratorical ability, and a glowing furnace for a spirit. In 1938 he began teaching a course in Bible at the college. Of course, the church and community had a long history of dual responsibility on the part of its pastors. Dr. J. A. Campbell had served as pastor of the church and head of the school, jointly, for almost a half century. After eleven years, in 1945, Dr. Howard resigned as pastor of the church and began devoting his full time to teaching and to evangelistic work.

In his teaching his students found him a hard taskmaster. He taught no crip courses. The knowledge that he required of them was massive. Yet, his classes, at times, were close to having the character of a revival meeting. Wherever Charles Howard was, there was evangelistic fervor. He came close, with apology to King Arthur, to asking every man he met if he had heard the story; and, if the man had not, Charles Howard would tell it loud and clear. In those days he was extremely conservative in theology and doctrine. This was not fully appreciated by sections of the student body, faculty, or administration. In its dedication, 1954, *Pine Burr* said:

> With a deep sense of gratitude for his love and loyalty to Campbell, the community, the church of Christ, the Bible, and Christ, we, the staff humbly and sincerely dedicate 1954 edition of "Pine Burr" to Professor Charles Barrett Howard.

It is doubtful that any teacher connected with Campbell College ever had a wider influence for the college. In his evangelistic travels, far and near, he told the story of the school, told it persuasively, inspiringly, and with great love. Through the teacher-evangelist multitudes came to know about the institution.

Dr. Howard has been influential in another way. Early in his career, long before his official connection with Campbell College, he started a "Christian education fund." At first it was from his own meager earnings as pastor of rural churches and as teacher in the public school system. But gradually as his influence widened and the help that he gave to students increased, he received help from others, including members of his own family. Often funds came from former students who had been helped. When they graduated and began working, they repaid the money they had borrowed and began contributing to the fund. They told friends about the project; the friends contributed. The fund grew and was increasingly used. In the September issue of *Reader's Digest* for 1973, the story of the Howard Fund for Christian Education is briefly told. The statistics read like fiction.

> Because the Howards have always chosen to remain at low-paying pastorates and schools where they've felt most needed, their combined yearly salaries (she has sometimes taught, too) have never exceeded $3,000. Yet, in 47 years they have assisted 1,692 students at 425 schools and colleges in 47 states and 92 foreign countries! They accomplished this amazing

feat by personally raising and managing—in their spare time—a revolving aid fund which has totaled just over $2 million. . . . Last year they gave Campbell sufficient assets to endow a chair of religion—and they put up most of the money for two scholarship funds of $30,000 each, the income from which will assist outstanding high school students in two counties.

When I wrote that story and sent it to the *Reader's Digest*, they questioned my veracity. They did it in a nice way, but they let me know that I would have to furnish proof of my amazing statements. So, I asked Dr. Howard to give me a personal statement as to the facts in the case. He did so, saying that everything that I had written was true and that his files were open and his auditors' reports were available. The *Digest* was not satisfied. Could they send a member of their staff to Buies Creek to interview Dr. Howard and me? That was arranged. Their representative came and stayed with us for a full week. He spent long hours with me, with the Howards, and with members of the college administration and faculty personnel. He interviewed students who were being helped. He talked with business, professional, and laboring people who had been helped when they were students. Toward the close of the week this representative of the magazine, a seasoned journalist, came to my office and asked if he might use my telephone to call home base. I asked if he wished to conduct the conference in private; he assured me that he did not. Then I heard his end of an unusual conversation. As I can now recall, this is how it went: "Well, I am at Campbell College in Buies Creek, North Carolina. I've been here all week. And, let me tell you, I've been in this business for thirty years. During that time I have interviewed statesmen, politicians, gangsters, and all the rest, but this Howard story is the (expletive ejected!) tale I've ever come across, and it's all true."

Aye, the Howard story and the Howard man are both true.

1940-1950

In 1944 President Leslie Campbell accepted an invitation to speak at a high school graduation service near Wilmington, North Carolina. He did not know the principal, Dr. G. A. Tripp, but later, in speaking of the experience, Dr. Campbell said, "We met as strangers. . . . But it was love at first sight. . . . Before the evening was over and we had started our journey back home, we had made an arrangement with Mr. Tripp to come to Buies Creek to look over with us a location here."

Professor Tripp began his work at Campbell College in the fall of 1944. He taught in the social science field and was, for a period of time, head of the department. He came to Campbell with a rich background of academic training, richer than the president of the college realized. That shows the modesty of Professor Tripp. He also brought with him a distinguished record of teaching and administration in the public schools of Tennessee and North Carolina. In 1941 he had been selected as the Principal of the Year in Tennessee.

Professor Tripp was interested in the individual student. My daughter remembers once he met her in the hall of the D. Rich Building and asked her to come to his office. She was timid and nervous, was not aware that he knew her name, wondered what she had done or had not done, that would cause him to want a conference. When she went for the conference, he asked how she felt about the grades she was receiving in his class. She told him that she was well pleased, the grades were better than she had anticipated making. He told her that he felt she was capable of doing better work; he would like to see her get better grades, and then he took time to advise her how she could improve the quality of her work.

In 1958 the *Pine Burr* was dedicated to Professor Tripp. The students saluted him as an enthusiastic interpreter of dreams, decisions, and deeds of America. They said that he was a sympathetic teacher and that he was constantly replenishing his ideas by pursuing the role of a student. He was, they said, a loyal supporter of all college activities, a devoted family man, and that "his interests extend from the classroom to the garden, the woods and the coastal waters." As a part of the dedication they quoted the lines from Sir Walter Scott:

> Breathes there a man with soul so dead
> Who never to himself hath said,
> This is my own, my native land?

1950-1960

Dr. Perry Q. Langston came to Campbell in 1950; his coming added to the reservoir of courage, goodwill, concern, and over-all

Christian discipleship. His home was Conway, South Carolina. He graduated from Clemson College in South Carolina and went on to Southwestern Baptist Theological Seminary in Fort Worth, Texas. There he received his Doctor of Education degree.

Dr. Langston was severely wounded in the African campaign during the Second World War. The fact that he lived seemed a miracle to his doctors and nurses, but the experience did leave him with a wheelchair as his constant companion.

His loyalty to the college, his deep care for students, his awareness of the growing edge in his own professional field, plus his willingness to go the second and third miles in all responsibility at the college and his church, have made him an indispensable member of the college family and the community life. He supervises his students as they do intern work in the churches. He confers with them about their studies, personal problems, and careers. He heads important committees for the faculty. Probably no member of the teaching staff at Campbell College is more deeply involved in the total life of the school than this man whose body is confined to a wheelchair but whose mind and spirit soar over difficulties and handicaps. Besides, his responsibilities go far beyond the college and college community. He is active in his denomination's life; he serves on some boards, commissions, and important committees. He attends long, short, exciting, and boring committee meetings where long-range plans are made for his profession. By his side, as his inspiration and helper, is his capable wife Clara with her dynamic spirit of helpfulness.

The 1957 *Pine Burr* was dedicated to Professor Langston. The students said that this was a man who ". . . wrests victory from defeat, triumph from tragedy, and strength from pain. . . . He radiates good cheer, enthusiasm and friendliness. He asks no quarter and represents a constant challenge to all able-bodied men and women." In 1971 Dr. Langston was singled out for his excellence in teaching.

Dr. W. Conrad Gass came to Campbell to teach in the department of social sciences. In 1963 he became head of his department. During more than twenty years students and faculty have recognized him as a fine teacher and a warm friend. He brought to the school an excellent academic background. He was magna cum laude graduate from Carson-Newman College in Tennessee. He received a degree from the Southern Baptist Theological Seminary, an M.A. degree from the University of Louisville, and his Doctor of Education degree from Duke University. He had practical experience before coming to Campbell: had pastored three churches in Kentucky, had taught three years in the public schools of Kentucky, and had taught two years at Campbellsville College in Kentucky, where he served as chairman of social sciences.

In 1970 Professor Gass was nominated for and received the award for excellence in teaching. In 1964 his students said of him, recalling the legend of the Great Stone Face: "For ten years this quiet, unassuming teacher, like a skillful potter, has been helping to mold the lives of countless young people on this campus whom he has taught and with whom as a friend he had associated and counseled." They said that in him they found remarkably well-balanced elements. They enumerated moral fortitude, temper with humility, insatiable eagerness for new truth with respect for sacred traditions, and firmness in upholding academic standards blended with the spirit of love.

Dr. Frank E. Weyer is an excellent representative of that small but significant group of teachers who retired from one teaching institution and then taught at Campbell. These persons, from all indications, have often done their finest teaching and made their greatest contribution under such circumstances. While they loved teaching, mandatory requirements forced their retirement; yet, still vigorous in body, alert of mind, and eager in spirit, they continued to serve. Dr. H. Broadus Jones and Dr. Cronje Earp are also excellent examples of this fine group.

Dr. Weyer had known a full and significant career at Hastings College in Nebraska, where he had served as dean longer than any other man in the history of the college, but along with this record, he had, at one time or another, held about every other post in the college from president, down, or up, to janitor! After retiring from Hastings Dr. Weyer spent a year in Lahore, Pakistan, where he was a Fulbright Lecturer, assisting the educational department of that country.

This fine educator and Christian gentleman was born and grew up on a ranch in Nebraska. He attended a one-room school. Later he rode a pony twenty miles each day to attend school. He received his A.B. degree from Hastings in 1911—the same year that J. A. Campbell and his two sons graduated from Wake Forest. When Dr. Weyer came to Campbell, it was with the idea that he would stay a year, possibly two. But that time was stretched to ten fruitful years. His purpose in coming to Campbell was to establish the department of education. He did this in such a splendid way that before his ten years were up, Campbell was furnishing more teachers for the public school system than any other private college in North Carolina.

This "Cornhusker" of Nebraska's interest and commitment extended far beyond the college. He became a vital part of the community's life, assisting, advising, cooperating in all movements of a constructive and creative nature. He immediately felt a tug of loyalty to the traditions at Campbell and to the area that nourished the roots of the college. He found a deep kinship with Leslie Campbell, under whose administration he came to the school. He was equally happy in his relationship with the administration of President Norman A. Wiggins. Always eager to prepare his students for the present day and the approaching tomorrow, he never lost sight of Campbell's significant heritage. And it is doubtful that any son or daughter of Campbell College appreciated the founder's dreams and ideals for the school more than this man of Nebraska soil.

So came the teachers with their mighty hearts. And, with due appreciation to Carlyle, the history of a school is but the biography of its great teachers.

9.
"FOR US THE LIVING"
—UNFINISHED BUSINESS

Is there some unbending path that leads superior students to Buies Creek? Or is it just the ordinary run of school timber that finds its way to the institution? I have often wondered why it is that Dr. Campbell is so successful with students, and why they "turn out" so well. At first glance it would seem that he has a "pick and choice." But I know that is not the case; he takes in some students that have not the "wherewith" to gain admittance to other halls of learning. Reverend Fred N. Day and other good men send poor boys and girls to Buies Creek for an educational lift that will make it easier for them to cope with life's battles. I know no better way to explain it than by saying that there's but one Buies Creek Academy. Such achievements can come only by divine will. Almighty God directs that institution, and J. A. Campbell is his willing servant.

Henderson Steele, Editor
Harnett County News
1925

J. A. CAMPBELL knew that when his school was weighed in the scales of adequacy, the tilt of the balance would be in the direction of the "average" student, not the "distinguished" or "outstanding" one. "Chiefs" were important; there would always be a few, but there were many "Indians." Who these "Indians" were and what they did as a result of having attended his school was a fair steelyard for evaluating his work.

Of course, he was aware that the "typical" student is a myth because there is no such person. Even to begin a description, you would have to determine a time-slot. The typical student would be different in J. A. Campbell's administration from such a student under President Leslie A. Campbell's administration. While under President Wiggins' administration the so-called typical student would be different from each of the former characterizations. More, the typical student selected would vary greatly within the same administration. The typical student selected from among that original sixteen pupils answering to the roll call on January 5, 1887, would certainly be different from such a scholar selected in the class of 1920.

Yet, if these variations are kept in mind, if it is understood that wide differences do exist, the typical student under J. A. Campbell's administration would be recognizable by all who were personally acquainted with the school. For one thing he was older than his counterpart in other schools, probably three to five years older. The Campbell student's education had been interrupted, sometimes due to faulty schools, occasionally due to hardship in the home, not infrequently to indifference on his part.

This so-called typical student's parents were farmers; they had little formal education and were members of a Baptist church in eastern North Carolina. They were good, moral, law-abiding citizens. They did not own the land they farmed, but with good luck and good seasons they would own it within the next ten years. There was little reading material in the home, perhaps only a half-dozen books; the county newspaper came once each week. They received the *Biblical Recorder,* Baptist state paper, and there was the Sunday School quarterly and other religious material brought home from the local church. Of course there was no television but in later years there was a radio. There was deep loyalty between members of the family but all sentiment was held within strict bounds.

From this typical student's birth his parents had dreamed of sending him to high school, and possibly—a wild idea—but possibly to college. They had worked hard and were willing to make sacrifices that the son or daughter might have a chance. Once they had heard Professor J. A. Campbell speak at a school commencement in their community. He had said that no student who had ability and character and was willing to work had ever been turned away from his school from lack of money. The parents liked that. Their son had ability; he had proven it in the local school. He certainly had character; there wasn't a finer boy in the community. As for work, he was born to it!

So, their son came to Campbell. The boy had never been away from home before. He soon learned that he was poorly prepared for the school work that was expected of him. But he found the teachers sympathetic and willing to help him. He worked in the dining room to help pay expenses. He made friends. There was some discreet dating of the opposite sex. He soon began to feel comfortable in his surroundings. He was becoming a "typical" Campbell student. He would graduate, not with outstanding honors but with credit to his efforts, to the sacrifices of his parents, and to the patience and competence of his teachers. And his life, the home he established, the church of his choice, the community in which he lived would all be better and stronger because he came to Campbell.

Those of us who were students during J. A. Campbell's administration recognize that young man. He has marked similarities to many of our friends, is not entirely foreign to my own story. Of course, there were other types at the school. There were some students from homes of wealth and culture, some were from broken homes, quite a few from orphanages, and a few came from other countries. But these were the exceptions, not the average or typical Campbell students. J. A. Campbell identified with these representative students in a way that he did not empathize with the unusual student, especially if that student was from a home of wealth and privilege. He would receive and help the student from the affluent home; he was glad to have a few students who could pay their bills! But it was for the "poor boy and girl" that he had built his school. He was more comfortable with these. He would—did!—give his life for these.

J. A. Campbell followed his graduates and took great pride in their achievements, whether those accomplishments were "great" or "small." And he was never too modest to claim some of the credit for his school! He talked about these distinguished sons and daughters of his school; he wrote about them. He invited them back to speak at his and their school. In the *Little River Record* for May, 1910, Dr. Campbell wrote, after listing the achievements of Herman Stevens, I. N. Loftin, and J. A. Clark: "Young brethren, Buies Creek is proud of you and rejoices with you in the services you are rendering your Lord."

The percentage of students graduating from Campbell College who achieved distinction was probably not so great as some other schools could boast. There were reasons. Shakespeare claimed that some men were born great, while others achieved greatness, and a few had it thrust upon them. Usually, the Campbell student had to "achieve" whatever greatness was his. His home did not give it to him at birth through wealth, prestige, social, educational, or cultural structures. His family ties did not link him with the great. His parents did not have "interlinking pulls."

At the same time, the Campbell pupil did have something in his favor. The very fact that this so-called typical student could not rely upon family fortune, prestige, and influence to speed him along meant that from the beginning he had been encouraged toward self-reliance. The school made its contribution. From the first day certain lessons were before him. He was a steward of his time, talents, and opportunities. He should rely upon his ability, hard work, and cooperation with his fellows. He would be held responsible by God and man for what he did with what he was, what he learned, and what he did. Education was not just a privilege; it was a responsibility: "To whom much is given, of him much will be required." Such teaching was as much a part of the Campbell bill-of-fare as was English, mathematics, history, and Latin. It was exemplified in classroom and on the school grounds; it was drilled into him in chapel and at church. The heroes held up to him were those who had "achieved greatness"; they had not been born into it, nor had life and circumstances thrust it upon them.

How does such a philosophy stand in relation to prestigious family names and fortunes? Difficult to say. Results would differ from time to time, from place to place and student to student. Who knows why one man succeeds and another man fails? Brothers will take different roads: one taking the "road less traveled," the other taking the road most traveled. We may be prompted to ask, "Upon what meat doth this Caesar feed that he has become so great?" or looking at another, admonish all who have tears "prepare to shed them now."

Along with other schools, Campbell has a list of "Distinguished Alumni." The list is not long; it was started only in 1965. The earliest alumnus on that list graduated in 1904. It is interesting to note that two men from that 1904 class have been so honored. At this writing one of the two lives and is active; the other is dead.

Dr. Herman T. Stevens of Newport News, Virginia, lives. Dr. J. B. Willis of Hamlet, North Carolina, died in 1974, seventy years after he graduated from Campbell.

After graduating from Buies Creek Academy, Dr. Willis received degrees from Wake Forest College and Southern Baptist Seminary. He pastored churches in Sanford, Jonesboro, Morehead City, and Hamlet, all in North Carolina. The last pastorate claimed his unique talents and commitment for a period of thirty-seven years until his retirement in 1965. During those years he became one of Hamlet's best-loved citizens. In a sketch of his life, shortly before his death, he was called "one of the grand old men of Hamlet," who had been, the journalist said, minister to "the whole town, not just to his church." In addition to his major field of religion, Dr. Willis made his contribution to the civic life of the area. He served more than once, as president of the local Rotary Club. He was chairman of the Richmond County Board of Welfare, chaplain and chairman of the board of trustees of Hamlet Hospital. He was active, also, in the affairs of his denomination. He served repeatedly as a member of the North Carolina Baptist General Board. For more than twenty-five years he was a trustee of Wake Forest University and in 1953 received the honorary Doctor of Divinity degree from the school.

In 1970, when Dr. Willis was eighty-seven years old, he began a trust fund at Campbell College to assist graduates from North Carolina Baptist Children's Homes to attend Campbell. Speaking of his love for Campbell College and his debt to J. A. Campbell personally, J. B. Willis wrote: "If I am ever able to accomplish anything in life, Buies Creek deserves the honor, for it was there that I first realized what it means to live. You have not only taught me the need for an education, but that which is far greater, the value of a Christian life."

Dr. Herman T. Stevens holds a unique place in the life of the school and among its alumni. He enrolled at the school in September, 1899, and graduated in the class of 1904. He lived in the Campbell home; was, in his words, "Professor Campbell's houseboy." It was he, as noted earlier, who stood with his arm about the shoulders of Dr. Campbell on that bleak December night in 1900 and saw the school building go up in flames. Then he spoke the words that have become a part of the rich heritage of the institution, "Don't cry, teacher. We are going to build you a brick school." Dr. Stevens graduated from Wake Forest College and did his theological studies at Southern Baptist Seminary. He received his degree from Wake Forest in law because, according to his explanation, he was not academically prepared to do the languages that were required for an A.B. degree. But he hastens to explain that his studies in law prepared him for the work that he would do, the work of building and developing churches. Few men have been more successful than Herman Stevens at that task. In the peninsula area of Norfolk and Portsmouth, Virginia, he led in the organizing of twenty-four Baptist churches. His knowledge of law made it possible for him to assist these new churches in securing property in the highly industrialized area.

Dr. Stevens was remarkably successful as a pastor of churches. He was serving with the Home Mission Board, and as Superintendent of Evangelism was sought after as an evangelist in North Carolina. He assisted Dr. Campbell in nineteen revival meetings. His denomination called upon him again and again for promotional purposes. At one time he was on the official staff of Campbell College as chief of its development program. And, at this writing, in his mid-nineties he continues to preach in revival meetings.

One of the best known men in the field of religion to graduate from the school was Dr. Kyle M. Yates, a native of Apex, North Carolina. After his student days at Buies Creek, Dr. Yates graduated from Wake Forest University, Southern Baptist Seminary, and the University of Edinburgh, Scotland. For thirty-six years he was professor of Hebrew and Old Testament at the Southern Baptist Seminary. Later, he was for many years professor of religion at Baylor University, Waco, Texas, retiring as professor emeritus. He wrote a dozen or more books, contributed to learned journals, and was a member of the committee that produced the Revised Standard Version of the Bible. He was popular as a Bible teacher and lecturer.

Dr. Ralph A. Herring was the son of missionary parents. He graduated from Buies Creek Academy in 1917. A brilliant student, he went on to graduate from Wake Forest and Southern Seminary. He was successful as pastor, teacher, author, and administrator. For twenty-five years he served as pastor of the First Baptist Church at Winston-Salem. Later he headed the extension work for the seminaries of the Southern Baptist Convention with offices in Nashville, Tennessee. Various institutions sought to have him serve on boards of trustees. He was a world traveler and Christian statesman.

The first woman in the field of religion to be honored with the Distinguished Alumni Award was Marjorie Spence of Lillington, North Carolina. Miss Spence graduated from Campbell, Meredith College, and Woman's Training School in Louisville, Kentucky. She was a Southern Baptist missionary to Chile for forty years.

Others in the field of religion who were singled out for this award were Eugene Olive, pastor of churches and effective leader in denominational causes; R. C. Foster, who made a useful contribution to the cause of religion in eastern North Carolina; Millard F. Booe, chaplain, pastor, and in later years businessman; J. Boyce Brooks, whose careful, consistent, and faithful work has made him a successful pastor and useful denominational leader; and J. Winston Pearce, the present writer.

At the time of this writing ten individuals in the field of business have been singled out for the Distinguished Alumni Award. They are: H. Spurgeon Boyce, W. Carroll Bryan, Lewis E. Burroughs, B. B. Creech, Robert A. Harris, William Grey Humphrey, James L. Johnson, Frederick Ralph Keith, Frank Spurgeon Masten, Miss Irene Mooney, and Milford Quinn.

H. Spurgeon Boyce left Campbell in 1917 to continue his studies at the University of North Carolina at Chapel Hill. He received two degrees from that institution. His loyalty to Campbell has surfaced in many ways. Probably no man has served more years as a trustee of the institution, served on more important committees for the school, and given more of his valuable time to its best interests. Mr. Boyce's home is in Durham where for many years he has been in the building supply business, operating under the title "Boyce Supply Company." He is active in civic, social, and religious causes. He has served as district governor of Kiwanis, a member of the Durham board of education, and chairman of the Durham County hospital commission. An active churchman he has made his contribution in almost every avenue open to a layman in his church; deacon, Sunday School teacher, Sunday School superintendent, chairman of finance committee, etc. He and Mrs. Boyce travel widely.

W. Carroll Bryan has served repeatedly on the board of trustees of Campbell. His business interests have been wide and successful, most of these being in Goldsboro and Jacksonville. President of the First National Bank of Eastern North Carolina, later chairman of the board, owner of a building supply company—these are among his many business ventures. Like Boyce, he is an active Kiwanian and a participating churchman. Recently asked his plans on retiring from business, he said, "keeping in good health, fishing, gardening, and trying for peace on this globe."

After leaving Campbell, Irene Mooney graduated from Meredith College and was a high school teacher for fourteen years. She then entered the business field where her interests have included being head of the Mayodan Coca-Cola Bottling Company and director of the Southern National Bank. She is a world traveler, active in civic and religious affairs, and a participating member of the First Baptist Church, Madison. Her interest in Campbell College has been an abiding one.

Dr. James L. Johnson is a native of Kipling, North Carolina, but his youth was spent in Buies Creek. He graduated from Campbell in 1940. He is also a graduate of the University of North Carolina and the University of Illinois. More than twenty-five scientific papers and treatises bear his name. For many years he held significant positions with the pharmaceutical company of Upjohn in Kalamazoo, Michigan, including directorship of its laboratory division.

Robert A. Harris, vice-president of Fieldcrest Mills, Eden, North Carolina, is a neighbor of Miss Mooney's. Lewis Edward Burroughs is with Burlington Industries, has served as a member of its legal staff, assistant general counsel, and associate counsel. Milford Quinn of Warsaw has his own wholesale grocery business, one of the largest in eastern North Carolina. Frank Spurgeon Masten was vice-president of a paint distribution firm in Richmond, Virginia. William G. Humphrey has served as president of the Fine Foods Division of Deering Millikin, Inc., director of Cotton Blossom Corporation, Magnolia Industries, Piedmont Motor Lines, and People's National Bank of Greenville, South Carolina. Frederick Keith, warm and loyal supporter of Campbell through the years, has many business interests including being a farmer, merchant, realtor, and mayor of St. Paul's, North Carolina. The fine golf course at Campbell bears his name. Barham Bryan Creech of Four Oaks, North Carolina, was a builder, merchant, realtor, and a principal developer of his town and community. For more than fifty years he was a deacon in his church, the First Baptist Church of Four Oaks.

As might be expected, one of the large groups in the Distinguished Alumni field is in education: teachers, administrators, presidents of institutions. In this group is the president of Campbell College himself, Dr. Norman A. Wiggins, so honored while he was professor of law at Wake Forest University. Mrs. Sarah Eakins Spivey graduated from Campbell in 1965 and in 1973 was chosen as North Carolina's "Teacher of the Year."

The group includes the son of the founder of the school, Dr. Carlyle Campbell. He taught at Buies Creek Academy and State College in Raleigh and was president of Coker College in Conway, South Carolina, and Meredith College, Raleigh, North Carolina. Mrs. Gladys Strickland Satterwhite, singled out elsewhere in this story, taught for twenty-eight years at Campbell. Her fields were English, French, Latin, and journalism.

Albert E. Clark, the only professional journalist on the list of Distinguished Alumni, graduated from Campbell in 1937, later studying at the University of North Carolina at Chapel Hill. His professional engagements were with the *Greensboro Daily News,* the *Raleigh News and Observer,* the *Charlotte Observer,* the *Baltimore Evening Sun* and the Associated Press. He has been with the *Wall Street Journal* in its Washington office. In 1953 Clark got his greatest scoop. President Eisenhower was scheduled to deliver a major address on the controversial Taft-Hartley Bill. The president never made the speech, but associates felt that the discourse should be released to the public. Clark was selected to do this because it was felt he would be fair in his dealings with all sides of the issue.

It may be surprising to realize that only one physician has been chosen to receive the favored alumni award. The single choice is Dr. D. Russell Perry of Durham, a graduate of the class of 1912. Dr. Perry is medical examiner for Durham County, and through the years he has been an active churchman at the Temple Baptist

Church of Durham. Through the three administrations, two Campbells and Wiggins, Dr. Perry has demonstrated his loyalty to the school.

Dr. William Robert Proffit might be listed in education or dentistry, for he is one of the nation's outstanding orthodontists. Dr. Proffit is a native of Harnett County and his mother was, for many years, a valued member of the faculty of the school.

Two men from the field of sports have been selected for the honor. They are brothers, James and Gaylord Perry, both major league baseball pitchers. James graduated from Campbell in 1959; Gaylord a year later, 1960. For years they have been in the front ranks of major league pitchers. For much of that times a controversy has raged over Gaylord and his "spit-ball."

While the above list completes the names of those who have received the Distinguished Alumni Award of the school, it does in no way complete the list of distinguished sons and daughters of the school. It is easy to add to the list, difficult to stop adding: Professor A. Lewis Aycock of the English faculty at Wake Forest University; Ned B. Ball, president and chief operation's officer of Merrill Lynch, Pierce, Fenner and Smith; Franklin Douglas Byrd, Jr., superintendent of Cumberland County Schools; Paul Green, dramatist; William A. Johnson, attorney, former Commissioner of Revenue; LeRoy Martin, vice-president of Wachovia Bank and Trust Company; Carlton T. Mitchell, professor of religion at Wake Forest University; Dan Stewart, vice-president of Carolina Power and Light Company; Roy Sowers, Director of Conservation and Development in North Carolina; Wayne Turnage, member of main company of the Metropolitan in New York; R. Kelly White, president of Belmont College, Nashville, Tennessee; Dr. B. P. Marshbanks, dentist; Alonzo Parrish, education and business; and the list grows more and more attractive as it grows longer and longer.

Let the last name on this partial list be that of one who was especially close to the founder of the institution and to the son who succeeded him, one who gave her life unselfishly and in a beautiful way to the school that she loved so much, Miss Ada Overby. For many years she served as private secretary, for years as registrar. In checking old accounts I have been astounded at the amount of pen work that she did in keeping all kinds of records.

In one of those books I found a page written in her own hand, where my school records were kept, including financial record. There were many entries where I was paid for serving meals, sweeping floors, firing boilers, etc. The amounts credited ranged from 30¢ to several dollars, never enough to cover the bills that I owed. But at the top of the page, in "Miss Ada's" own hand, are the words, "Do not send statement." Distinguished Alumni? By any and all measurements her name needs to be included, included for her own sake, but also for that great group of dedicated people who serve in the background and without whom the institution could not have become what it is today or was yesterday.

A favorite teacher once commented on an announcement that is often seen in connection with forthcoming plays: "Casting problems are holding up production." This simply means that while the play is written and ready, the producers are having trouble finding actors who are capable of playing the parts. Campbell College's record for preparing performers in the art of living—both "typical" and "distinguished" students—is an inspiring score sheet! J. A. Campbell believed, with Lincoln, that "it is for us the living . . . to be dedicated to the unfinished work."

10.
"PLUS THE CARE OF
ALL THE CHURCHES"

The story of illustrious men cannot be too often retold. Like great
outstanding mountain-peaks, these men invite description but elude
definition; they provoke examination but defy exhaustion . . . we
grasp so much of the spirit as we can comprehend . . . and as
there are infinite gradations of comprehension, so there are infinite
varieties of portrayal.

David S. Muzzey

DR. C. Oscar Johnson, long-time pastor of the Third Baptist
Church in St. Louis, Missouri, loved to tell of a visit he made to
a little rural church. During his student days he had been the pastor
of the church and of two other small churches at the same time.
Third Baptist in St. Louis was one of the largest and most influential
churches in the country, and his own ministry was recognized on
the national level. But he was back visiting one of the churches
he had served in a part-time pastorate of student days. During the
noon hour one of the old men of the church, a man who had been
a deacon when Dr. Johnson was student-pastor, came showing
sympathy and concern. Dr. Johnson wondered what the problem
was. Finally the old man said: "Oscar, they tell me you have only
one church now; we had high hopes for you, son. What happened?"

J. A. Campbell was a pastor for nearly fifty years, forty-eight
years to be exact. Yet he was never pastor of a "full-time" church.
That is, he was never pastor of a church to which he gave all
of his time and talents. He was always pastor of more than one
church, dividing his time between them, as well as giving time
to his school work. He was pastor of as many as five churches
simultaneously. For many years, the major portion of his ministry,
he was pastor of both Buies Creek Baptist Church and Spring Branch
Baptist Church. A close look at a map of the area plus a consid-

eration of the day's modes of travel, buggy and horseback, will give cause for wonder, near amazement. The following are churches he served as pastor, listed in alphabetical order:

Averasboro
Benson
Buies Creek
Cannan Grove (less than a year, 1888)
Coats
Dunn
Duke (Erwin)
Friendship
Green Level

Hector's Creek (Chalybeate Springs)
Holly Springs
Mount Tabor
New Life (Angier)
Baptist Grove and Pine Forest (records not clear on these two; he might have pastored)
Spring Branch

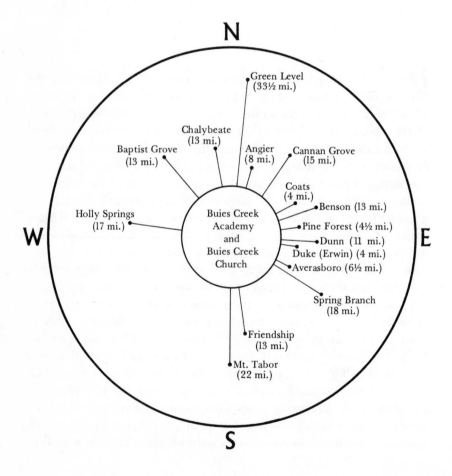

Most of these pastorates were brief, from two to fifteen years. Two of the churches had his ministry for more than forty years, Buies Creek and Spring Branch.

J. A. Campbell believed in the ministry of the spoken word. From the beginning he had made vocal expression a vital part of the curriculum of his school. Through quoting of Scripture, declamations, orations, drama, and debate, he had sought to prepare all of his students to express themselves before audiences. As for religion, to him, whoever said "gospel" said "preaching!" "Jesus came preaching." Jesus said, "The spirit of the Lord is upon me for he has anointed me to preach . . . ." "This gospel must be preached . . . ." J. A. Campbell loved to quote those words to his ministerial students. Preaching was a high and holy calling; a man should give it his best.

His ability as a preacher is shown in his first sermon of record. It was during the Christmas holidays of 1885, while he was a student at Wake Forest College. The place was Piney Grove Baptist Church and the pastor was his dear friend, the Reverend J. M. Holleman of Apex. Young Campbell's text was John 8:32, "And ye shall know the truth and the truth shall make you free." The title of his sermon was "Truth Delivers from Slavery." He divided his discourse into two major divisions: (1) In what respect are men in bondage? (2) What is the truth that makes men free? In the conclusion of the sermon a third question was asked and an affirmation was given. (1) Are you a slave to either of these (political or religious forms of slavery)? (2) You can be free by knowing the truth and living it.

Remember, it is his first sermon, so far as any records show. He is a first-year college student and has not had the first lesson in homiletics, the art of preaching, so far as we know. It is a biblical sermon; he takes a text and stays close to its deep and basic meaning. But the text is not used for its own sake anymore than a searchlight is. The purpose of a searchlight is not to call attention to itself but to throw light upon dark problems and troublesome areas.

J. A. Campbell was my pastor and school-head for four years. Sunday after Sunday I heard him preach; day after day I heard him in chapel messages. Consistently he would begin with a clear question, a definite problem, a humorous anecdote, a difficulty that was faced by student, teacher, citizen in general. Gradually he would begin to focus the light of the Scriptures upon these difficulties and help us work toward a creative solution or, if no solution seemed possible, to point to resources that were adequate for bearing and carrying purposes. His approach in chapel and sermon talk seemed to be: (1) This is where we are; (2) This is how we got where we are; (3) This is the way to get out of, away from, where we are to where we really ought to be. A large number of his sermon outlines have been preserved. These date from his student days to his declining years. Through the years he developed maturity and skill as a preacher and teacher but, basically, his method remained the same. The Scriptures, the great truths of theology, were searchlights to be focused upon the problems, joys, victories, failures, and successes of life. His sermons were firmly structured. His outlines were easy to follow and hard to forget.

In his funeral sermon on George Whitefield's death John Wesley observed, "It was the 29th (December) that he first preached without notes." Wesley must have thought it significant; so did J. A. Campbell. He never used a manuscript in his preaching; he seldom used notes. When he did, the brief outline was often on the back of an envelope or a small piece of paper taken from a loose-leaf notebook. He looked his audience in the face, "eye ball to eye ball." He knew how to put great truths into simple language and small packages. His sermons abounded with illustrative material. Again and again you would hear, "For example," "for instance," or "let me illustrate," or "I remember." Often his audience was rested through some delightful touch of humor. Clear, "tight," and easy to remember, were characteristics of his preaching. Kierkegaard said that when he asked Hegel for a street address in Copenhagen, the philosopher gave him a map of Europe. J. A. Campbell would never have done that!

To him the preacher was a messenger. He did not originate the "message"; he simply delivered it. The preacher was a witness. The business of a witness is to tell what he has seen and heard, not manufacture rumors. Something had been done, something had been said. The preacher had firsthand knowledge of this; it was his business to tell. This was an awesome responsibility but at the same time a joyous privilege, and J. A. Campbell felt both.

He believed in evangelism as it found expression in the well-known "revival meeting," but it is interesting to observe that he did not "hold" or conduct revival meetings himself. He did affirm their place in winning people to a personal commitment of their lives to Jesus Christ. He saw to it that revival meetings were held in his churches and that they were conducted in his school. He was careful in the choice of those he invited to conduct these services. Again and again he returned to those whom he knew, to persons who had been with him in services before, whose heads were clear and hearts were warm, who loved the Lord and loved the people, who proclaimed the gospel as he understood it and had been able to communicate these great biblical truths to the people. Two men were with him again and again for these special services. They were Herman T. Stevens and Fred N. Day. One was a pastor, the other was a jeweler and an evangelist. Dr. Stevens' name has appeared in this history many times. Mr. Day was a close personal friend of Dr. Campbell, probably his closest friend. In personal relationships they were referred to as David and Jonathan. When they were together they were boys again; each released in the other the spirit of youth and gaiety.

As a lay evangelist Mr. Day was remarkably successful. During forty-one years, between 1897 and 1938, he conducted 522 revival meetings. In those services 9,500 persons accepted Christ and were baptized into Baptist churches. The freewill offerings in those 522 meetings amounted to more than $32,000. Mr. Day donated every dollar of the sum to religious causes, particularly Christian education, paying his own expenses from his jewelry business. A large portion of these offerings came to the school that his friend J. A. Campbell headed. On thirty different occasions Mr. Day was with Dr. Campbell in revival meetings. The two men made a successful evangelistic team.

Dr. Campbell was an effective preacher and promoter of evangelism, and, more, he was a compassionate and beloved pastor. It is possible to be one without being the other. He cherished the words of Jesus, "Feed my sheep." Early in his ministry he sought and found the shepherd heart. When I was a high school student at Buies Creek Academy, he recommended me for the pastorate of the Coats Baptist Church. No one should question the influence

John Henry Day

Dr. Herman T. Stevens

he had over those people when it is known that I was called as pastor of the church! Shortly after, there was a death in the church family. It was to be my first funeral service. Understandably, the family requested that Dr. Campbell participate in the service. That funeral service took place almost fifty years ago but I remember. Dr. Campbell stood to speak. There was a long, long, long silence as he simply looked at the grief-bowed family. Slowly his eyes became misty, a tear trickled down his cheek, then, another and another. Still he did not speak. Finally, with a slight quiver in his voice: "I would much rather come and sit by your side." I do not remember what else he said. I doubt that the family did. But that was enough. The family knew that he understood and that he cared. "Sympathy" means to "suffer-with."

On another occasion, in the same church, the crowds had come. It was the funeral service for a distinguished and honored citizen who had taken his own life. Row after row, rank after rank of flowers filled every foot of space at the front of the church. When Dr. Campbell stood to speak there was, again, that long silence, then: "If the flowers of appreciation had been given in life, if the words of love had been spoken then, we would not be here now."

He "sat where they sat." He understood the people because he was of, by, from, and for the people. He never forgot that. The people were always aware of that. Some years ago a senator was nominated to become a member of the banking commission. The nomination had been confirmed by the senate. But the examiners bore in: did he think he was qualified to serve on that important commission? He did. Was he a bank officer? He was not. Was he, or had he ever been, a board member of the bank? He had not. Had he ever been employed by a bank? He had not. Then what made him think that he was qualified to serve on the banking commission? The senator said: "Because I was a depositor." J. A. Campbell was a depositor in the commission of life.

The same strong, creative, and constructive promotion that he brought to his school he brought to the churches that he served. He knew how to "speak to the children of Israel that they go forward." And, forward they did go under his leadership. Church buildings were remodeled; new church houses were constructed. Gifts to all causes increased, especially to missions, education, and child welfare. Youth work flourished. The churches that he served were always on the cutting-edge of ministering to youth.

From a letter dated October 16, 1905, to the membership of the Buies Creek Church I quote:

> Last year our church surpassed all former records of our church. This year we must undertake to do better things. Already 61 have been baptized into our fellowship and 25 more await baptism. This is indeed a glorious record, one that should fill us with gratitude and prompt us to greater undertakings for the future. The Sunday School and Prayer meetings have been the best in our history, but are yet a long way from what they ought to be. Be loyal to Christ, your pastor, your church and the lost.

Yet he was patient with the people. Year after year he preached and taught, counseled and wisely administered. He kept vital and needy causes before the people. Often it was years before the congregations were able to see the need and respond to his challenge. He was patient. He knew that in some respects the pastor is like a locomotive. The railroad engine could go faster alone, but its business is to pull the freight cars.

Of course, the Baptist Church at Buies Creek, the first Baptist church, the only Baptist church there as long as he lived, is of primary concern in its relationship to the school. In 1933 Dr. Campbell wrote the following:

> In the year 1872 there were in Harnett County five white Baptist churches—Cumberland Union and Neill's Creek on the northside of the

Cape Fear River and Friendship, Lillington and Antioch on the southernside of the Cape Fear. Lillington was organized in 1870 and in 1872 had not more than 25 members. . . .

In 1874 Rev. Allen Betts began a Sunday School in a small schoolhouse located on what is now a part of Campbell College campus, the plot near the present Kivett Building. A revival meeting was held in the fall of 1875 and a church was organized, Rev. Allen Betts, A. N. Campbell and J. M. Holleman constituted the presbytery. Mr. William Pearson (Mrs. Campbell's father) and Reddin Byrd were active, with their families and others, in organizing the church and erecting a house of worship. An acre of land was given for the church and another acre for the schoolhouse, lands adjoining, by Mr. and Mrs. James H. Gregory, members of this church to the time of their death. What a stream of blessing they set in motion for all eternity in donating and dedicating the lands upon which to build the church and the school! . . .

Rev. Allen Betts was called to be pastor of the church and served for three or four years. Upon his resignation the church called Rev. J. M. Holleman, who served until the close of 1890. Upon his resignation the church called J. A. Campbell who began his services in the beginning of 1891 and resigned at the close of 1895. Rev. William Page was called and served for one year, 1896, being followed by Rev. A. N. Campbell, who served for two years as pastor. The church called J. A. Campbell again to the pastorate in 1898.

There it is. From 1898 until his death in 1934, J. A. Campbell was pastor of the Buies Creek Baptist Church. Add to that the five years that he first served and you get forty-one years. Church and school, school and church, side by side, hand in hand, heart by heart, pastor and principal, teacher and pastor. They were "lovely in their lives and in their death they were not divided." As stated, Mr. and Mrs. J. M. Gregory gave the land for both the school and the church. The first day of school the schoolhouse was not ready; school met in the church. For a number of years the church was not large enough to accommodate the people. The church met in the school, the Kivett Building, using the classrooms for Sunday School.

From the same brief history of the church quoted above, Dr. Campbell says:

In 1914 the church decided to undertake to build a house for the Lord, our present beautiful house of worship. Mr. William Pearson, the honored deacon and builder for the years, broke the ground for the new house. Appropriate services were held for this great undertaking in October 1914. The Sunbeams of North Carolina gave $500.00 for the new church and the Home Mission Board of the Southern Baptist Convention gave $1,000.00. The Carnegie Corporation contributed $1,000.00 toward the purchase of

our pipe organ. And our good women, from their own sacrifices and solic-
itation of help from others, gave another $1,000.00. Much credit is due
Prof. W. F. Snoddy, member of our church, director of music in our school,
for his activity and leadership in securing the organ and raising from among
his friends $500.00 for the organ. The men and women of our community,
out of their scant means, gave money, worked with their own hands,
furnished teams, gave and gave again and again to erect this temple to
the glory of God and dedicated it when completely free of all indebtedness.

In the brief history Dr. Campbell then speaks of things that were
more dear to him than all else:

During these nearly forty years it has been the pastor's privilege to baptize
his own three children and one grandson and 1,350 others, 1,354 in all.
Many of this number have gone on to glory, while hundreds of others
are marching toward the Holy City with songs of victory in their hearts,
praises for the king on their lips. From this church the gospel has been
sounded out to the ends of the earth. From this treasury the orphans have
been clothed and fed. The aged minister has been comforted. The sick
and the suffering in hospitals have been visited. Many struggling young
men and women have found mental and spiritual equipment for service.
Many here have found light for the valley and shadow. Here we have
brought our dead to bear them to their last resting place, while our tears
have mingled with the tears of those whose hearts were broken, whose
homes were left lonely, and here ere long they will bring our lifeless bodies
and then bear them out to await our Saviour's coming. Thank God afresh
for his church placed here, for folk who love it and keep it holy unto
the Lord. Thank God anew for our young men and young women who
worship here and upon whom we and our Saviour must depend to make
this church go and grow and glow. Let us preserve for them a great spiritual
church, in which Jesus shall live and dominate our community life. . . .
But it remains for another to pick up the story here, as it will for still
other subsequent historians to write what we trust will become a still more
glorious church history.

So, side by side he ministered to the school and the church, the
academy and the community, each receiving his best. He believed
in each with an intensity that brooked no rivals. Recall that the
text for his first sermon was, "Ye shall know the truth and the
truth shall make you free." In that sermon he made it clear that
the "truth" was a special kind of truth, not simply facts, but truth
as revealed by God through Jesus Christ his only Son. He did not
believe in keeping education in one compartment and religion in
another. He was as concerned that Christ be honored in the
classroom as he was that he be honored in the church house. However, he believed that special times and special places and special

emphases were necessary. And that if Christ was to be honored everywhere, then he had to be honored somewhere. That special "somewhere" was the church of the living God. In sermon and song, in revival and personal counseling, he sought to lead his students to a firsthand knowledge of and an open commitment to Jesus Christ as Lord. In the churchyard by the school he baptized the converts. It pained him greatly for any student to leave the school without having made a public profession of Jesus Christ as Lord and master of his or her life.

The roll of the church reveals the names of hundreds of students who were baptized into its fellowship while they were attending the school. He felt, expressed it over and over again, that a trained mind without a dedicated spirit was a danger that he did not wish to be a party to creating.

One measure of a man's success as a pastor is the regard in which he is held by other pastors and by people in other churches. By this measurement, J. A. Campbell stands tall. In matters of morals, civic righteousness, political integrity, and the common good, he worked closely with all churches and denominations. As stated earlier, his school was never sectarian. But in his religious affiliations and ecclesiastical allegiance he was always unapologetically Baptist. He believed in close cooperation with his fellow Baptists. The grass root area of that cooperation was the local association, the Little River Baptist Association. It was composed of the Baptist churches within the radius of roughly fifty miles. He became clerk of that organization when he was a young man, in 1880. He held that office until 1932, more than fifty years. One of the significant things about that, in addition to the long term of service, is the particular office that he held, that of clerk. It is not considered the top office of the association; that would be moderator of the association. Indeed, the office of clerk carries more work and drudgery than it does honor and prestige. It is a tedious, time-consuming, patience-trying job, and its holder is mainly in the background. Yet, it is the office that J. A. Campbell held for more than fifty years. He never held the top office of moderator.

That this was of his own choosing and not the wishes of his peers there can be little doubt. Again and again, in various ways, people revealed their esteem for him. For example between the years of

1887 and 1930, a period of a little over 40 years, he was invited to preach one of the two major sermons at the annual meeting of the association 31 times. To read the records of that body is almost like a "stuck record": "J. A. Campbell was elected to preach the annual sermon." In addition to the major sermon, consider the following. Eleven times during these years he spoke on Baptist periodicals; eight times he spoke on Christian education; eight times on temperance, eight times on state missions, eight times on foreign missions, four times on home missions. Six times he spoke on the orphanage, six times on associational missions, six times he spoke on general subjects. JAC believed in team work, joint effort. The churches in the association were, for the most part, small; the pastors were limited in education, often their vision was limited, but JAC believed in working with his brethren. George S. Halas, longtime coach of the Chicago Bears football team, said, "Football is a team game. There never has been a one-man team. But sometimes the addition of one man can make all the difference in a team."

11.
BENEFACTORS AND A
FAVORABLE BALANCE OF TRADE

One night in the city of London—the night being one of most dismal fog—a man was feeling his way through darkness. . . . The man was reciting to himself, as he went, the closing words of Scott's Marmion. He was keeping up his heart with a song. He was facing the darkness by the force of his indomitable soul. He had reached the line, "Charge, Chester, Charge!"—He had just uttered the words when a voice answered him out of the darkness, completing the line, "On, Stanley, on!"—and another wayfarer in the fog, another pilgrim of eternity, emerged from the mist. Under a lamp they met, those two. . . . They looked into each other's face, grasped hands, passed on, each in his own high-hearted way.

Lockhart
Life of Sir Walter Scott

W HERE do you begin if you wish to write about the benefactors of Campbell College? Shall it be with William Pearson who at the close of a day invited J. A. Campbell to spend the night in his home and talked to the young man about the possibility of beginning a school in the Buies Creek community, then canvassed the community, raising $350 for the school building?

Or will you begin with Sheriff Johnson who on the first morning of school sent money with which J. A. Campbell paid outstanding bills and found encouragement? You might choose young Josephus Daniels who spoke at the first commencement of the little school in the spring of 1887. From that day he gave his friendship and the support of his newspaper to the young Scotsman and his struggling school. You could choose J. W. Bailey, editor of the *Biblical Recorder*. He wrote as eloquently of J. A. Campbell's relationship to his students as anyone ever did, thereby, letting parents know that the son or daughter who went to Buies Creek Academy would have a capable teacher plus a warm and wise friend.

It would not be amiss to begin with Herman Stevens who, as

a student, stood by the young teacher's side on that cold December morning and watched the school building burn to the ground and, placing an arm about his teacher, said, "We students are going to build you a brick building." Again, one might begin with Mr. Kivett who stood by the bed where young Campbell had thrown himself following that fire, and said, "Get up, Jim Archie; there's work to do. You are a Campbell; get a hump on you!" He then burned the brick and put up the fine school building which still stands as a monument to his friendship and beneficence.

Wherever you start, it will be possible to go further back. Whomever you list as benefactors there will be others who deserve the title also and, it may be, deserve it more than those whose names are chosen. Still in a story of the school there is need for listing the names of individuals and families whose generosity assisted in making the school what it is.

In the fall of 1900 Secretary John E. White of the Baptist mission board in Raleigh, wrote a letter that was to be the first contact with a wealthy man who was to become one of the school's benefactors. The man's name was M. C. Treat of Pennsylvania and California. Mr. Treat had assisted needy ministerial students in schools in western North Carolina. Dr. White wrote suggesting that he consider lending money to worthy ministerial students at Buies Creek Academy. When he received an encouraging reply from Mr. Treat, Dr. White wrote to Dr. Campbell: "I have given him [Treat] some of the special character of your school. I would suggest that you write to him. Put something definite before him."

The letter was written and the result was a life-long interest in the school on the part of Mr. Treat. The following year, 1901, the first loans were made "to boys and girls of good habits who are preparing for the ministry in the Baptist Church." The loans were made with the understanding that they were to be repaid within four years. However, if the loans could not be repaid at that time, as soon as possible. Mr. Treat wrote: "Many will pay it back; many will not. Yet the good will come to them in either event. When the money is returned, it will go to aid others. I am taking this money from my little income and believe it goes five times as far to endow men as to endow schools." If a student died before the money was repaid, it was considered paid. Mr. Treat was always interested in the quality of the student rather than the numbers helped.

This was the beginning of the "M. C. Treat Loan Fund." The fund never contained large sums of money but it did serve a real need for many years. The main advantage of the transaction, however, was to establish a contact and a relationship with a man who did other and greater things for the school. Centuries ago, Aristotle commented that benefactors seemed to love those they benefited. This was certainly true in the case of M. C. Treat the benefactor and J. A. Campbell the receiver.

The great fire that destroyed the school buildings in December, 1900, put this theory to the test. On April 8, 1901, Professor Campbell received the following letter, quoted earlier, from Mr. Treat:

> Dear Mr. Campbell: I want to make an offer for your consideration. If you can raise $10,000 for building during 1901, I will pay one tenth of it, or you will have but $9,000 to raise. . . . Tell your people that this comes from the North, from one you never met, from a business man who is a large borrower of money himself, and yet interested in your work.

In the *Little River Record*, March-April, 1901, Professor Campbell shared this good news. He wrote of how the letter was read before classes, how there were tears of joy and prayers of thanksgiving. But he was realistic. He wrote, "Can we meet the conditions? Can we raise the $9,000? I cannot, and I do not know anyone who can." Yet, anyone who knew James Archibald Campbell, the red-haired Scotsman, could have prophesied that he would move a bit of earth and storm a few of heaven's gates before he let that $1,000 go by-the-board.

Every gift was welcomed and acknowledged. Many schemes for raising money were promoted, from oyster suppers to "Brick Envelopes." Each envelope contained fifty "bricks." So, an envelope was worth $5.00. People could buy single bricks, fifty bricks or more. Newspapers were generous with space for telling the story. The school raised its $9,000. Mr. Treat's offer of $1,000 was the spur that was needed.[1]

The Little River Baptist Association met with the Antioch Baptist Church on the morning of November 6, 1909. Before the opening session that morning Dr. W. R. Cullom, Professor G. E. Lineberry, and Dr. Campbell were on the grounds talking together. Dr. Campbell voiced his concern that his school had great need for a dormitory for girls. Their numbers were increasing and facilities for housing them in the community were limited. As the three men talked, Dr. Cullom made the suggestion that the association should build a dormitory for girls at the school. Professor Lineberry approved the idea and made suggestions as to how it could be accomplished.

The second week in December, following, Dr. Campbell attended the Baptist state convention meeting in Wadesboro. On returning from the convention, Tuesday morning, December 9, 1909, he wrote to Mr. Treat telling him of the great need for a girls' dormitory. Four days later, Saturday, December 18, Dr. Campbell received the following note from Mr. Treat:

> Will give you $1,000 to build dormitory at Buies Creek, providing you will raise $3,000 by Saturday, December 25th. You have until 10 p.m. for this work. If it strikes you, get busy.
>
> M. C. Treat

The man seemed to take a fiendish delight, or angelic, in throwing out difficult challenges. As stated, the communication was received on Saturday. Dr. Campbell was preparing to go to his preaching appointment at Duke, now Erwin. He secured G. T. Mills to supply the pulpit for him at Duke. Campbell headed for Raleigh. When he arrived, the hour was late, and it was Saturday, but with the assistance of his brother-in-law, J. S. Pearson, he found a printer who agreed to work on Saturday night. By three o'clock on Sunday morning they had more than a hundred letters in the post office. Many of these were sent special delivery. He sent telegrams to pastors so they would have the message before going into their pulpits on Sunday morning. The *Raleigh News and Observer* allowed him to place his message in the Sunday edition of the paper.

At eleven o'clock Dr. Campbell worshiped at the First Baptist Church in Raleigh. The pastor, Dr. Tyree, allowed him to make an announcement. The congregation gave $350. At the evening service he was allowed to present his cause at the Tabernacle Baptist Church in Raleigh; the congregation gave $200. He spent Monday in Raleigh canvassing friends. Monday evening he arrived home in Buies Creek. Mr. G. E. Lineberry, educational secretary for the Baptist state convention, came and on Tuesday and Wednesday canvassed the Buies Creek community. He secured almost $1,000 in cash and pledges. Dr. W. R. Cullom, who had made the suggestion that the Little River Baptist Association erect the building, canvassed the people in Dunn; he secured $500. The Reverend G. T. Mills worked in Angier, Antioch, and other places. The Reverend I. N. Loftin telephoned a message pledging $100. Buies Creek Academy boys at Chapel Hill and those at Wake Forest sent generous subscriptions. Letters began to come bringing encouragement and hope.

By ten o'clock on Christmas night, December 25, 1909, $3,219.50 had been given and subscribed. The challenge had been met. The school would receive Mr. Treat's gift.

Dr. Campbell said the experience had increased his faith in God and promised greater things for Buies Creek Academy. He was sure that in all the state no school had more loyal friends. There were more than four hundred persons who had helped. The smallest contribution was 25 cents "from a poor boy in Raleigh." Dr. Campbell wrote, "As God sees the unknown giver it may have been 'more than they all.' "

The plan was to begin building in early spring of 1910. What kind of building? There were those who felt that it should be of brick. Dr. Campbell wrote that he would like to use brick but there was not enough money. "If we had $7,000 we would undertake a brick building." He continued, "Hundreds of our friends did not know of the effort and consequently did not help. If $3,000 more should be secured we would build of brick."

Bricks were used, and the first one was laid on June 5, 1910. Dr. Campbell wrote that the mills were cutting the lumber, the yards were making the brick, and the masons were busy at their task. The dormitory was two stories high, with basement. It would be 116 feet long and 44 feet wide. It would have 32 rooms besides the basement where there would be a cook room, dining room, heating plant, storage room, and assembly hall. Ultimately the building cost not $4,000, the original goal, but $20,000. The unit was ready for occupancy in 1913. It represented a new day for Buies Creek Academy.[2]

Under the name Buies Creek Academy, Inc., twenty trustees were elected by the Little River Baptist Association. These would control the dormitory that had been made possible through the friendship, generosity, and prodding of the school's first major benefactor, M. C. Treat.

From the beginning, the primary department of the school had been housed along with the academy. The Kivett Building was so crowded that a unit for these primary grades was desperately needed. This time the benefactor was Harnett County. In 1915 the county lent Dr. Campbell money with which to construct a building for the younger children. The loan from the county was to be, and was, repaid by teaching the public school for the district. The building was named the William Pearson Hall in honor of Mrs. Campbell's father who had started it all by proposing to young Campbell that he begin a school at Buies Creek. The death of Mr. Pearson came on May 25, 1915, the year the building was completed; it was the third permanent building on the campus. The Pearson Building stands and is still in use, as are the first two brick buildings, Kivett and Treat.

In February, 1920, Evangelist Fred N. Day purchased a nine-room house near the Treat Dormitory, known as Beaver property. Mr. Day paid $3,000 for the house and land and presented it to Buies Creek Academy, Inc. It was known as the Fred N. Day Annex and housed fourteen girls.

To D. H. Senter of Chalybeate Springs, lifelong friend of the founder of the institution, goes credit for beginning an endowment fund for the school. In the early twenties Mr. Senter contributed $1,000 for this purpose. In 1924 W. C. Ellis of Greenville, South Carolina, suggested an endowment insurance plan. His idea was that each alumnus take out a ten-year endowment insurance policy payable to the school in the amount of $100 up. In this way the class of 1925 subscribed $5,000 to the fund.

Following the end of World War I in 1918, the school grew rapidly. By 1923 the enrollment had reached 620, including the primary grades. Again, there was need for additional living space for students, especially girls. That year Mr. Day, the jeweler-evangelist, again came to the rescue. He bought a nine-room residence for $2,000 and presented it to the school to be used by girls who had to pay their own way through school. In case of great need, married students would be allowed to live there. Later this building would become the first Home Economics Building.

Also, the "Boys' Dormitory" was built in 1923. It was a two-story unit with forty-five rooms. "Because of the 'singular service to Christ' rendered by Mrs. Joel G. Layton of Lillington, North Carolina, and her late husband, and because of their generous support of the institution through the years, the Board of Trustees on March 22, 1951, unanimously directed that the main section of the building be henceforth known as the Layton Dormitory." [3]

Two other buildings came into existence during the year 1923. The Mathematics Hall, used for many years as a gymnasium, was built. A generous gift came from D. Rich, wealthy manufacturer of Winston-Salem.

Mr. Rich was secretary-treasurer of the Reynolds Tobacco Company. He had been introduced to Dr. Campbell through Fred N. Day. Mr. Rich was an active Christian, a member of the First Baptist Church of Winston-Salem. He approved of the way Dr. Campbell was operating his school and, as noted, had already made a substantial contribution toward the erection of the gymnasium. Mr. Day approached him with the suggestion that he give a much-needed library building to the school, and that the building be in memory of his first wife, Carrie Rich. Mr. Rich was pleased with the idea and asked what such a structure would cost. The figure quoted was $25,000. Mr. Rich immediately protested, saying that no library building worthy of the memory of his beloved Carrie could be built for any $25,000! He said if he gave such a memorial he wanted it to be as "flawless and beautiful as was the character of the woman in whose memory it was given."

Indicative of Mr. Rich's resolution, when the building was nearing completion, he came down to see it. On the front of the building, as agreed, were the words "Carrie Rich Memorial." Mr. Rich saw that the name "Carrie" began on one stone and extended to a second stone; the spacing of the letters was correct but they were not all on the same stone. He called the builder and informed him that such an arrangement would not be accepted. The two stones would have to be removed and one large stone, adequate for the full name would have to be used. His directions were followed. His contributions for the library building went beyond $60,000, more than twice the originally suggested cost. The larger figure resulted in a building said to be second to none in the state for beauty and usefulness for the school at that time.

The night of September 26, 1923, was a significant date in the life of the school. Mr. D. Rich spent that night in the home of Dr. J. A. Campbell. I recall hearing Dr. Campbell tell of the experience. The Campbells were nervous for they were not accustomed to having millionaires as their guests. When Mr. Rich came down for breakfast in the morning he was asked the usual question, "Did you sleep well?" The answer was disturbing: "No. I slept very little." But, he went on, "No, I did not sleep well. Jesus and I talked together most of the night. And, Jesus told me, 'Buies Creek must live.' "

Later that morning Mr. Rich spoke at chapel and told the same story, adding, "If I live to get home I shall change my will." It has been said the man was borne on wings of prayer as he returned to his home in Winston-Salem! Mr. Rich died on October 21, 1924, just over a year after that "conversation with Jesus" when he was told, "Buies Creek must live." The family found that he had left one eighth of his estate to the school at Buies Creek. One half of that sum, approximately $160,000, came to the school immediately. The money was used to erect the large memorial administrative building that bears the benefactor's name. The remaining half would come to the school on the death of a relative.

One of the great needs of the school in 1926 was a modern sewer system. In 1923 Alonzo Parrish of Benson, an alumnus of the school and a member of the board of trustees, gave the school a deep-well pump with a 15,000-gallon water tank. A deep well was sunk which gave ample water for all the school's needs at that time and in the foreseeable future. But no funds were available for completing the sewer lines and equipping the buildings with necessary sanitation appliances.

Contact was made with B. N. Duke, the North Carolina tobacco philanthropist, now with his headquarters in New York City. Dr. Campbell was given an appointment with Mr. Duke and told that he would be allowed fifteen minutes in which to present his cause. At the suggested hour Dr. Campbell was present. He had prepared what he wanted to say, felt that it could be covered in fifteen minutes, the time allotted him. But, so interesting was the story and so graphic were the needs presented that, at Mr. Duke's request, the interview lasted an hour.

Shortly thereafter, Mr. Duke sent his representative, Alex H. Sands, Jr., to Buies Creek to look over the school. The first person he approached on arriving at the campus was Professor Edgar Lynch. Mr. Sands introduced himself and the man with him, revealing that they wanted to see the school at Mr. Duke's request. Professor Lynch expressed his regret that Dr. Campbell was away. Whereupon Mr. Sands assured him that he had not come to see Dr. Campbell; Mr. Duke had already talked with him. "We want to see what you've got here and how you are taking care of it." Mr. Lynch called Professor Marshbanks to show the men over the campus. Reporting the story from personal memory, Mr. Lynch tells how he tagged along behind the three men. He says that Mr. Sands had a walking cane and that again and again he would stop, open doors to closets and classrooms. Once he said, "You can't help being poor, but you *can* be clean. I want to see how you take care of what's given to you."

After they had made a tour of the grounds and buildings, Mr. Sands asked Professor Marshbanks, "Now, you want Mr. Duke to give you money for the water and sewerage system. If he agrees to help you, how much money do you think it will take?" Professor Marshbanks, known for his conservative approach to all financial matters, said, "Well, Mr. Sands, we have a little money. I believe if we had $25,000 we could get the job done." They walked on across the campus and Mr. Lynch heard Mr. Sands say to his companion, not knowing that his words were being overheard, "This is a bigger job than the one we saw yesterday. They wanted $40,000. I think Mr. Duke should help these people. I'm going to recommend that he do it."

I have heard Dr. Campbell refer to that incident. He always believed that it was Professor Marshbanks' careful and conservative approach that impressed Mr. Sands and helped, at least in part, to win Mr. Duke's support. I have before me a copy of a letter—not the first—that Mr. Sands wrote to Dr. Campbell. The letter is dated January 21, 1927, and reads in part:

> Dear Mr. Campbell: I am again being given the great pleasure of being directed to send you the enclosed check of Mr. Duke to the order of Campbell College for $10,000.00. This present check makes a total of

$50,000.00 which Mr. Duke has given your school. Need I say anything more about the way you are operating your school than that I have heretofore said and that this check from Mr. Duke expresses? The only condition Mr. Duke would impose upon you in connection with this present gift is that you let no one outside those necessary in your organization know of its receipt.

With kindest regards,

Sincerely yours,

Alex H. Sands, Jr.[4]

In addition to making possible the water and sewer system of the college, Mr. Duke's gifts were also used in 1928 to add an annex to the Layton Dormitory for boys. This unit contained eighteen rooms. The records indicate that altogether, Mr. Duke's gifts to the school amounted to about $60,000. And, it seems reasonable to believe, based upon correspondence, business transactions, and the mutual admiration that had grown up between Mr. Duke and Dr. Campbell, that had the philanthropist lived longer (he died in 1929, two years after the above letter was written) his contributions would have been considerably larger.

The interest of the Duke family continues, however, through his distinguished granddaughter, Mrs. Mary D. B. T. Semans, who through the Mary Duke Biddle Foundation continues the interest in and the contributions to the college. In 1971 the college bestowed upon Mrs. Semans the honorary Doctorate of Humane Letters.

In the early thirties Miss Evelyn Snider, professor of English, was looking over the campus hoping to find a place where she might stage a unique May Day production. She decided upon the space between the D. Rich Building and the gymnasium, referred to earlier. The location, the terrain, the trees, and shrubs all served her purpose so well that she began to envision an outdoor theatre on the spot. In keeping with Miss Snider's enthusiasm and promotional abilities the project was soon under way.

During the school sessions of 1933, 1934, and 1935 Paul Green, distinguished alumnus, began developing the site for an outdoor theatre. He was given the expert advice of his friend, Dr. H. R. Totten of the University of North Carolina. I have always cherished the memory of being allowed to see Paul Green, Pulitzer Prize winner, Guggenheim Fellowship participant, playwright, poet, novelist, short-story writer, and academically oriented Dr. Totten in overalls and muddy shoes with blistered hands, using shovels, rakes, and hoes as they supervised and led in the manual labor required for the construction of the beautiful little theatre! In size, location, and beauty it was, according to informed critics, unsurpassed anywhere in the state. In the replacement of the old gymnasium, destroyed by fire, it became necessary to include the space occupied by the little theatre. Planning is under way for assigning and constructing a new Paul Green Outdoor Theatre.

J. A. Campbell's work was done, primarily, among and for the poor and less fortunate. His benefactors were, in the main, from the same group. He did not have the assistance of large numbers of wealthy patrons and big foundations. Yet, in the desperate hours of the life of his school he found the help that was necessary. Through agony and travail he, his school, and those who helped became great together. There is a passage of Scripture (Rom. 5:3-4) which speaks to the condition. The King James Version says: "Tribulation worketh patience; and patience, experience; and experience, hope." But another translation gives it this way: "The pressures of life develop staying power, and staying power develops competence, and competence develops hope." It did for J. A. Campbell.

Notes

1. *Little River Record,* January, 1910.
2. Ibid, June, 1911.
3. Catalogue, Campbell College, 1962-1963, p. 31.
4. Archives, Campbell College

12.
A SCHOOL BY
ANY OTHER NAME

Let him die without pity, who will not quench his thirst at the river,
because he cannot come in at the fountain.

Thomas Fuller

$\mathbf{F}$ROM the first day of school, January 5, 1887, J. A. Campbell could claim the school as his own. William Pearson had said that he did not think the community could pay the young teacher $40 per month and suggested, instead, that young Campbell operate the school as his personal project, getting whatever he could from its operation. The community would undertake the construction of a building.

Two points: one, J. A. Campbell "owned" the school; two, the community owned the building in which the school was housed. It is well to keep those differences in mind. It is doubtful that young Campbell would have stayed with the school if it had not been his own operation. It is certain that he could not have provided the building on his own.

From the opening of the school in 1887 to the "great fire" in 1900, the above arrangement continued: J. A. Campbell owned the school and the community owned the buildings. From the small one-room building in which the school was started to the spacious administration building 136 feet long and two stories high, containing six large classrooms, Art Hall, Commercial Hall, Library, Society Halls, to the large tabernacle, 80 × 90 feet, used for commencement exercises and other public gatherings, all, all this, was public property, not the possession of J. A. Campbell. He had a school; the people provided a place for him to put it.

Then, in 1900, came the fire. All but the open tabernacle and one small and separate building was destroyed. At this point another

149

significant decision was made. Professor Campbell decided to launch a building program of his own. The records do not confirm but it was probably the only way that such a program could have been launched and brought to a successful conclusion. The name of J. A. Campbell had become a household word throughout the area; the people believed in him and what he was doing. To know that they were giving to him, as well as to his school, would have given additional leverage to the financial campaign. So, the Campbells purchased from the school board, school committee, the land on which the old buildings stood. The date was May 28, 1901. The land had been given for the school by James Gregory and wife. N. A. Stewart was chairman for the committee for the school "district No. 1, white race, Neill's Creek Township, Harnett County and State of North Carolina." The price was ten dollars—a fair price as land was selling in those days. To this property the Campbells added modest acreage over the coming years. So, the fine structure, later to be named "The Kivett Building," came to be the first building on the grounds in the name of J. A. Campbell. The unit was dedicated in 1903.

However, J. A. Campbell was never interested in accumulating buildings; he was interested in the school within the buildings. So, as early as 1911 he began to place the physical equipment of the school under the guidance and ownership of the Little River Baptist Association. That year, 1911, Buies Creek Baptist Academy, Inc., was organized, with a body of twenty trustees appointed by and responsible to the association. From that date, as one dormitory after another was built, they were placed under the supervision and ownership of the Baptist denomination. From that time there was a Buies Creek Academy, unincorporated, and a Buies Creek Academy, Incorporated. The first, the unincorporated, owned the school; that was J. A. Campbell. The second, the Incorporated, was the Baptist Association; it owned the dormitories and other buildings.

For example, the Carrie Rich Memorial Library was opened for use in the spring of 1925. This lovely building was given to Buies Creek Academy, Inc., that is, to the Baptist denomination, as represented by the trustees of the Little River Baptist Association. About this time Dr. Campbell began to think about and to move toward giving the entire school, all parts of the physical institution, to the Baptist State Convention of North Carolina.

There were a number of reasons for this, some documented, others axiomatic. First, there was the basic purpose of J. A. Campbell in beginning, developing, and promoting his school, not for personal gain or recognition but for the benefit of boys and girls, mainly poor boys and girls who might, otherwise, be denied the opportunity for an education, especially an education under the guidance and influence of Christian teachers. Second, there was the strong conviction that people would support an institution that they felt they had some guidance in, control over, and stewardship for; in short, an institution that in some real way belonged to them. Third, there was the knowledge that there was more permanence in a religious body, a Christian denomination, than there was in a single individual or the family of a single individual. Fourth, an element of competition was emerging that had not been present before, namely the great movement toward a free public school system. Many private high schools, academies, were falling by the wayside; others would fail. J. A. Campbell rejoiced in this public school movement; he had worked to bring it about. But he saw that the action had serious implications for his school. His institution needed the undergirding of a great denomination. He was already thinking of extending his academy into a junior college. For that, resources would be required that an individual and a single family could not cope with. He was past fifty years of age. He had always been aware of history, of "time's chariot wheels" rumbling in the distance. Fifth, in close connection with the above, he saw that if he was to secure the interests and gifts of wealthy benefactors the school would need to be more than an individual project. Mr. D. Rich had shown this when he placed the library building under the guidance and ownership of Buies Creek Academy, Inc., that is, under the denomination. Sixth, he believed in the mission, the teaching and purpose of his denomination. He trusted his Baptist brethren.

If he was going to divest himself of the long-range responsibility for the school, the group to receive it was, of course, the Baptist State Convention of North Carolina. The Convention had already donated some money for the operation and continuance of the school, but it had never had control of the school. In the early

1920's the school had been asked to give $5,000 toward a great fund-raising campaign for the denomination with the assurance that when the campaign was completed, the school would receive $40,000 as its allotted share of the campaign. The two senior colleges, Wake Forest and Meredith, already owned by the Convention, were asked to give $10,000, with the understanding that their allocation would be in proportion.

Campbell pledged its $5,000. And on the basis of the promised $40,000 Professor Campbell made plans for constructing the first dormitory for boys, the building that later would bear the name Layton Dormitory. The campaign was not wholly successful and Buies Creek received $20,000 instead of the $40,000 promised.

In 1924 Dr. Campbell went to the General Board of the North Carolina Baptist State Convention and offered to sell Buies Creek Academy to the Convention. After full and free discussion, it was proposed that a committee of three study the property and give an evaluation. The committee of three was to be appointed in the following way: the Convention would appoint one member and J. A. Campbell would appoint one; these two members would appoint a third member as umpire. The findings of two members would be final. In the 1924 Baptist State Convention a report was given by the Board of Education listing the assets of the school. The report said:

> There is a Buies Creek Academy, Incorporated and Unincorporated. Buies Creek Academy, Incorporated, is the property of the denomination, the title being invested in a board of trustees appointed by the Little River Association. Of the seven buildings now at Buies Creek, five are owned by the denomination. Buies Creek Academy, Unincorporated, with property consisting of two buildings and sixteen acres of land is owned by J. A. Campbell. Upon his holdings the Convention has an option properly recorded, which may be exercised at the discretion of the Convention. Under the terms of this option, through a generous provision on the part of Rev. and Mrs. J. A. Campbell in the interest of Christian education, the Convention is to pay them half of the actual value of their holdings less $6,000.[1]

On the above terms the appraised value of the property held by Dr. and Mrs. Campbell, Buies Creek Academy, Unincorporated, was valued at $56,000. Dr. Campbell, true to his agreement, slashed through the figure and came up with $28,000 and his agreement to complete the Layton Dormitory on his own.

The minutes for the Baptist State Convention, 1925, pp. 106-7, tells the story:

> It will be remembered that at the beginning of the 75 million Campaign, Reverend J. A. Campbell and Mrs. Campbell gave the Convention an option on their interest in Buies Creek Academy, said option to be exercised when the Convention so ordered. Also, the Convention of 1924 passed the following action: "The Board of Education is empowered to receive the Buies Creek Academy property, should it become necessary or thought desirable to make the transfer before the next session of the Convention." In January, 1925, it became apparent that it was desirable to make the transfer because of the wish of D. Rich, who made such a generous donation to the institution, that the Convention own all the property and not merely a part of it. Accordingly, the Board of Education, at a special meeting on January 30, 1925, adopted the report of the committee in accordance with the terms of the original option which provides for such a committee. The report of the committee follows: "With reference to the purchase of Buies Creek Academy, Unincorporated, that is, that part of the buildings and grounds now owned by the Reverend J. A. Campbell and wife, it is recommended that the Board of Education pay to J. A. Campbell for his holdings $28,000. . . ." By referring to the terms of the purchase herein outlined, it will be seen that J. A. Campbell and family have made a handsome contribution to Christian education in property.

It was done. The transaction had taken place. The report was approved. The Convention owned the school and trustees were appointed. Few informed people ever doubted J. A. Campbell's sincerity or questioned his motives where his school was concerned. But none could do so now. In thirty-eight years, 1887-1925, he had given his life as few men had ever given their lives. He had built an institution valued at almost a half-million dollars, even in those days. Yet, he had agreed to part with it for $28,000—actually the final figure was much less because the completion of Layton Dormitory cost more than was anticipated. True, the final transaction, the conferring of that part of the school listed as "Buies Creek Academy, Unincorporated, valued at only a little more than fifty thousand," the rest of the institution, Buies Creek Academy, Incorporated, had already been given to the denomination, building by building, as they were constructed. But it was all the same. He had given a school valued at almost a half million dollars to his brethren through the Baptist State Convention and he had received less than $25,000 in return for the transaction. He said: "For all these years we have had an aim. It has not been to make money or to win the praise of our fellow men. It has been to serve God by serving our fellow men. To reach our aim, the one thing for which all other things have been sacrificed, we have been compelled to use money and have sought to win friends."

Dr. Campbell's next undertaking was to persuade the Convention to permit the raising of the academy, providing elementary through high school classes, to junior college status. His motives were apparent, mostly the same as for selling the institution. Conditions were very different from what they were in 1887 when he began his school. More young people were seeking education; those who were seeking were desiring more. The public school program was moving onto the scene. State-supported high schools were the order of the day. He believed the time had come to move a step ahead.

On March 4, 1926, Dr. Campbell and a number of his trustees appeared before the board of education of the Baptist State Convention. It was a special meeting of the board, called for the purpose of considering Campbell's request that he be allowed to raise the school to junior college status. The opposition from certain prominent and influential Baptist educators immediately arose. There was objection on financial grounds; it was one thing to operate an academy, another thing to operate a college. The additional expense would be great. If the move was made, these educators doubted that the school could attain accreditation. If the move was to be made at all, it certainly should not be taken until the type of school could be developed that would assure acceptance from other fine schools.

Opposition was not new to J. A. Campbell. He was in his element when fighting for his beloved school. Now he marshaled his arguments and presented them: Why did he think the action could be taken? How did he think it could be done, and done effectively? He concluded by saying, "All I am asking is that you give me a chance." The board of education took the following action:

> Resolved: That the Board of Education authorize Buies Creek Academy, Incorporated, to offer for the session 1926-27 one year of work above the high school grade, the Board of Education recommend to the 1926 Baptist State Convention that Buies Creek Academy be raised to the rank of a junior college, beginning with the session of 1927-28: *Provided first,* that Dr. J. A. Campbell, to whom Buies Creek has been leased, will assume all additional financial responsibility until the session of 1929-30, unless in the meantime the Board of Education shall be relieved of at least half of its present burden: *Provided further,* that our approval is conditioned upon the organization of the college in such a way that it can secure

standard rating with the State Department of Education (Refer to Division III Recommendations.)

That reference reads:

> Sec. 2. The Board recommends that Buies Creek be raised to the rank of a junior college, beginning with the session of 1927-1928, in accordance with the motion passed by the Board in its meeting on March 4, 1926. (See Division I, Section 6.—That refers to the statement quoted above.)

So, J. A. Campbell had asked for a privilege and been given a responsibility! Financial responsibility was his and his alone for moving to junior college status. If he decided to assume the financial responsibility, he would have to accept the responsibility for quality education. But J. A. Campbell was not afraid of the first. He certainly would have offered no other type of education. So, again, he looked to the motto of his school, *Ad astra per aspera*—"To the Stars Through Difficulties."

On March 5, 1926, the following appeared in *Creek Pebbles*, the school paper:

BUIES CREEK TO BECOME JUNIOR COLLEGE
Baptist Education Board Gives Plan Unanimous Approval

> To those who were responsible for this outcome we owe our deepest love. Many of the members of the Board made heavy sacrifices of time and money to stand by Buies Creek. Several pled effectively and spoke words of encouragement when the debate was doubtful. We must mention the name of Hon. J. C. Clifford, attorney for our trustees, who without hope of reward spoke eloquently in our behalf. To the faculty and students of the school should go much credit for the victory. No more touching thing in the plea of the superintendent was expressed than the pledges of support made at the chapel hour just before the meeting. To all, we pledge to match your sacrifice with the best that is in us.
>
> The victory won is only preliminary. We have just won a chance to fight. The promised land lies before us inhabited by gigantic problems and dangers. But having passed through the wilderness, passing up.

Another significant event took place in that same 1926 Baptist State Convention meeting in Wilmington, November 16-18, 1926. A motion was made by the Reverend A. C. Hamby and read:

> In view of the fact that our brother, Dr. J. A. Campbell, working strenuously and untiringly through a period of forty years, has built a great school at Buies Creek, known through the years as Buies Creek Academy, Inc., and recently changed to Buies Creek Junior College, and,
>
> Whereas it is eminently fitting that such devotion to the cause of education should be kept in memory perpetually and the name and work of

Brother Campbell be preserved as a cherished memorial of North Carolina Baptists, be it

Resolved, that the Baptist State Convention now in session, request the Board of Education and the Board of Trustees of Buies Creek Academy, Inc., to change the name from Buies Creek Academy, Inc., to Campbell College.

The motion was not based on impulsive thought. Outstanding citizens, including educators from other schools, had given it serious consideration. Dean D. B. Bryan of Wake Forest College was one of the first to suggest that the name should be changed, and there were others. The trustees were entirely favorable. In fact, had it not been for Dr. Campbell's own objection, it is probable that the trustees would have taken the action at their first meeting after the Convention raised the school from an academy to junior college level.

Another significant event for James Archibald Campbell came in 1926. Wake Forest University, his alma mater, bestowed upon him the honorary degree of Doctor of Divinity. From his childhood days on his father's share-cropping farm when he had been known as "the little Campbell boy who loves to read," he had been a student. Because of home conditions he had dropped out of Wake Forest after a year and half. He had done some work by correspondence and had been given his A.B. degree in 1911, along with his two sons, Leslie and Carlyle. Now he was being recognized as an outstanding educator and one who was a credit to his old school.

Voices of approval for the advancement of the school to junior college status and for the recognition of Dr. Campbell as a leading educator were quick to appear. Sanford Martin, respected editor of the *Winston-Salem Journal* wrote:

To those who know the history of this institution there will be no more inspiring occasion in the educational life of North Carolina this year than the formal opening of this new junior college. . . . It is the fulfillment of a great dream of a great man. . . . He dared to be a pioneer in a work which the State of North Carolina did not. . . . Most college presidents have their colleges ready-made for them. Not so with Dr. Campbell. . . . He has achieved the unique distinction of having built the college which he heads. . . . Winston-Salem is especially interested in the progress of this institution because it was a Winston-Salem man, the late D. Rich, whose generous donations really made it possible for Dr. Campbell to raise the standard of Buies Creek from a high school to a junior college. Another Winston-Salem man, Rev. Fred N. Day, a trustee of the institution for years, has been one of its most faithful and helpful benefactors. . . . With a plant and equipment worth nearly a half-million dollars the new junior college will open under the most favorable auspices possible. Already there are twice as many applications for registration as were on file at this time a year ago. There ought not to be and there probably will not be a happier man in America next Tuesday than Dr. J. A. Campbell—the man who built a college in the backwoods of North Carolina.

Ben Dixon McNeill of the *Raleigh News and Observer* wrote in his distinctive style of the school and its president whom he admired:

He preached to them on Sunday and through the week he taught them. . . . The red-headed teacher-minister gave everything. . . . His school grew, the encircling forests began to melt away and farms to spring up. . . . Boarding pupils began to come in from the outer edges of the circle of Campbell's influence, and were cared for in the homes of the neighborhood. . . . The circle widened. Pupils came from farther away. . . . Dr. Campbell feels that his school is on the threshold of new and greater things for the young people of the State. . . . "We have kept it democratic," Dr. Campbell said, "We have kept it within the reach of the great mass of people of the state who have never been able to pay for the frills that go with education. We have tried to give to them good solid instruction, keeping at the forefront the religious feature of training, and with the expense of it kept down to the lowest possible figure."

The middle twenties were eventful years. Between 1924 and 1928 J. A. Campbell gave away a school that it had taken him a lifetime to build, and then he raised that school from academy to junior college level. The name of the school was changed to honor the founder, and the founder was given an honorary degree by his old college in recognition of outstanding achievement in the world of education. The school he founded was given a large bequest, a bequest that still stands, after half a century, as one of the institution's largest gifts. A library building was dedicated, a structure that for beauty and adequacy for the need at the time was second to none in the state. And the school saw the enrollment of its first college class. Eventful years indeed. But the rumble of those "chariot wheels of time" were drawing closer and closer for J. A. Campbell.

Note

1. Minutes, Baptist State Convention, 1924, p. 98.

13.
THREESCORE YEARS AND TEN PLUS TWO

It is no disparagement of any other school to say that there is probably not another institution anywhere in the South that has rendered so much of the kind of service as has been rendered by Buies Creek Academy and its remarkable head, Reverend J. A. Campbell, whose influence and encouragement and the inspiration of whose life have touched and blessed the lives of tens of thousands of young men and women since that day in 1887 when he first opened the school in what was then a "dark corner" of Harnett County, but which today is one of the most enlightened and progressive rural communities in the state.

J. H. Paraham, Editor
Charlotte Observer
June, 1925

IN 1901, when he was thirty-nine years old, J. A. Campbell wrote, "Those who know me know something of how hard I have worked. I cannot carry for the next ten years what I have borne for the last ten. But, I am willing to give my life to this cause."

He could not know that for thirty-three more years he would remain at the head of his institution and that the burdens would not lessen, only change in form. But at the end of the spring term in 1933 his "latest sun was sinking fast" and his race was nearly run. In September of that year he suffered a heart attack. His family and the college community were concerned but optimistic. Headlines taken from *Creek Pebbles* for the next six months tell the story:

September 23, 1933	DR. CAMPBELL IN HOSPITAL
October 7, 1933	DR. CAMPBELL IMPROVING
November 11, 1933	DR. CAMPBELL GETTING REST AT COKER

November 25, 1933   HAPPY DAYS HERE AGAIN
                           (Dr. Campbell returned home
                           from hospital)

December 16, 1933   DR. CAMPBELL AT CHAPEL
                           AGAIN

January 13, 1934   ALUMNI AND FRIENDS
                           CELEBRATE FOUNDER'S
                           SEVENTY-SECOND BIRTHDAY

February 3, 1934   WINSTON PEARCE
                           ASSISTANT PASTOR
                           DR. CAMPBELL IS GIVEN
                           LEAVE OF ABSENCE FOR
                           SIX MONTHS

March 10, 1934 `   DR. CAMPBELL CARRIES ON

March 24, 1934   BELOVED FOUNDER-
                           PRESIDENT PASSES AWAY
                           DR. J. A. CAMPBELL LAID
                           TO REST; GREAT CROWDS
                           PAY TRIBUTE TO HIM;
                           BEAUTY AND SOLEMNITY
                           MARK THE FINAL RITES
                           POTEAT, MADDRY, STEVENS,
                           GARDNER, PEARCE & OTHERS
                           HAVE PART IN SERVICE

Dr. Campbell died at Pittman's Hospital in Fayetteville, North
Carolina, on March 18, 1934. He was attended by Dr. R. L. Pittman,
himself a former student of Dr. Campbell's. His head nurse was
Grace Alderman, another of his students. She had grown up in
the Spring Branch Church where Dr. Campbell had pastored for
forty years; he had baptized her. His family was near during his
last hours. One remembers how he died: "It was early morning.
Dr. Campbell turned toward the window through which the rays
of the sun were beaming. The smile of joy and peace that flooded
his face surpassed anything that I have ever seen. His countenance
glowed. Then, as I watched, there came a slow and gradual transfor-
mation; the gleam left his face, and, he was gone. This is how
he died."

The funeral service was held on Tuesday, March 20, in the D. Rich Memorial Building. The large chapel was filled; far more people were outside than were able to find space within. It was estimated that four thousand were present for the service. The Reverend I. T. Newton, who had assisted in the ordination of Dr. Campbell to the gospel ministry in 1886, had preceded him as pastor at the Dunn Baptist Church and at Spring Branch Church, and had been a close friend for half a century, led the opening prayer. The hymn, "Jesus, Saviour, Pilot Me," was sung. It had been sung at the opening of every school session since 1887. The writer, serving as assistant pastor of the Buies Creek Baptist Church, read the first Psalm. It, too, was a part of the tradition of the school, having been read at every opening service from the beginning. Tributes were paid by three friends: Dr. William Louis Poteat, Dr. Charles E. Maddry, and Dr. Herman T. Stevens.

These men were well qualified to speak. Dr. Poteat was president emeritus of Wake Forest College. He had been a young professor at the college when J. A. Campbell was there as a student in 1885-86. Dr. Campbell was a member of the board of trustees of the college when Dr. Poteat was elected president in 1905, serving as a member of that body until Dr. Poteat retired in 1927. It was under Dr. Poteat's administration that Dr. Campbell had received his degree from Wake Forest along with his two sons in 1911. And it was under Dr. Poteat's tenure that he had been awarded an honorary degree.

Dr. Poteat began by saying, "He was my friend. I loved him and he loved me. I know for he often told me so." He went on to praise the work that the good and great man had done in Christian education. He said, "He did not despise the day of small things. He began here with nothing. And look about you today. He knew of a truth that one shall find his life if he loses it, and he will just as surely lose it if he is bent on finding it. My soul! Who would despair of this generation when one remembers that the spirit of such a great man lives on in thousands of lives he touched?"

Dr. Charles E. Maddry, the second person to speak, was then Executive Secretary of the Foreign Mission Board of the Southern Baptist Convention. In 1921 he had been elected General Secretary of the Baptist State Convention of North Carolina, in which position he served for eleven years. During those years he and Dr. Campbell worked closely. He had come to understand what Buies Creek Academy, later Campbell College, meant to the world program of missions. For around the world he had seen those who had received their education and love for Christ at the school. His subject at the memorial service was, "J. A. Campbell as a Denominational Leader."

He called Dr. Campbell another Barnabas—a discoverer and an encourager whose record is written in a second "acts of the apostles." "Dr. Campbell was a great servant of God because he early had a divine experience of the saving power of Christ. He loved his fellow-men, and he had a divine insight into the hearts of young people. Love is costly," he said. "Because of his great love for others, he literally wore himself out serving them, giving poor boys and girls the chance of an education; verily he loved unto death. He was thoroughly missionary at heart, loving people not only at home but unto the uttermost parts of the earth. He always saw a future of service in his boys and girls."

It was altogether fitting that the third man to bear his testimony was Dr. Herman T. Stevens, a student by his side at the "Great Fire," as an evangelist by his side in more than a score of evangelistic meetings, as a friend by his side through "fair and foul" weather, with his school through good and through hard times. It is doubtful that any student knew J. A. Campbell more fully or appreciated him more deeply than Herman Stevens. His subject was "J. A. Campbell as a Safe Guide for Youth." "To me," said Stevens, "he was a safe guide in suffering, in self-control, in service, in seeking the lost, and as a shepherd of those entrusted to him." As he spoke briefly on each of the divisions, head and heart were combined in unique eloquence.

At the graveside, a quartet sang, "The City Foursquare." Dr. J. R. Jester, minister of the First Baptist Church, Winston-Salem, led in prayer. The Reverend E. N. Gardner, minister of the First Baptist Church, Dunn, spoke a brief closing word. He said that when the roll was called and the name of J. A. Campbell pronounced, someone might answer, "Not present, but accounted for; he is with the risen Lord." Then Mr. Gardner read Oxenham's poem, "Fold Up the Tent," and pronounced the benediction.

Following the service the crowds lingered. They seemed reluctant to leave "the yellow stricken sands" where the body of their friend lay and over which his feet had gone on missions of light and learning. Groups remained at and near the graveside. Other small groups made their way back to the campus grounds; they mingled, talked, wept softly, and laughed gently. The young and the old, the rich and the poor, the student and the teacher were remembering. And to "re-member" is to be "membered-back, or again." As they remembered J. A. Campbell, his life and his work, they lived again; again they became a part of him and their experiences with him.

His life had been a sort of looking glass in which they saw how to adjust and guide their own lives. Again and again when life had been hard and pressures strong, they had looked into that mirror and asked, "What would Professor Campbell do?" The answers they found were not easy ones for J. A. Campbell never allowed the stupid to appear intelligent, the vain humble, nor the foolish dignified. He did not dwell on petty peculiarities, on physical shortcomings, on erratic and unworthy behavior, on the mighty at the expense of the helpless, on questionable gain as over against honest poverty, or on cultural veneer as opposed to deep character. He knew the difference between the real and the mere seeming as few men did. He liked the ad in the county paper: "For Sale, Bloodhounds $20; Part Bloodhounds $5." He said you could always get the inferior at a reduced price.

They remembered how he had fought against alcohol, tobacco, gambling, permissiveness, and all forms of corruption in high and low places. He had not forsaken the injunction that those who love the Lord should hate evil. One remembered how Dr. Campbell had been responsible for Highway 421, between Lillington and Dunn, coming by Buies Creek. A movement had been under way to locate the highway on the west side of the Cape Fear River; that would have isolated Buies Creek. Dr. Campbell measured the distance proposed, compared it with the distance if the highway came by Buies Creek, proved that it was actually nearer, by a fraction, to bring the road by Buies Creek. Marshaling his facts and his arguments and casting all of his persuasive powers impregnated by the well-known Campbell charisma, he won his day in

THE EDUCATORS: Leslie H. Campbell, President of Campbell College; Mrs. Bessie Campbell Lynch, head of Music Department, Campbell College; Mrs. J. A. Campbell, wife of founder; Carlyle Campbell, president of Meredith College. Above them: picture of Dr. J. A. Campbell, founder of Campbell College.

court, and the thoroughfare came by Buies Creek.

They could recall that like Jacob of old wrestling with his adversary at the Jabbok, Dr. Campbell would release no antagonist until a blessing had been received. From every hardship and sacrifice J. A. Campbell learned valuable lessons. It has been observed that the great victories of his school came through what at the time seemed like failure and often even tragedy; it was true of his own life as well. At the beginning, the community was unable to pay him a salary for teaching. So, he took the school on his own; he was able, thereby, to shape and mold the academy as he would never have been able to do had it been a part of the regular public school system. When the great and "awful flames" consumed the school buildings in 1900, a new and greater school arose from the ashes. Failing in a romance that he was fully convinced would lead to marriage, he found a companion whose love, loyalty, ability, and endowment made it possible for him to achieve personal strength and accomplish greatness for his school in a way that, seemingly, would not have been possible with another. The closing of the bank of which he was president allowed him to show every depositor that his integrity was superior to any economic distress; he made friends thereby. When the state began to cover the land with high schools, his own private academy appeared threatened. But it was out of this competition that his junior college, that would later make possible the four-year school, was born. His institution, birthed in poverty and developed in hardship, learned to major on essentials and forego frills, thereby keeping student expenses at the lowest possible sum. He could understand the hiking pioneers who trimmed the edges from their maps that all extra weight might be eliminated. But out of this background of simplicity and frugality his school came to be known as a place from which no boy or girl was ever refused admittance for lack of funds.

There had been antagonism and some open opposition to him and his efforts from the beginning. This resistance was indicated when William Pearson canvassed the community in 1886 to raise money for the construction of the school building. There was one family in the community that refused to contribute. It was symbolic. He could expect help from the majority; there would always be the opposing minority. At best this group would stand on the sidelines; at worst they would openly resist. Writing in the *Little River Record* for January, 1900, he said: "In some instances we have met with active opposition, and in many cases with indifference. We had to contest every inch of the ground we are holding, although our object through the years has been to serve the people and honor the Lord." At times he expressed his utter inability to understand why he was opposed in his efforts. It was never easy for him to see that the very persons who most need leadership are, often, the ones who resent leaders determinedly, that the criticism aimed at an educator is never hindered by ignorance, that while only God could make a tree, and it took him generations, any angry man with an ax could cut the tree down in a few minutes. Yet, when you listen closely to the heartbeat of J. A. Campbell's life, when you read with care what he wrote, you will find that he gave very little time or effort to his opposition, whether the opposition was loyal or disloyal. He sought to distill all possible good from every adversary and from each criticism; then, he went on to the positive.

In the days following Dr. Campbell's death the secular press, as well as the religious, was generous with words of praise. From the *Winston-Salem Journal* for March 20, 1934:

> When Dr. James Archibald Campbell died there passed one of the mightiest forces for education and righteousness North Carolina has produced. . . . Man's greatness is measured by his achievements. . . . Dr. Campbell erected his own monument—Campbell College. His memory will be perpetuated in the lives of a great host of young men and young women who have tasted knowledge under his guidance. . . . North Carolina has not witnessed a more inspiring career than this man carved for himself in the woods of Harnett County. . . . Dr. Campbell gave his life to Christian service and to the youth of North Carolina, "Greater love hath no man."

As that editorial indicates, Dr. Campbell's greatest contribution was in and to the lives of his students, not in buildings and grounds. Still, if there is to be a school, you need somewhere to put it. And shortly before his death Dr. Campbell gave a brief summary of the material assets. He said:

> At this time the property of Campbell College, owned and controlled by the Baptist State Convention of North Carolina, consists of 32 acres of land, on highway no. 60, between Dunn and Lillington, with seven brick buildings, together with equipment, all valued at more than four hundred twenty-five thousand dollars. The only debt upon this property is $9,000, a balance due on money borrowed to complete the dormitory, payable

$2,000 per year with interest. For the faculty only devout men and women are sought. Twenty-eight men and women in the faculty, with college degrees, heads of departments with master's degrees, have served 224 years, an average of eight years each. Five members of the faculty have served 99, an average of nearly 20 years each. . . . Our student body for the year has been satisfactory, financial conditions considered. We have an enrollment of 198 college students, 256 high school students, making a total of 454 in these two departments, representing eight states and more than seventy counties. Nearly three thousand students have been graduated from the institution, during these forty-three years, and its sons and daughters are scattered throughout the world. Nearly one hundred of them are to be found in the pulpits of North Carolina alone. Since 1900 it has been the privilege of the president to baptize into the fellowship of the Buies Creek Baptist Church 1,272. . . . Our faces are turned to the future with great and glowing outlook. The glorious history of the past is but a prophecy of the more glorious future. Let the friends of the institution throughout the world say heartedly, in the spirit of our greatest benefactor, "Buies Creek must live." [1]

On April 1, 1971, James Archibald Campbell's name would be entered into the North Carolina Educational Hall of Fame. At that time not more than 500 names were included for the entire nation. As for the small and select list from North Carolina, his name joined those of Governor Charles Brantley Aycock, James Y. Joyner, Edward A. Alderman, Calvin Wiley, Charles Duncan McIver, Edward Kidder Graham, William Louis Poteat, and William Preston Few. The citation would be accepted by his son, President Carlyle Campbell of Meredith College. It read:

North Carolina
Educational Hall of Fame
Founded in 1957

Be It Known to All Men:

That, in recognition of outstanding contribution to Public Schools in this state, the North Carolina Chapter of the Horace Mann League of the United States of America, Incorporated, and the Board of Directors of the North Carolina Association of Educators do hereby add the name of

JAMES ARCHIBALD CAMPBELL
to the
North Carolina Educational Hall of Fame

In witness whereof the signature of the Presidents thereof are hereto affixed. Given on this the First Day of April, 1971.

William Buie McIver,
President
North Carolina Chapter
The Horace Mann League

Jerry D. Paschal,
President
North Carolina Association
of Educators

And, now, his body rests hard by the school that he founded, in the little village cemetery that gently slopes toward the west. A simple stone stands at the head of his grave, midway between the grave of James Archibald Campbell and Cornelia Pearson Campbell. A small stone at the foot of each grave gives pertinent facts:

REV. JAMES ARCHIBALD
CAMPBELL
1862-1934

"The Steps of a Good Man Are Ordered
of the Lord." Ps. 37:23

CORNELIA PEARSON
CAMPBELL
Nov. 19, 1865
Nov. 19, 1963
Wife of
James Archibald Campbell

With reverence and recognition let this word be affirmed: "And James Archibald Campbell died in a good old age, full of riches, and honor; and Leslie, his son, reigned in his stead."

Note

1. *1830-1930, The Growth of 100 Years of North Carolina Baptists* (Bynum Printing Co., 1930), pp. 71-74.

14.
THE PAST
PROCLAIMS THE FUTURE

Campbell College came into being because the soul of a community needed it and because there was a man who had a vision of how to fill that soul's need. From its humble beginnings more than fifty years ago, the institution has grown in character and strength, and today its influence for truth and creative living is felt throughout the state. Tomorrow that influence can reach farther still if we the alumni and friends who have benefited so deeply from the school come forward now with our loyalty and support for its president and faculty and the work they are so devotedly carrying on. This is an opportunity for each of us to do something that really counts. And that's what every man wants in his heart—to make his life count for the best, count for something that abides after he has gone into the grave.

Paul Green, 1944

JAMES Archibald Campbell died on March 18, 1934. Eight days later, on March 26, Leslie Hartwell Campbell, his son, was elected to succeed him.

The board of trustees met at the Carolina Hotel in Raleigh on that date, March 26, 1934. A paragraph from the minutes of the meeting reads as follows:

> B. H. Taylor of Dunn nominated Professor Leslie H. Campbell for a successor for his father, Dr. J. A. Campbell, and the nomination was seconded by Mr. H. M. Holleman of Asheville. The chairman awaited other nominations but no further nominations were made. Expressions of confidence in the ability and noble Christian character of Prof. L. H. Campbell were made by various members of the Board. Rev. A. P. Stephens made a motion that said nominee be elected by acclamation which motion was duly seconded and the motion was put upon a rising vote which was unanimous.
>
> B. F. McLeod, Chairman
> Miss Mattie Bain, Secretary Protem

On March 28, 1934, Harvey Holleman wrote to the new president:

> Prof. L. H. Campbell,
> President

168

Campbell College
Buies Creek, N. C.

My dear Leslie:

Reaching home this morning. Glad I could attend the special meeting. Arrived in Raleigh at 7 A.M. gave me time I desired to interview other members as they arrived for the session.

I was privileged to second your nomination—and there were no other nominations. Your election was unanimous.

I wish to offer my congratulations and to say that all of the Trustees pledged themselves to support and assist you in every way possible, and help in all ways to make your administration successful.

With best regards, I remain

Sincerely yours,
Harvey Holleman[1]

It is interesting to note that Mr. Holleman had a vital part in that transaction. It was in his father's home in Apex, North Carolina, in 1880, that J. A. Campbell had boarded during his year of schooling in Apex. Reverend Mr. Holleman, the father, had been present when J. A. Campbell was ordained to the gospel ministry and had delivered the charge to the young minister. Harvey Holleman had, himself, been present on that cold January morning, January 5, 1887, when J. A. Campbell opened his little school for the first time; young Holleman was the first boarding student to enroll. Through the years he had been a close friend of Dr. Campbell and Leslie, and he had always been a loyal alumnus of the school. He was now serving as an additional link between the past and present administration, between father and son.

B. Herbert Taylor, the man who made the motion to elect, was also a longtime friend of the Campbells and of the school. His loyalty and generosity would be recognized in naming the athletic field "The B. Herbert Taylor Athletic Field."

The speed with which the special meeting of the board of trustees was held, the dispatch and smoothness of the election, the singleness of the nomination, the unanimity of the vote to elect—all these say much for the way Leslie Campbell had conducted himself and led in the affairs of the school. There seems to have been no serious question in the mind of any of the trustees as to who would be the new head of Campbell College. The new president had been born within a mile of the campus. Other than for his years in college, he had lived in the village. Aside from his brief period of business he had been actively affiliated with the school since 1911, when he graduated from Wake Forest College. He was no "newcomer," no unfamiliar and untried hand.

Because the school term was nearing its close, the inauguration would have to wait. The date of January 31, 1935, was chosen. It would be near two significant dates in the life of the school: J. A. Campbell's birthday was January 13; the anniversary of the beginning of the school was January 5. The occasion would mark a threefold cause for celebration.

Dr. M. L. Skaggs of the faculty presided over the Founder's Day program, beginning at 2:30 P.M. An address was delivered by Dr. John R. Jester, pastor of the First Baptist Church, Winston-Salem. Afterward, there was a brief flower service at the grave of Dr. J. A. Campbell; a large wreath of flowers from the faculty was placed on the grave. Professor John E. Ayscue was master of ceremonies for this impressive service. An "Inaugural Dinner for Guests" followed. The Reverend E. Norfleet Gardner, minister of the First Baptist Church in Dunn and teacher of Bible in the college, presided.

The inaugural ceremony began at eight o'clock that evening. Professor Marshbanks, business manager, and for a brief time, dean, presided. There was a series of brief addresses:

> "On Behalf of the Baptist State Convention,"
> Dr. M. A. Huggins, General Secretary
> North Carolina Baptist State Convention
>
> "On Behalf of the Campbell College Alumni,"
> Dean D. B. Bryan, Wake Forest College
>
> "On Behalf of the Church Colleges,"
> President Charles E. Brewer, Meredith
> College
>
> "On Behalf of the Junior Colleges,"
> President Annie D. Denmark, Anderson
> College, and, also, President of the
> Southern Association of Junior Colleges for
> Women
>
> "On Behalf of the State Colleges of North Carolina,"
> President Frank P. Graham of the University
> of North Carolina
>
> "On Behalf of the State of North Carolina,"
> His Excellency, Governor John C. B. Ehringhaus.[2]

President Leslie H. Campbell

The introduction of the new president was made by the president of the board of trustees, B. F. McLeod. President Campbell expressed his appreciation for the large and distinguished group of guests who represented great political, educational, and religious groups; the assembled Campbell clan including family, trustees, alumni, and honored members of remote sections of the commonwealth; and the neighborly greetings from the faculty, community folk, and students. He said that the occasion was more truly a tribute "to the Sainted Founder of this institution and to others like Rich, Day, Treat, and Kivett who have here a monument more lasting than bronze. The events of this hour constitute only a link between a past set with marvelous achievements and a future calling for our wholehearted endeavour."

He stated in scholarly and earnest words the place and need for the junior college. He said that this, in his mind, established a place, a place of humble service, for Campbell College. He was mindful of the group that Campbell had ministered to in the past; it was a group that Campbell would continue to minister to:

> Years ago the founder established here in this quiet community an institution dedicated to the service of the forgotten man. From the cotton mills of this state and from the most backward rural communities have come thousands of poor boys and girls, counted now among the state's finest citizens. To be sure the doors of this institution have ever been open to those of independent fortune. Cheapness is in itself no virtue and must not characterize the quality of work offered. We rejoice in every improvement in equipment, and every new touch of beauty on the campus. The scholastic standards must continue to rise under the direction of educational experts. At the same time we must never forget the true dignity of humble service. In a democracy like ours raising the standard of living from the bottom is a no less glorious field of service than serving at the top. In that endeavour, we seek not your pity, but solicit such cooperation and support as the undertaking seems to merit.

If from "the other world" there is sight and knowledge of what goes on in this one, then the "Sainted Founder" must have smiled and said, "Well done, Leslie; I am proud of you." But the approval from that "other world" would have been no less strong with the next emphasis that the new president voiced. He said:

> Campbell College has been and must be a Christian institution. The ruling passion in the mind of the founder of this college was to make it Christian to the core. Loyalty to him whose spirit still guides here and fidelity to a great religious brotherhood, by whom this work is sponsored, demand

that we brook no compromise of this principle. But an even mightier imperative comes from the witness of your spirits with ours, that Christ is the supreme need of a storm-tossed world today.

He was aware of responsibility resting upon the president of such an institution. That responsibility could not be shifted. He said that among those responsibilities was the never-lifted responsibility of keeping the college upon its charted course. His would be the responsibility to see that the bad and the nonessentials were excluded, even as the essentials and the good were included. His would be the final responsibility for the selection of his associates on the faculty, final decisions in matters of discipline, and the proper interpretation of the spirit of the institution.

He expressed deep and moving appreciation for his faculty. He said that his heart prompted him to pay tribute to the men and women of other years who had breathed into the physical walls of the school a spiritual reality known as Campbell College. "Worthy successors to these you are," he affirmed, "who with sacrificial spirit through dark days of depression have borne uncomplainingly extra duties with no thought of compensation. May a grateful institution in days ahead more richly reward you."

He called upon his trustees for wise, courageous, dedicated administration, and leadership. The institution had desperate need for additional sources of income to preserve the equipment and to pay those who served an honest wage. He pleaded for their attention to be given to the matter of endowment. In hope and prophecy he stated that the institution had enabled many to rise from a condition of dependence to one of economic security. Unselfishly the institution had extended its services to those of all creeds and conditions of life. "I will not believe," he emphasized, "that a grateful constituency will fail us."

Then, in a final thrust, Leslie Campbell, the new and second president of Campbell College, sounded a note that bore a deep significance, a significance that all persons charged with the affairs of the college in years to come would live with, whether gladly or regretfully. He said: "This is no coronation day. Rather it witnesses the solemn dedication and surrender of all there is in our life to a holy cause." [3]

Leslie Hartwell Campbell meant those words, and all who knew him in any thorough and intimate manner during the next thirty-three years of his administration will attest to how he lived the words. Abraham Cowley said it: "His way was chosen, he forward thrust outright, nor stepped aside for dangers or delights."

And, so, Leslie H. Campbell was officially inaugurated as the second president of Campbell College. On the day of his inauguration all that remained of that far-off January 5th day in 1887, the first day of school at Buies Creek for his father, was the old well on the grounds near the Kivett Building. It was no longer in use but its waters were still fresh and clear. So were the traditions, convictions, and principles that had guided his father in his first days of teaching.

Much has been said and written, justifiably so I believe, of the hardships and difficulties encountered by young J. A. Campbell in the early days of his school. In many ways the experiences of his son, the second president, paralleled the experiences of the father. At least a part of the Gloria Patri was in order: "As it was in the beginning, is now . . ." In the year he was elected came the dark, gray clouds billowing and swirling from the dust bowl in the Midwest. The next year, August 14, 1935, Congress would enact the first Social Security legislation. His election came just ten months after President Franklin Roosevelt's closing of all banks. And while the strong and swift action of Roosevelt had brought hope to the nation, in many quarters hope was about all that it had brought. Eastern North Carolina was largely dependent upon farming. The area was especially hard-hit. Many small colleges closed. Some reopened later; some never opened again.

Speaking of those days the president would say:

> It was all we could do to hold things together at the time. We even used the barter system and many students helped pay for their tuition by bringing us potatoes, corn and other foods. We had to tell our teachers that if they would stay, we would have to pay them on the basis of their sharing their salaries in proportion to what we could collect. Enrollment dropped to less than three hundred, and most of the students were working their way through school.[4]

There is before me a record of produce that a student brought to the school to be applied on his board bill. It is typical of what happened repeatedly during the dark days of the depression in the 30's:

12 lbs. of flour
5 lbs. of Irish potatoes
4 lbs. of butter beans
3 lbs. of string beans
3 lbs. of shelled beans (butter beans)
14½ lbs. shelled string beans
2½ bushels corn meal
5 biddies weighing 8 lbs.

The above described articles were accurately weighed, and the young man was allowed a fair price for each article, and was given credit on his year's expenses for the same.[5]

The time came when it looked as if it would be impossible for the school to continue. One evening the president called the small faculty together, all nineteen of them. He faced them and with choking voice said, "It looks as if we shall not be able to make it." There was silence for a brief time and then a member of the faculty stood and said, "Well, Campbell may not make it but let us die first." It was the word that was needed, the articulated sentiment of the group. The person who related the incident said that in and through that experience he was led to begin praying that God would allow him to return to the college every dollar the school ever paid him in salary. He said that through and by the assistance of many he had been able to do that more than six times.

Then came a fire. It destroyed the Fred N. Day Annex, making it imperative that a girls' dormitory be built. During the depression years no financial help had come from the Baptist State Convention, owners of the school. But in 1937 the school received $14,900 from the Convention for the operation of the college. A part of that amount was payment for the debt incurred when the Convention took over the college. The next year, 1938, the school received only $2,500 from the Convention.

During the lean and hungry years of the depression one source of small but sure relief was the county school system. The new president explained the arrangement:

My father had an agreement with the Convention by which he was to keep up the property at his own risk—that is, he had leased the school from the Convention, thus operated it as a private school. Then Harnett County had a contractual agreement with the school by which the county furnished all the public school teachers, paid their salaries and also paid rent.[6]

Campbell College began to climb out of the depression toward the close of the thirties. Then in 1941 the country was hurled into World War II. Campbell College, as all other institutions, suffered from wartime shortages. Materials and effort were being poured into the war. Little or no building, not directly related to the war effort, was possible or allowed. During those years there was little upkeep of buildings and equipment. Consequently, when the war was over, the physical plant of the college was in deplorable condition. Too, as a result of the wartime draft and essential wartime industry there were few male students. The enrollment of women increased and some of these had to be housed in the annex of the boys' dormitory.

Then came the end; the war was over in 1945. Now the veterans wanted "in." They crowded classrooms and called for dormitory space. The first step was to remove the public school classes from the campus. Since the opening of the Kivett Building in 1903, the public school had called it home. The contract that the school had with the county school system came to an end. A public school building was erected in Buies Creek from county and state funds. This ended a source of income to the school, but it also eliminated what had often been a source of irritation and controversy related to the doctrine of the "separation of church and state." And there was additional space for college students. It looked as if the school at last had the green light for advancement. But just as the college began to accelerate, another serious obstacle loomed in its path.

In Greensboro on July 30, 1946, the Baptist State Convention voted to accept the financial offer from the Z. Smith Reynolds Foundation, Inc. and move Wake Forest College to Winston-Salem.[7] That meant good news and bad news for Campbell College. First the bad news; good news later. With the removal of Wake Forest College the old campus in the town of Wake Forest would need to be reassigned for usefulness or disposed of. It was a valuable piece of property with associations and traditions clustering about it.

The session of the Convention that voted to move Wake Forest College voted to offer the old campus for a junior college. There seems to have been no clear idea as to what would be involved in such a decision nor how the decision could be implemented and brought to fruition. Immediately various ideas were projected as the pages of the *Biblical Recorder* became the forum. There were those who felt, from the beginning, that the property should be used for a Southern Baptist seminary. There were seminaries at Louisville, Kentucky; Fort Worth, Texas; New Orleans, Louisiana; Kansas City, Missouri; and Berkeley, California. There was no seminary on the East coast. One was needed, and now was the time to get it. Among persons advocating this position were W. K. McGee, Perry Crouch, and Nane Starnes.[8] It was proposed that the property be given to the Negro Baptists of North Carolina.[9] Dr. George W. Paschal proposed that the property be used for a great secondary school patterned along the line of the fine preparatory schools for boys in New England and the north. He would let the choice students go to the public schools for their first two years of work and then come to the Wake Forest school for the final and finest preparation that could be secured for the superior colleges and universities of the country.[10]

But the Convention had said the property was to be offered for a junior college. That action was on the records. Then on November 13, 1946, M. A. Huggins, General Secretary of the Baptist State Convention, had a strong article in the *Recorder* giving his support to the junior college idea. He proposed that Campbell, Chowan, and Wingate give up their present locations, move to the Wake Forest campus and form from the three schools one strong junior college. It was not the first time this idea had been proposed, but the fact that Secretary Huggins now endorsed the idea gave it added weight.

While the typical Baptist in North Carolina could view the whole matter with relative objectivity, that was not the case with President Leslie Campbell. His life was so involved with the life of the school that even he could not tell where one stopped and the other began. As stated, the physical equipment at Campbell was in serious need of repair and upgrading. The faculty needed enlarging and academic improvement. Veterans were crowding the doors. But how could any of this be done? It all called for money, great sums of money. Who would give significant amounts of money to an institution when the parent institution, the Baptist State Convention, was seriously considering closing the school and moving it to another location? Even if the president of the school, his trustees, and friends were far-sighted, or foolish, enough to believe that the school would not be moved, large contributors would certainly hesitate to commit their resources until the question had been finally resolved. The records show that from the beginning of the war in 1941 to the final decision on the disposition of the old Wake Forest property, only one building was constructed at Campbell, Britt Dormitory in 1948.

President Leslie Campbell was caught-in-the-middle. He felt a special responsibility for the school. He was a servant and employee of the Baptist State Convention. All of his roots, traditions, and heritage were at Buies Creek. Yet, he wanted to fairly represent the wishes of the Baptists of North Carolina. He conferred with the members of the committee appointed by the Baptist State Convention to bring recommendations as to the disposition of the Wake Forest property. He listened to his neighbors and friends in the Buies Creek area. Of course, the reaction here was to strongly oppose moving the college from Harnett County. An editorial in the *Harnett County News* for December 1, 1949, is typical:

> When it comes to the actual moving of Campbell College out of Harnett, away, even, from the very spot where Dr. James Archibald Campbell put it, the *News* is dead set against it . . . as our friends might expect us to be. . . . There are others, many, in Harnett County who feel as we do about the matter. We have heard it said that if Dr. Campbell were living today he would agree to abide by the decision of the State Convention in seeking the removal of his college to Wake Forest. Maybe so. But we doubt it. Dr. Campbell held in his heart and soul a great love for his school as it was when he departed for the Good Heaven, and where he stands now. . . . No, Campbell College should not be moved! It's a monument, and it's a dreary practice to move monuments.

In 1949 the Baptist State Convention voted that the Wake Forest College property be used for a strong junior college and the Convention registered its sentiment to ask Campbell, Wingate, and Chowan to form this new institution. This seemed fairly definite. Although the Convention had not given a final verdict about the removal of the three schools, it had only registered its sentiment. And it was well known that movements and discussions were continuing to other ends.

Then, finally, at a special called meeting in Charlotte, April 27,

1950, the North Carolina Baptist State Convention voted to rescind the motion it had passed saying that the old Wake Forest property should be used for a junior college. The Convention then voted that the Wake Forest property be offered to the Southern Baptist Convention for the purpose of establishing a seminary. The Southern Baptist Convention accepted this offer.

So, finally, the matter was settled. Campbell College would not be moved from its ancient spot in Harnett County. The new president, Leslie Campbell, had endured, endured the lean and hungry days of depression, the hot winds of a burned dormitory, the devastating destruction of war, and the debilitating indecision caused by the controversy over what to do with the old Wake Forest property. The Baptist State Convention was beginning, modestly, but beginning, to assist the college financially. It was time for a forward thrust, an aggressive building program, and a general upgrading of the quality of education at his beloved school. The next quarter of a century would see what was close to an unparalleled development. A closer look at the man who would head this foreward movement is in order.

Notes

1. Archives, Campbell College.
2. Ibid.
3. Archives, Campbell College (A copy of the Inaugural Address preserved).
4. Archives.
5. Archives.
6. Archives.
7. Minutes, Baptist State Convention, appropriate years.
8. *Biblical Recorder,* February 11, 1948, February 19, 1947.
9. Ibid, October 9, 1946.
10. Ibid, October 16, 1946.

15.
BUILDING ON
THE HUMAN HEART

Better that we should know a painter only through his vision or a poet by his song, than that the image of a great man should be marred and made mean by the clumsy geniality of good intentions.

Oscar Wilde

AN ancient Chinese proverb says that wherever an uncle kisses a nephew for the first time there shall he gain special ability. For example, should the uncle kiss the nephew on the forehead the child might become a great thinker; if on the throat, a great singer; if on the foot, a great runner. Where did the uncle place his kiss on Leslie Campbell?

In him the elements were mixed. He had the hands of a farmer and the eyes of a poet and mystic. He had the grin of a comic jester, but he often had the stance and stare of an Old Testament prophet. His endowment included no particular charisma, but his clarity of thought and directness of speech compelled attention. He loved peace and he sought harmony but he was no stranger to warfare; with extended nostrils, piercing eyes, and humped shoulders he reminded you of a determined football lineman ready for a do-or-die stand. He was a good husband, a concerned father, a loyal citizen, a wise educator, a determined builder, a successful president, a devoted churchman. And, he was a practical dreamer.

Leslie Campbell had a goodly heritage and he was grateful for it; increasingly grateful as he grew older. Following his retirement he and Mrs. Campbell took a trip to Europe. The highlight of their travel for him was their visit to Scotland. He wrote from Edinburgh of being aware of "those far off days when chivalry and knighthood were in flower." They stayed at the Caledonian Hotel in Edinburgh. He quoted from Scott, "O Caledonia! Stern and wild. . . . Land

180

of mountain and the flood. Land of my sires." He was thrilled by an invitation from the Duke of Argyll, ancestral home of the Campbells, to visit him. In *The Highland Call,* Paul Green has Peggy MacNeill say, speaking of her loyalty to the Scottish clans and their traditions:

> . . . the strength of my people, all their history and glory grips me. . . . You don't know what it means, this clan feeling . . . this kinship. Back in Scotland they knew what it was, they still know what it is. It's something that holds these Highlands together stronger than life, stronger than death.

Leslie Campbell could appreciate that.

His gratitude for and his loyalty to his parents were well known. In his inaugural address he referred to "the sainted founder of this institution." He spoke of the difficulties that faced the new administration, but he said, "Fortunately, a rather intimate and extended association with our Founder-President, a genuine feeling of veneration well becoming in a son for a noble father, and a knowledge of the past struggles of this institution offer a profitable basis for shaping a future policy."

He was grateful for the traditions of the school. He knew impatience. There had been times of rebellion on his part over what he thought were ways and methods that needed changing. This did not mean a lack of appreciation for what had gone before. In the early 1960's Campbell College experienced some unrest among its students, much less than many colleges and universities, but some unrest. The students were demanding changes, quick and drastic. The president faced the issue. To his trustees on July 26, 1962, he said:

> Some laws and customs, like style in clothing that changes overnight, are of little consequence. In my opinion, however, Campbell College possesses sacred traditions and behaviour patterns that must not rely for preservation upon the popular vote of any single student generation. In other words, I am convinced that privileges granted must, in so far as possible, meet the test of consistency with demands of the college program upon the student, the willingness of the student to accept responsibility for the wise use of such privileges by the group, and the broad cultural and spiritual objectives of the college.

There speaks, in restrained and cultural tones, a spiritual descendant of old Naboth, saying to the young Ahab: "God forbid that I should give the inheritance of my fathers unto thee!"

Leslie Hartwell Campbell was born at Buies Creek on April 3, 1892. His schooling, until college, was received at Buies Creek Academy. In the fall of 1908 he and his brother Carlyle, entered Wake Forest College. They roomed together, took the same courses, graduated in three years, each magna cum laude. Majoring in social studies, Leslie received his A. B. degree in 1911. The following letter indicates his interest:

Dear Homefolks:

This is Sunday night. We are well and hope you all are. Hope you have had a pleasant time today. I have had a fine time. After Sunday School and preaching this A.M., I got the best dinner I've had since I've been up here. We had chicken, banana cream, Irish potatoes, and several good things.

Well this has been a notable week. The debate Thursday night was fine. The Randolph-Macon fellows were simply outclassed. They were very young and I suppose inexperienced. When the decision was rendered, three in favor of the Negative, the fellows just went wild almost. I have heard of great enthusiasm before but I've never seen anything to equal this. The fellows jumped over the seats, ran to the rostrum and got Collins and Martin on their shoulders and this continued for many minutes. When they finally got out then they paraded the streets; stormed the B. U. W. and played all manner of things. Some of us got home on a fast train which consented to stop. When we got here we found the fellows that had remained (there were only about a dozen) had found some barrels and had them afire along the walk up to the dormitory and library buildings. Just between the two was a great heap of wood blazing as high as the buildings.

The next day there was no school. Had a mass meeting at nine o'clock to prepare for the coming of the speakers on train #38. We got dinner at 11:30 in order to get there on time. After we got down to the depot all the students lined up in single columns on each side of the walk from the train into the campus. Several marshalls were appointed to place the speakers and Dr. Poteat in the carriage which was placed just inside the campus. The carriage and wheels were ornamented with old gold and black. There were four horses all covered almost with old gold and black; on the two foremost sat the stately person of Dr. Tom and Uncle Jake. After the speakers and Dr. Poteat had been placed in the carriages we all followed them up faculty avenue up to the Athletic Park and then back to the big chapel. Where after a short speech by Dr. Poteat, Dr. Lynch followed in a very witty speech which I suppose you saw in the *News and Observer*. Then the alternate speaker Hipps was called and then came the speakers, Collins and Martin. This ended the program. The students rose up and called for Prof. Carlyle but he said he was suffering from headache and wouldn't speak.

This ended the great celebration. I never have seen anything like it.

Your Boy,
Leslie

In 1916 he was awarded the M. A. degree. Later he did graduate work at the University of North Carolina and at Columbia University. Wake Forest awarded him the honorary LL.D. degree in 1955.

Following his graduation from Wake Forest in 1911 both he and his brother Carlyle returned to Buies Creek Academy to teach. They were warned against doing this by one of their college professors, who said: "Now, boys, let me give you some advice. Your father will want you to come back to the school and settle down there and teach. If you do you will never be anything but 'Leslie and Carlyle' all your lives. You will be just 'J. A. Campbell's boys.'" But they did return, apparently had never seriously considered doing anything different. As stated, neither had a regular salary. They lived at home, taught in the school, and went to their father for money whenever they needed it just as they had done before leaving home for college. It is interesting to note that while Leslie and Carlyle were at Wake Forest, each was given the authority to write checks, according to need, on the father's bank account. Interesting, too, that Leslie's handwriting was so similar to that of his father's that no one, not even the father, could distinguish between signatures! Both were young: Leslie was eighteen, Carlyle was only sixteen. Still, to be college graduates, teaching, with no salary but simply drawing on their father as the need arose, is unusual and shows something of the relationship that existed between parents and children.

Leslie began his teaching with the eighth grade but he taught "up-and-down-the-line" wherever he was needed. With a brief interruption in business, about three years, and for further schooling, he gave his full attention to teaching until 1926. That was the date the academy became a junior college. Leslie then became dean but continued to teach. He was dean from 1926 to 1934, the date when, on the death of his father, he became president of the school. He was president from 1934 to 1967, a period of thirty-three years. His father had headed the school for forty-seven years. But in terms of total service, Leslie had the longer tenure. He was with the school a total of fifty-six years, with time out for the brief business interlude.

In 1914 he was married to Viola Haire who lived only a few

years. One child, a son, A. Hartwell Campbell, was born. In 1925 Leslie married Ora Green, a teacher in the academy and a native of Harnett County. To this union four children were born: Catherine McLean, Elizabeth Pearson, Ora Green, and James Archibald Campbell.

The new president was an active and practicing Christian. He had deep convictions and rich emotions, but he seldom traded on sentiment. To him religion was a way of life growing out of deep and abiding principles that were anchored in a personal relationship with Jesus Christ. This relationship and these convictions did not need to be paraded; they needed only to be lived. They were to influence and guide every phase of a man's life and conduct. He believed in the place and significance of the local church. During his life he held about every office and place of leadership open to a layman: Sunday School teacher, superintendent, deacon, chairman of large and small committees. He was active in the local association and was its moderator for seventeen years. Wider fields claimed his time and talents, in 1930 he was vice-president of the Baptist State Convention. There was never any question in his mind that Campbell College should be a Christian institution and therefore different from schools that were not religiously oriented.

In his report to the board of trustees on July 26, 1962, he asked that they not be unmindful of the almost certain fact that the school would have ceased to exist but for the affiliation with the Baptist State Convention. He said that he was equally sure that the school, at that time, could not long exist but for the generous support that it received from a uniformly benevolent denomination. He said he hoped the school ever merited that loyal support by faithfully "supporting all other agencies of the Convention in the promotion of every Christian endeavor."

In 1966, when his desire to retire had been made known, he was asked by the trustees of the college to address them on "Campbell's Future." He agreed and on May 18 he said:

> In some way the ideals, affections, resolves and will power of coming generations of youth must be lifted. I know of no such regenerating dynamic to be found outside the Christian concept. If Campbell College and other church-related colleges fail in their Christian witness, the future of the church and our whole society may well be in jeopardy.

That Pegasus principle was disciplined and harnessed to the plow of everyday practice for Leslie Campbell. During my own student days at Campbell I saw it in operation. A series of revival services was being conducted on the campus. Shortly before, a serious problem had arisen in the life of the school. It concerned students, faculty, and administration. Feelings of anger and rebellion ran high. The visiting minister for the revival services preached a message of "good news and good will," but the students were not hearing the message. Ears were closed to love and forgiveness; retaliation was uppermost in their thinking. We came to the last day of the public services. A group of students was asked to meet with "Professor Leslie" in one of the Society Halls during the hour of worship. The memory of that hour has remained fresh with me through the years. Our leader revealed his deepest desires to us that day. He spoke freely of how disturbed he was over the atmosphere and spirit on the campus, how important it was that we know love and good will, that we experience and grant forgiveness, that the gospel of Christ be heard and accepted. He told us that he frankly did not know where the blame for our current problem should be placed; he felt that we had reached a point where that was not the issue. It was, rather, who was willing to go the "second mile" in magnanimity. He was perfectly willing to accept total blame for the unfortunate situation; would we join him in that spirit? We would and we did. Result? During that very hour a dramatic change came over the service of worship that was then in progress; lives were transformed. The campus knew a new birth of freedom, good will, and caring. The Pegasus of high principles was pulling the plow of practical Christianity on our campus, and Leslie Campbell was between the plow handles.

The man was honest and truthful. He played by the rules and he wanted others to do likewise. When one of his peers failed to do so, especially if that peer was a professed follower of Jesus Christ, Leslie Campbell was deeply disturbed. His honesty and truthfulness went beyond the academic and philosophical, reaching out into business and commercial affairs. His brief business venture has been referred to. He opened a general mercantile store and, close by, a drug store. Neither undertaking was successful. He decided to give up the venture and return to teaching. But there were those who had put money into the business undertaking, believing in Leslie Campbell even if they had questions about his business pursuits. He personally assumed full and complete responsibility, saw to it that no contributor lost a dollar on the venture; although, it took him years to discharge all obligations.

He stood by his teachers, academically. Once a teacher was selected, a teacher with Christian principles and commitment, that instructor had Leslie Campbell's support. He defended his teachers against criticism and pressure from without and from within the school. This often cost him but he stood his ground. He wanted teachers who were Christian, responsible individuals; then he wanted them to be free to pursue truth as they saw it. This did not mean that he was insensitive and unguarded about what was taught. Under certain conditions, he could be demanding; he felt that this was his responsibility. Having assumed that responsibility himself, he did not welcome it from others.

A teacher who was on the faculty before Leslie Campbell became president and remained on the faculty throughout his entire tenure as president says that the outstanding characteristic of his life and his administration was vision. He was a dreamer. "Behold this dreamer cometh," was said of young Joseph in the Bible story; it might have been restated of Leslie Campbell. His visions and dreams occasionally produced problems for him, even as they did for Joseph, for dreamers are not always practical. The person who follows a vision may not be appreciated by the persons or trustees who have to translate the vision into bricks and stones and buildings. He once said, "To plan too small for the future of the college may be as reprehensible as to plan too optimistically." He believed that. And all who know the history of the school would admit— perhaps grudgingly—that but for Leslie Campbell's visions and dreams, visions and dreams that trustees and business associates often deplored, much of the upgrading and expansion of the school would never have become a reality. Arthur O'Shaughnessy saw it: "We are the dreamers of dreams. World-loosers and world-shakers. . . . Yet we are the movers and the shakers of the world forever, it seems." And, with visions, dreams, and shakings, the college did move forward.

Observe: 1934, Paul Green Outdoor Theatre;[1] 1937, Fred N. Day, central section;[2] 1940, Remainder of D. Rich bequest;[3] 1946, B. Herbert Taylor Athletic Field;[4] 1947-48, Britt Dormitory opened;[5] 1952, Carter Gymnasium;[6] 1954, Jones Hall;[7] 1955, Blackmon-Hatch Carillon and Kitchin Dormitory; [8] & [9] 1956, Size of library increased; [10] 1957, Marshbanks Dining Hall renovated; [11] 1959, Baldwin Dormitory for Men;[12] 1959, Campbelltown Apartments;[13] 1960, John S. Pearson Infirmary;[14] 1960, Powell Dormitory;[15] 1960, Erwin Forest;[16] 1961, James E. and Mary Z. Bryan Hall;[17] 1961, James A. Campbell Administration Building;[18] 1962, Strickland Hall;[19] 1962, Saul's Hall;[20] 1962, Leslie Hartwell Campbell Hall of Science;[21] 1963, Turner Chapel;[22] 1963-64, Music Buildings;[23] 1963, Northeast Hall;[24] 1964, Baggett Acres;[25] 1964, Tyner Chair of Bible;[26] 1965, Godwin Maintenance Building;[27] 1967, Hedgpeth Hall;[28] 1967, Bobby Murray Hall.[29]

Under his administration the institution rose from a small junior college with an enrollment of 312 students to a four-year senior school with 2,200 students, facilities valued at $7,000,000, and an operating budget of $2,700,000. It may be safely affirmed that few men presiding over the fortunes of a small college located in an isolated village in a rural community with so few alumni having attained wealth, with a paucity of friends in places of power and influence, ever led their schools to greater physical expansion in so brief a time.

But Leslie Campbell was more than a builder of buildings. He was a great human being and he was kind. The outsider sees buildings that vision and dreams have much to do with erecting, but friends and neighbors remember him for his humility, his neighborliness, and his utter lack of pretense. A member of the faculty recalls that when her mother died, the president soon was at her door asking, "Can I help?" "No, Dr. Campbell, I do not know of anything that you can do; thank you for coming." "Well," said the president, "these may be helpful." He handed her plane, train, and bus schedules that he had checked, verified and marked.

A student from the Far West received news of his father's death. Soon the president was at the door of the student's mobile home. "Is there anything that I can do? Do you have money to go?" Another recalls that when she and her husband first came to Buies Creek, they moved into a rented house. The weeds and grass in the yard were a foot high. President Campbell assured her that the maintenance department would come to mow the grass. Several days passed and the mowing was not done. Each day the president checked himself, not his secretary, to see if the grass had been cut. Early on Saturday morning she heard the mower and said to her husband, "Well, finally, that maintenance department has sent a man to mow our lawn." A little later she looked out her window and was amazed and embarrassed to see the president mowing her lawn! Robert Browning once advised, "Would you have your songs endure? Build on the human heart."

His kindness was bestowed upon me as a student. He was interested in me as a person as well as a student. Although he was, at the time, dean of the school, and taught only college courses, he taught one summer a high school course that I needed—and I was the only person in the class. Later he taught a course when only two of us were in the class, because of our need. When the time came for me to leave Campbell he took me to Wake Forest College, helped me find a place to live, assisted in the selection of courses, talked to my professors, vouching for me all the way. Later he even served as "best man" at my wedding!

One of his extracurricular activities in my student days was coaching our debate team. We traveled widely, always going in his car. Although budgets were close, his thoughtfulness and consideration of us will remain a source of gratitude. William Lyon Phelps of Yale said that the business of a teacher was not to supply information but to create a thirst. In his teaching, counseling, coaching, and friendship Leslie Campbell created thirsts. The areas of our interests and intellectual appetites were enlarged. Kipling spoke for him:

> I have eaten your bread and salt.
> I have drunk your water and wine.
> The deaths you died I have watched beside
> And the lives you lived were mine.

His colleagues were aware of their president's deep commitment to the school. In April, 1959, the college celebrated Dr. Campbell's sixty-seventh birthday and his twenty-fifth year as president. Speaking for the faculty and administration, Dean Burkot said that above everything else the president was a man completely dedicated to his task. He said that the burden of presiding over a church-related college was extremely heavy, that not even the president himself could estimate the sleepless hours, the countless miles, and the endless dreams he had lavished on Campbell College during the quarter century he had served as its president. And, whatever credit might come to his colleagues and helpers, the final responsibility always rested upon the president.

The dean was voicing the approval and conviction of his peers and the president's host of friends who had observed and marveled at his commitment. Every ounce of his energy, every affection of his spirit, every desire of his life were in some way connected with the welfare of the college. Not even his father at his best ever gave a deeper commitment of life and fortune.

Notes

1. Started under J. A. Campbell's administration, referred to earlier, finished under President Leslie Campbell's tenure as president.

2. In 1936 one of the two frame buildings, used for girls' living quarters, was destroyed by fire. This was the spur that resulted in the construction of the central section of the Fred N. Day Dormitory for Girls. It gave housing to thirty young women. In 1956 wings and portico were added, making it possible to care for 72 girls.

3. In 1940 the remainder of the estate of Mr. D. Rich came to the college, $151,700. It was primarily in the form of stocks and bonds. The entire sum was immediately added to the endowment. The value of this part of the bequest has varied, of course, depending upon the state of the portfolio at the time but for this particular gift the school would have found it exceedingly difficult to operate. In his vision, Mr. Rich said Jesus spoke to him saying, "Buies Creek must live!" And, through generous stewardship, "he being dead yet speaketh."

4. Mr. B. Herbert Taylor, Dunn businessman, long-time friend of the Campbell family, made it possible for the school to have much-needed athletic facilities. In 1946 a six-acre plot of land was purchased for outdoor sports and athletic events. Mr. Taylor underwrote the equipment, lighting and landscaping. The area was named the B. Herbert Taylor Athletic Field.

5. When Britt Dormitory opened for the school year 1947-48, it was the most modern and best equipped hall on the campus. The funds needed for construction were supplied by many friends, some at great sacrifice. The trustees agreed that the building should bear the name of "Britt," honoring W. S. Britt of Lumberton, the building's largest single benefactor. Mr. Britt was an alumnus of the school.

6. The Carter Gymnasium, completed in 1952, honors the N. H. Carter family and the significant services of Harry C. Carter of Greensboro. Harry Carter had served as president of the Board of Trustees of the school, had been a generous benefactor and effective in his leadership in the financial community. At the

time of its dedication, and for succeeding years when Campbell was a junior college, the playing floor, the equipment, the offices, the classrooms were adequate for the physical educational needs of the institution.

7. Jones Hall, opened in 1954, was also arranged in suites with connecting baths. It had provision for 72 young women. The name honored William Hubert Jones and Lula Bostic Jones, both of whom had served faithfully as trustees of the school and generous benefactors.

8. In 1955 funds were donated by the Reverend J. F. Blackmon and Mrs. Blackmon for the installation of a carillon system and placed in the tower of the Kivett Building. The system tolled the hours, amplified daily vespers, and had provision for sending out over the campus recitals from the chapel organ.

9. Campbell College has had no warmer friend nor more consistent benefactor than J. F. Kitchin of Norfolk, Virginia. He graduated from Campbell in 1925, just as the school was merging into junior college status and being taken over by the Baptist State Convention of North Carolina. Mr. Kitchin made a significant contribution toward the school's becoming a four-year institution. Kitchin Dormitory for men gives recognition to the help that he has given.

10. This addition to the original structure, given by Mr. D. Rich in memory of his wife, increased the size of the library by three times and gave adequate space and facilities for more than 200 students in the reading rooms.

11. The B. P. Marshbanks Dining Hall was constructed in 1933 and would care for 400 students. In 1957 the hall was completely renovated; three additional dining rooms were added, new storage space, equipment, modern cafeteria counters, and facilities to care for 1,000.

12. Baldwin Dormitory for Men was built in 1959, named in 1964. The name honors O. Hampton Baldwin, Lizzie Luther Baldwin, his deceased wife, Delphia Baldwin, his sister and O. Luther, his deceased son. The hall accommodates 130 men.

13. The Campbelltown Apartments are twelve duplex houses built in 1959 for married students and faculty families, attractively designed, with built-in modern facilities.

14. The John S. Pearson Memorial Infirmary was opened in 1960 and honors the brother of Mrs. J. A. Campbell. Mr. Pearson was business manager for the *Biblical Recorder;* later, for many years, business manager for the *Progressive Farmer,* influential farm journal. A generous challenge gift from Mrs. J. A. Campbell started the project. Offices for college physician were added in 1963. The building houses the Blackmon Medical Center dedicated to Junious F. and Katye Hatcher Blackmon, parents of Dr. Bruce B. Blackmon, college physician and his sister, Mrs. Bradeene Blackmon Vail.

15. Powell Hall for Women was opened in 1960, three-story dormitory, accommodating 60 girls. It joins Treat Hall by connecting lobby and reception room. The trustees named the building Powell Hall in honor of Misses Mabel and Nell Powell, faithful and devoted teachers of the college.

16. In consideration of the long and friendly relationship between Erwin Mills, Inc. and Campbell College and "their joint promotion of the economic, social, cultural and religious development of their constituency," Erwin Mills donated to the school a valuable tract of timberland, approximately 150 acres. The trustees of the college designated this "The Erwin Forest." The timberland lies adjoining other college properties along the Cape Fear River. The gift was made in 1960.

17. The James E. and Mary Z. Bryan Hall was opened in 1961. It has a cluster of twelve one-story apartment units, grouped around an interior court and joined by an exterior wall and roof. Each of the units has four bedrooms, living room and bath, and accommodates eight young women. One section provides a lounge, guest room, and quarters for the faculty counselor. This part of the building is dedicated to Carroll Bryan and his wife, Lanie. Carroll Bryan is the son of James E. and Mary Z. Bryan. In his remarks at the dedication of the building President Campbell said: "For some ten years Carroll has filled at one time or another almost every post a faithful trustee of the college could fill. But at his side at every turn has stood his devoted wife sharing cheerfully and fully in the assignment. In the full consciousness of what that friendship and help have meant to me personally and to the college, I rejoice that the lounge in this beautiful dormitory will continue to commemorate their years of distinguished service."

18. Opened in 1961 the James A. Campbell Administration Building was dedicated to the founder of the school, Dr. James Archibald Campbell, and his widow, Cornelia Pearson Campbell. It is a two-story structure and, at the time of its completion, as complete and modern as any structure on the campus.

19. North Dormitory for Women was completed in 1962, a three-story structure, located just behind Bryan Hall and consisting of apartment units with a total accommodation for 96 young women.

20. South Dormitory for men opened in 1962 also. It, too, is a three-story building adequate to house 131 men. The rooms were arranged in apartment-units consisting of five bedrooms, a living room, and bath. This modern building became "Sauls Hall," honoring E. P. Sauls, Campbell's generous friend.

21. A third major building opened in 1962, the Science Building (later to be named the Leslie Hartwell Campbell Hall of Science). Great care was taken in the planning and construction of the three-story structure. It contains 44,000 square feet of space for physics, biology, chemistry, and home economics.

22. "In October 1961 the Board of Trustees, prompted by the deep desire to exalt worship as the preeminent function of the auditorium of D. Rich Memorial Building, as well as by the intention to associate permanently with its chapel the names of two distinguished Baptists, long-time friends of Campbell College, voted unanimously to name the chapel in honor of Dr. J. Clyde Turner and his wife, Bertha Hicks Turner. Such action called for complete renovation and installation of improved facilities prior to the formal dedication exercise on January 25, 1963."

23. In the summer of 1963 and 1964 two additional frame structures were built to provide for the expanding music program of the college.

24. Northeast Hall for Men was opened in 1963. It consisted of air-conditioned apartments for 32 men.

25. In 1964 Mr. and Mrs. Deke E. Baggett and Mr. and Mrs. Deke L. Baggett gave, as a memorial to the late Dr. Leamon Baggett, approximately 130 acres of land in Horry County, South Carolina. The gift was made with the purpose that it be used for field studies by the departments of biology and geology.

26. The Lewis Edward and Martha Barnes Tyner Chair of Bible was launched in 1964 by their grateful children, who said, "for the Christian precepts of their home and for their superior educational advantages afforded by their parents."

27. The O. W. Godwin, Sr., Maintenance Building was opened in 1965, named

for the man whose "invaluable planning and assistance in construction of this massive structure provided long-needed space for storing large quantities of supplies purchased at the lowest available prices."

28. The last year of President Campbell's administration the New Hall for Women was completed. The same year, 1967, the building was renamed Hedgpeth Hall to honor R. A. and Elsie Hedgpeth of Lumberton, both of whom served as trustees for the school and were generous benefactors.

29. Also in the last year of President Campbell's administration, 1967, a new residence hall for men was completed. This adequate building was named Bobby Murray Hall, honoring the dynamic businessman and faithful friend of the college. These last two buildings were constructed under the administration of President Campbell but first entered during the tenure of Dr. Wiggins.

16.
"THE PEAK OF FIFTY YEARS OF UNSELFISH SERVICE"

And the more I learned about Oliver Wendell Holmes, Jr., the more insupportable it became to think of him as dead, cold and motionless beneath that stone in Arlington. I found myself possessed by a witch's frenzy to ungrave this man, stand him upright, see him walk, jump, dance, tell jokes, make love, display his vanity or his courage as the case might be.

Catherine Brinker Bowen[1]

WHEN the Baptist State Convention voted in 1950 to offer the old Wake Forest campus to the Southern Baptist Convention for a seminary site, that ended the speculation about moving Campbell College to the town of Wake Forest. Then an aggressive program of development was begun immediately on the Campbell campus.

Then in 1956, the year Wake Forest College was moved to Winston-Salem, the Reverend Douglas Branch, pastor of the First Baptist Church in Rocky Mount, later to become General Secretary of the Baptist State Convention of North Carolina, introduced a motion before the State Convention to the effect that a four-year Baptist college be set up in the eastern part of the state. Another tizzy!

Even before that, alert individuals were calling attention to the educational "vacuum" that would be left in eastern North Carolina with the removal of Wake Forest College to the west. Dr. Clarence Poe, editor of the *Progressive Farmer*, respected farm journal, pointed to this. He said that there were a half dozen states with a smaller area than eastern North Carolina had, a dozen states with smaller populations, a dozen states that did not have the resources, soil, and climate opportunities that this eastern section of the state had. He affirmed that there was already an appalling lack of college facilities east of Raleigh and that when Wake Forest

193

College made its move the need would be accentuated. A map of North Carolina was drawn with Campbell College pinpointed. It could be seen that if a line was extended from Campbell out in a hundred-mile radius, swinging round, it would take in the center of the state geographically and would include "the center of an area progressive in spirit with unexcelled potential in civic and economic development."

On May 5, 1956, the Baptist State Convention heard Dr. Branch's motion, and a "Committee of 25" was appointed to study the matter concerning a four-year college in the east and to bring recommendations.[2] This committee employed professional help and in May, 1959 proposed the following resolution:

> That the Trustees of Campbell College, in the light of the rapid expansion since 1950, the need for a co-educational Baptist college in the east, and the enthusiasm of its alumni concerning the future of the school, consider converting the institution into a senior college as soon as they think desirable and possible to do so.[3]

Campbell's trustees met on May 14, 1959, ten days after the Convention passed its motion, in a crucial session. A careful reading of the extensive minutes reveals that the group was well aware of the heavy stakes at issue. President Campbell said to the group, "This issue, which I take to be inescapable, presents to you and to me responsibilities for making perhaps the most far-reaching, destiny-shaping decision in my professional career." The trustees faced the issue and approved the following motion: "That the Trustees go on record as being wholeheartedly and highly in favor of our becoming a senior college as soon as possible to do so, and that proper committees be set up to implement this action." The motion was made by the Reverend Ernest P. Russell and was seconded by Mrs. J. Hunter Strickland, Mrs. Martha Layton Winston, and Mrs. W. E. Nichols.[4]

At that meeting a steering committee was appointed, composed of representatives from the board of trustees: Claude Bowen, Mrs. J. Hunter Strickland, Howard Dawkins, and H. Spurgeon Boyce; and from the alumni association: A. Hartwell Campbell, J. F. Kitchin, and Norman A. Wiggins.

The alumni of the college had been busy. It polled the opinion of the North Carolina alumni and found that the vote was approximately 20 to 1 in favor of making Campbell into a senior college. Attention was given to reports from Pfeiffer College that was in the process of becoming a senior college. A study was inaugurated to determine the necessary requirements for changing Campbell's status from junior to senior college status.

The president and the dean of the college submitted in person what the college proposed to do to the Executive Secretary of the Commission on Colleges and Universities of the Southern Association, and, also, to the members of the Committee on Standards and Reports for Senior Colleges. The administration planned from the beginning to be guided every step of the way by those who were responsible for accreditation. The proposals submitted to the above groups were looked upon with approval. It was felt that the goals and plans for reaching them were realistic and adequate.

It was planned to begin immediately to enlarge facilities to care for an enrollment of 1,250 students. Strategy was mapped for reaching alumni, friends, civic and business groups, especially those immediately affected in the home area of the college. Blueprints were drawn for a financial campaign to secure the necessary funds required for senior college status. Proposals were developed to improve the standard of work within the college itself, raise faculty salaries, seek faculty members with higher academic qualifications, and improve the technique of teaching.[5]

The express was on the tracks and moving toward its goal; all who would help were invited aboard. At a later steering committee meeting the following actions were taken. The president and dean of the college were asked to confer with officials of the Southern Association of Colleges and Secondary Schools and of the North Carolina College Conference, asking for guidance and cooperation of these agencies in meeting all requirements in attaining acceptance and accreditation. The Council on Christian Education and the General Board of the Baptist State Convention were to be informed of the necessary steps for receiving accreditation as a senior institution. These groups were asked for assistance and given assurance that they would be kept informed.

As soon as the word went out that a move was under way to make Campbell a four-year institution, friends, well-wishers, and camp followers began to rally. The following words from the *Golds-*

boro News-Argus are typical:

> Wake Forest College, which has served North Carolina from the forests of Wake County since 1834, will move this summer to its new plant in Winston-Salem. Its removal will leave the great eastern half of the state without a four-year, co-educational, liberal arts college. Meredith College is for girls only. Campbell College is co-educational, but it is a junior college.
>
> Removal of Wake Forest 150 miles farther west will reduce the number of eastern Carolinians, percentage-wise, in its student body.
>
> It is natural and logical, then, that discussion is already being heard on Campbell College becoming a four-year college.
>
> Immediately it would appear that this would be a wise move and the best way to continue to serve those who have looked to Wake Forest but will no longer be able to look that way because the college is moving west.
>
> Campbell is an old, stable, respected, and growing institution. It has an accepted reputation for high standards.[6]

As this preparation express was moving into high speed there came, all within a period of a year's time, significant indications of the esteem in which Campbell was held by the educational community. A committee from the board of trustees of Pineland College, Salemburg, North Carolina, thirty-seven miles away, came to ask that Campbell College take over the operation of that institution. A second appeal came from a delegation of military people from Fort Bragg army base, twenty-five miles away. The group asked that Campbell set up a four-year degree-granting branch there with assurance that such an operation would be financially rewarding. The third offer came to the college from representatives of the town of Red Springs, seventy-five miles away, and from the Red Springs Development Corporation. This group offered the General Board of the Baptist State Convention all the real property of old Flora McDonald College, together with such dormitory and classroom equipment left on the property, for use by the Baptists for the establishment of a new junior college to serve the southeastern area of the state. President Campbell was appointed chairman of a committee to look into the offer. He and his group found an offer of the property, forty-three acres of land plus an offer of more than $100,000 pledged from local citizens plus $40,000 in additional assets.

Each offer was appreciated, carefully investigated, and rejected. It was felt that the college already had all that it could wisely undertake in advancing Campbell to senior status.[7]

From the beginning President Campbell was realistic about the task before him. He determined that if Campbell advanced it would advance worthily. He said, "We are not interested in changing from a first-class junior college to a second-rate senior institution. . . . We intend to go first-class all the way." He knew the task facing the college was a major one:

> The transmutation of Campbell into a senior college is a far more meaningful and involved process than superimposing the junior and senior years upon the already existing junior college. Just as the transition from old Buies Creek Academy to a junior college, begun in 1926, in many respects involved the rebirth of a new institution, so now becoming a senior college will result in many modifications in administrative policy and in the program of this institution.[8]

He reminded his college family that greater student participation in self-government would be an opportunity for there would be a more mature student body. It would be possible, and necessary, to provide a better laboratory for the practice of democracy. Higher academic standards would require a reexamination of entrance requirements. A more realistic appraisal of operating costs from year to year would become a necessity. In the past it had been necessary to base the courses of study on the philosophy of institutions to which the students would go for their final two years of college. He felt it would be a "thrilling adventure" to form the policies and to establish curricula in an institution based upon its own philosophy of education needed to prepare young men and women for life. He made it abundantly clear that selecting the ingredients of this new curriculum would be based upon Campbell's historic position:

> . . . that emphasis should be placed not upon the accumulation of things nor upon the outward state of one's being so much as upon man's own *being*. More important it is by far that man be free in spirit, be intelligent, be wise as to the truth concerning his own nature and well being, and as to the infinite relationships between himself and his environment; and, finally, to be good in terms of the divine principle of life built into the nature of all creation. In other words, in its highest sense, education must be grounded in the liberating arts. . . . More basic still is Campbell's philosophy of life that in Christianity is to be found the only moral behaviour that can ultimately liberate mankind. In Christian education, therefore, is to be found the only complete preparation for life here and hereafter. . . . As a member of the family of Baptist colleges,

> Campbell acknowledges her just obligation to serve the denomination in every way consistent with the function of a Christian college. It would seem to be self-evident that such a college would seek every opportunity to win others to Christ and his way of life, to teach the great doctrines of the Christian faith, and to train Christian leadership for tomorrow.[9]

Friends rallied. A campaign to raise $2,000,000 was launched—a large sum for that time and that place and that school with its modest background in fund-raising. But, the campaign was well launched. The president's son, Representative A. Hartwell Campbell, was general chairman of the drive. He linked the past and the present when he referred to the crisis in the life of the little school in the long ago, when the buildings lay in ashes and a student placed his arms about the bowed shoulders of the founder, Dr. J. A. Campbell, and said, "Don't cry, teacher; we're going to build you a brick school house." Placing his arms about the shoulder of the present president, his father, the son said, "Don't you worry, Daddy; we're going to build you a four-year college and it will be a good one, too!"

There was a breathless quality about those preparatory days. One had a feeling that time was taking account not of breaths taken but of heartbeats missed. Writing in the *Durham Morning Herald*, Alan Whiteleather, staff writer, said: "Buildings are going up faster than weeds at Campbell College. One dormitory was completed in 90 days flat. The number of teachers, the proportion of Ph.D.'s and teachers' salaries are going up rapidly." [10]

Spearheaded by Lieutenant Governor Lloyd Philpott, June 18, 1961, was declared "Leslie Campbell Day" throughout North Carolina. Lieutenant Governor Philpott said that such a day was fitting for "few North Carolinians have done more for educational progress in North Carolina. . . . None has battled greater odds over the past half century to do it." A TV documentary was featured by stations over the country on June 22. The program was titled, "To the Stars. . . . ," making use of the school's motto: *Ad Astra Per Aspera*, "To the Stars Through Difficulties." [11]

Soon the school was at the time to receive its first junior class, third-year college class. It was the fall of 1961. The class numbered 160 students. The total enrollment for the year was close to 1,300 and there was a faculty of 70. For his faculty, at the beginning of the term, President Campbell reviewed milestones in the school's 74 years of existence, academy and junior college. He called on his teachers for high efficiency and worthy standards. He sounded his theme again, "Campbell does not intend to give up being a first-class junior college to become a second-class senior institution. If I know where we are going, we intend to go first-class all the way."

The president was realistic; he knew changes would come: "We are bound to lose something, just as a child loses something when he grows into manhood. But the college will remain a small, liberal arts school. Teachers and advisors will continue to be close to the students." Commenting on the inevitable changes, President Campbell used a forceful local example of conversion. He said that there had been a famous buggy made over in Wilson, just a few miles away. It was called the "Hackney Buggy." It was a good buggy; it was known and used far and wide. But times changed and the company that made Hackney buggies had to change. "Now," he said, "if you will look at almost any school bus, you'll see the name 'Hackney.'"

That first junior class entered in 1961. To say "college and the 60's" is to imply far more than what is said in words. For the sixties brought into existence disturbance and rebellion and revolution on the college and university campuses of America. Campbell came through with almost no difficulty. There was excitement over the newness of the program. Faculty and administration were straining at the traces to prove that they could do, do well, what many had said would be impossible to do at all. Students responded affirmatively. There are indications that with the eagerness to measure up to expectations by accreditation agencies, the teachers required more and better work from their charges than they would later require. Yet, the students came through in a creditable way.

The junior class advanced to senior class, and by May 31, 1963, there were 132 "ready, able and willing" for graduation, the first four-year class to graduate from Campbell College. Dr. Sankey L. Blanton, distinguished clergyman, at that time director of public relations at Meredith College and a long-time close friend of President Campbell, was the baccalaureate speaker, and Dean William Hugh McEniry of Stetson University delivered the literary address.[12]

As the students were ready to march into Turner Auditorium for their graduation a dramatic incident took place. Carroll Leggett said it was perhaps the only unanimous action the class ever took! It was an impromptu act. After the class was in line someone remembered that President Campbell would not be at the services. He was in the hospital due to an eye injury. A mortarboard, symbol of senior dignity, was passed down the line as a collection plate. The offering was adequate, a telegram was drafted and flowers were sent. The seniors told their president that his absence was felt and that the class that first reaped the fruits of his work appreciated the fact that he had not only built castles in the sky but had dedicated his life to putting foundations under them on earth.[13]

As stated, President Campbell and Dean Burkot never allowed the school to forget that their goal was not just a four-year college but a fully accredited institution. They "went by the book" every step of the way and were often ahead of the book in their achievements. Therefore, in the minimum length of time, three years after the school became a four-year college, the Southern Association of Schools placed its full approval upon what had been done and was being done. The meeting of the association at which the favorable action was taken was in Miami, Florida. President Campbell and Dean Burkot returned from Miami early on the morning of December 2, 1966. When the train came to a stop in Dunn at 2:30 in the morning, having been delayed for more than an hour, the sight that greeted their tired and sleepy eyes went far to rejuvenate them. For there at the station, having waited in the cold for the delayed train, were 500 students, members of the faculty, and friends of the community to welcome them. The demonstration was sponsored by the student government of the school. Jimmie Jordan, student government president, speaking for the group, said that they had come to show their gratitude to the two men who had been chiefly responsible for bringing about the achievement in which all students would participate. He mentioned that Dr. Campbell had announced his retirement and surely securing full accreditation for the school was the peak of what he had done for the school in his fifty-five years of unselfish service for the college.[14]

Notes

1. President Campbell would retire the following summer. *Adventures of a Biographer* (New York: Little, Brown and Co., 1946), p. 47.

2. Minutes, Baptist State Convention for 1956, p. 64.

3. Minutes for Baptist State Convention, 1959, p. 69.

4. Trustee minutes, May 14, 1959.

5. Summary of Trustee Minutes

6. This clipping is in the archives of the college, date not clear.

7. From a paper by President Leslie Campbell, original in college archives.

8. *Creek Pebbles,* September 12, 1961.

9. Founder's Day Address, March 6, 1961, and Remarks to New Teachers, *Creek Pebbles,* September 12, 1961.

10. *Durham Morning Herald,* May 13, 1962.

11. Clippings in files of archives.

12. Archives.

13. Ibid.

14. Ibid.

17.
THREESCORE YEARS AND
TEN PLUS EIGHT

After spending more than ten years in a detailed study of the life of Robert E. Lee, Douglas Freeman said, at a testimonial dinner given in his honor:

> "I have been fully repaid by being privileged to live
> . . . for more than a decade in the company of a great
> gentleman."

PRESIDENT Leslie H. Campbell retired in June, 1967. He had been president of the school since 1934, a period of thirty-three years, the longest tenure of office for any college president in the state. He was seventy-five years old. The school had been in existence only five years when he was born. At the time of his retirement he had witnessed the erection of every building on the campus. As teacher, dean, and president he had served the school for more than half a century.

It took his father, James Archibald Campbell, thirty-nine years to bring the school from academy to junior college status. It took the son, Leslie Hartwell Campbell, thirty-six years to bring the junior college to senior-college status. It took twenty-five years to achieve accreditation for the junior college but only four years to gain accreditation for the senior college.

When President Leslie Campbell succeeded his father as president of the school, his annual salary was less than $1,000 per year; the enrollment was three hundred and twelve students; when he retired, the enrollment was 2,200. The increase in his salary was less dramatic. Total assets of the school in 1934, when he became president, were $435,456. When he retired, the resources of the school were $8,164,803. At the beginning of his administration there were twelve buildings on the campus; some of these were wooden structures that had been dwelling places. When his successor was chosen, there were twenty-seven buildings of substantial materials and the campus contained more than 570 acres. At the beginning his faculty had numbered twenty-two; at the close it was 110-plus, and the school had more than two hundred employees.

Under Leslie Campbell's leadership his school had become the third largest private college in North Carolina; only Duke and Wake Forest having larger enrollments. The last year of his presidency there were 124 students preparing for some form of church-related work, the largest number in any one of the seven Baptist colleges in the state. And Campbell was sending more teachers into the educational system than any private school in the state.

On his retirement Leslie Campbell was optimistic about the school's future. He gave a significant report to his trustees, a sort of rehearsal of "the ways of God with men," as those men related to Campbell College. He spoke of tangible and intangible assets and of primary needs. He thought that such an evaluation would be of interest and value to a prospective new president. He saw two serious handicaps; they seemed handicaps to him and he thought a prospective president might consider them in the same light. First, while North Carolina Baptists had been generous in the percentage of their funds given to higher education, there were seven colleges plus other vital missionary causes for which the Convention was responsible. Second, there was the Convention's consistent denial of the college's right to share in the "avalanche of Federal funds in prospect for buildings and constructional needs." And, to him, there was a third consideration that was also a handicap; it was the Convention's unwillingness to allow non-Baptists and out-of-state Baptists to serve on boards. This placed serious restrictions upon the ability of the college to promote rewarding financial contacts.

He said that apart from these three negatives everything was on the positive side. It had been amply demonstrated, he felt, that the smallness of the Buies Creek community was no barrier to securing students. On the basis of his experience of the past thirty-two years no president would find greater freedom of action. The board of trustees, twenty-eight members, was unusually strong. He analyzed and evaluated it. There were four dedicated and capable women, five able ministers; one of these had served as president of the Baptist State Convention. Four members of the board were in government service; one was a United States Congressman; one was a private secretary to a Congressman; one was a mayor of a fine eastern North Carolina city; another was a member of the North Carolina General Assembly. There was a skilled doctor and surgeon on the board, and there were thirteen businessmen, one being a member of the Radio and Television Commission of the Southern Baptist Convention. The retiring president felt that it was of real significance that all major industrial centers in the eastern two-thirds of the state be represented on the board.

Of course, any administrator would be vitally interested in the caliber and spirit of the faculty. He pointed to the fact that in 1960-61, as a junior college, the school had only five faculty members with doctor's degrees; now there were thirty-six. This was more than was required by Southern Association standards for accreditation. The average teacher's salary at Campbell for the coming year, if broken down according to ranking, approximated the mean average salaries paid by other North Carolina privately-owned senior colleges. The school ranked between the 40th and 75th percentile of colleges in the Southern Association in expenditures for four key items, listed as Total Educational and General Educational Expenditures.

He continued with his resumé. As for the financial status of the college, he said that it had been necessary to borrow rather heavily in order to provide for the rapid growth in student enrollment and at the same time make the big transition to senior-college status, but he felt that the financial obligations could be met. To him it was significant that with all of the rapid growth and expansion, the school had not failed to keep a comfortable surplus in the annual operating budget during the previous fourteen years.

The retiring president took pride in calling attention to the long and harmonious relationship with the Baptist State Convention and its agencies. A close relationship had existed, too, between the administration, faculty, and students. A strong degree of academic freedom existed in classroom and throughout the campus. He was grateful for the spirit of adventure and experimentation in evidence as the school moved toward senior-college status. And, finally, he paid tribute to "the rich traditions of an institution that give it character and stability in a time when the world seems now and then to be 'gone with the wind.' "

He said:

> As I look back reflectively upon the past fifty-six years since my brother and I returned from college to our home community to become associated with our father in the operation of Buies Creek Academy, my predominating impulse is to give thanks for God's unspeakable blessings, for thousands of forgiving friends who have accepted me for what I, at my best, aspired to be, and for enriching opportunities in a most rewarding life occupation.[1]

Earlier he had spoken to other friends:

> On this observance of Founder's Day we stand on a pinnacle from which we have seen in retrospect glimpses of the unfolding drama of this institution . . . drama filled with intense struggle, accompanied here and there with temporary reverses; with gropings frequently, toward some promised land of destiny, partially hidden behind the ranges; but, thank God, with occasional vistas of inviting new tablelands of thrilling achievement just beyond.[2]

When Dr. Campbell announced his retirement in March, 1966, Dr. Donald Moore, vice-president of the board of trustees and a member of the executive committee of that body, described the retirement as: "A tremendous loss both to Campbell College and to the cause of Christian education, but a retirement richly deserved through over half a century of devoted, outstanding and distinguished service." [3]

Words of approval were many and varied. Ted Malone, editor of *Creek Pebbles*, the college newspaper, wrote:

> As editor of the newspaper, as an Episcopalian, and as an individual I have had occasion to disagree with the policies of the administration and of Dr. Campbell, but as one who appreciates a job well and sincerely done, I feel compelled to pay this tribute, small and inadequate as it is, to a man who has spent his life for the advancement of things held universally dear by all men.[4]

The dedication in *Pine Burr*, college annual, for 1956, was thoughtful, perceptive, and beautiful:

> Heir to an unfinished task on the death of his beloved and illustrious founder-father in 1934, Dr. Leslie Hartwell Campbell has literally given his life to Campbell College and the cause of Christian education. With each passing year, the burden of his responsibilities becomes more complex and the pace which he sets for himself more grueling. Evidence of his durability lies in the fact that, almost without exception, he has outserved all college presidents in the state and region.

Forty-five years mark the span of his official connection as teacher, dean and president. As architect in the realm of ideas and dreams, he has converted them into realities and they stand about us, monuments of brick and mortar and steel. A navigator on the pathway leading to eternity, he has helped chart the course of countless lives in the direction of high ideals and noble living. An earnest student who grows in wisdom and stature.

What manner of man is he? A Christian gentleman, faithful in his witness. A loving father, zealous in his trust. A responsible guardian, tireless in his concern. A generous citizen, responsive to every need. A loyal friend, ready to lend a hand. A willing servant, humble in the extreme. A human being, aware of his limitations.

It is our privilege and honor to wish for him more years at the helm of the craft which he would guide "To the stars through difficulties." [5]

And, one more time:

State of North Carolina
Department of State

To All to Whom These Presents Shall Come, Greeting:

I, Thad Eure, Secretary of the State of North Carolina, do hereby certify the following and hereto attached Four (4) sheets to be a true copy of Resolution No. 54., Session Laws of 1967, a joint resolution honoring Dr. Leslie Hartwell Campbell upon the occasion of his retirement as President of Campbell College.

The original of which is now on file and a matter of record in this office.

In witness thereof, I have hereunto set my hand and affixed my official seal.

Done in office, at Raleigh, this 31st day of May in the year of our Lord 1967.

Thad Eure
Secretary of State[6]

President Campbell retired in June, 1967, and was made Professor Emeritus. In the following year he and Mrs. Campbell moved to Raleigh. They kept their house in Buies Creek open and usually returned to the village on weekends. By leaving the community and college he was away from endless calls, conferences, and requests. He knew, too, that it would give added freedom to the new president. Also, by being in Raleigh he and his brother, Carlyle, could be near each other. During the two years the Campbells lived in Raleigh, until President Campbell's death, he and Carlyle were together as they had not been since they were young men in college and for the brief time they served together on the faculty of old Buies Creek Academy. They talked, traveled, reminisced, planned, and played golf.

Because the Campbells usually returned to Buies Creek for the weekends, he continued to be deeply involved in the new Memorial Baptist Church that was organized on July 14, 1968. The church was at the center of his interest from the time of its organization to his death. It brought him great joy and vast sorrow. He had, of course, been intimately related to the original Baptist church in Buies Creek. In speaking to that congregation in 1969 he said:

> Sixty-five years ago this spring, at eleven years of age, I was attending school in the old tabernacle, the only building on the school campus at that time. One morning that spring, during a revival meeting, I walked down the aisle and confessed Christ and a few days later they took me down to Kivett's pond and baptized me into the membership of the church . . . from the standpoint of membership I am probably the oldest living member. My grandfather Pearson, then its oldest member, threw the first shovel of dirt in the excavation for erecting this building and I was chosen to throw the second.[7]

His father had been pastor of the church for almost half a century. Leslie could not remember when he began attending its services, having been carried there in the arms of his mother. He had been particularly active in the life of that church. His five children had all been baptized into its fellowship; it was there that four of them had been united in marriage. It had been—always—the spiritual home of the college. The church had always been vital in his own life. But for five years there had been open friction between a strong element in the college and the leadership of the church. The college opposition included students, members of the faculty, and members of the administration, including President Campbell.

The unrest seems to have sprung primarily from two sources. The group in the college, joined by a considerable group in the community, felt the church was giving inadequate attention to, and leadership of, youth in the church, including college and community young people. The group also felt that there was a lack of democratic procedure in the administration of the business affairs of the church. People on both sides were unhappy about the condition. President Campbell sought to the best of his knowledge and ability to lessen the friction, to narrow the gap, and to bring a creative solution. There were those in places of leadership of the church who earnestly desired the same result. No one was happy with the situation; yet the tension increased and the gap widened to a parting of the ways.

When groups began to meet in homes and community buildings to discuss the advisability—to them the necessity—of organizing another church, Dr. Campbell did not meet with them. He took no active part in that direction. He knew that the spiritual needs of the college community were not being met as he earnestly desired to see them met. But he could not bring himself to cast his vote for the organization of a new church.

However, once the decision to organize a new church had become a reality and the constitution of the church had been approved, he gave himself to its establishment and promotion without reservation. He attended its services, served as its moderator, was chairman of its building committee, was a member of the pulpit committee to secure a first pastor, and was serving as chairman of the deacons when he died. In the church's worship he found comfort and joy; in its promising future he experienced inspiration; with his new pastor he felt satisfaction and hope. In that closing period of his life his church, again, spoke effectively to his spiritual, intellectual, and emotional needs.

And he lived to see evidence of God "working together for good" with those who love him. He saw each church with a more harmonious fellowship than the one church had known, each church reaching individuals and elements in the college and in the community that the one church did not, probably could not, reach.

In March of 1970 Dr. Campbell suffered a heart attack. He came through the experience, regained some of his strength, and was able to carry on much of his former activity, especially his church interests. But he died in Rex Hospital, Raleigh, on November 25, 1970. Funeral services were held on November 27 in Turner Auditorium, the same chapel that had served for the memorial service for his father thirty-six years earlier. The Reverend Henry B. Stokes, his pastor, Dr. Charles B. Howard, President Norman A. Wiggins, and Dr. Donald Keyser of the department of religion participated in the simple service of dignity and beauty.

In his memorial message Pastor Stokes referred to the incident of an elderly man who played baseball with some young boys. The old man said, "I made a two-base hit. When I got to second, my breath was on first, but my heart was on third." Mr. Stokes said:

> As I knew Dr. Campbell in the last part of his life this described him. He was always looking ahead, down the road and doing everything in his power to get there. Being incapacitated did not mean a lessening of interest. During his illness I received letters from him concerning the work and life of his church which contained suggestions for its progress.

It remained for a former student, a *Pine Burr* editor, Lois Byrd, to give one of the finest words:

> There was nothing simple about Leslie Campbell; in fact, he was a very complex person. But there was one underlying thing that made him tick. He believed absolutely, and to the bone, in Christian education in any age, any circumstance—and for any person who desired it. . . .
>
> Dr. Leslie Campbell was a man skilled in the use and the writing of the English language. As a public speaker he sometimes groped for words, but when he took pen in hand the words flowed. He was one of the most gifted letter writers of his day, and a letter in his beautiful Spencerian handwriting was one to treasure, for both its appearance and content. Anyone lucky enough, or unlucky enough, to submit proofs to him for publication could be certain that what appeared to be perfect would return looking like a literary battlefield, but immeasurably improved.
>
> Almost unbelievable energy enabled him to work consistently fourteen hours a day, but he loved it.
>
> The thing that set him apart was his interest in people as individuals and his capacity for friendship. He would cross any room to speak to a friend he had not seen for years, regardless of the place, the time, or the company.
>
> He had integrity, business acumen, and a streak of toughness known as plain old-fashion guts. A college president once told this editorialist a story which perhaps is typical of Leslie Campbell. He said that, at a meeting, the question of teacher's certification came up. A group including Campbell had agreed the night before on a policy, but when it reached the voting stage the next day, "the only man who voted as he promised the night before was Leslie Campbell. That's when I began to appreciate Leslie Campbell," the college president commented. . . .
>
> Campbell's interests were wider than many knew, limited only by his demanding job. He was a skilled musician, gifted in amateur theatricals, and he liked golf. He could have made a living doing any number of things.
>
> He never worried about being compared with a father who was a college president or his brother Carlyle, who headed another college, Meredith. Leslie Campbell simply saw nothing wrong with working in the same school in the same rural place where he was born and strived to make his school one of the best in the nation.
>
> There is no wonder that thousands of poor boys and girls to whom Campbell College presented opportunity returned the favor when they were no longer poor, and were delighted to help Dr. Campbell in his task.[8]

And Leslie Hartwell Campbell resigned in a good old age, full of riches, and honor; and his student, Norman Adrian Wiggins, reigned in his stead.

Notes

1. President's Report to the Board of Trustees, April 15, 1966.
2. Founder's Day, March 6, 1961.
3. *News and Observer*, March 23, 1966.
4. *Creek Pebbles*, March 28, 1966.
5. *Pine Burr*, 1956.
6. Archives.
7. Ibid.
8. Written for *Sanford Herald* by its state editor, Lois Byrd, Campbell graduate of 1931, reprinted in *Campbell College Prospect*, January 1971.

18.
"THE OLD ORDER CHANGETH"

The old order changeth yielding place to new;
And God fulfills himself in many ways,
Lest one good custom should corrupt the world.

Tennyson

On March 7, 1966, President Campbell had announced that he would retire at the close of the spring semester in 1967. On April 15, following President Campbell's announcement, a committee was named to recommend his successor: Fred L. Taylor, James C. Cammack, Mrs. J. Hunter Strickland, Howard J. Ford, W. Randall Lolley, R. A. Hedgpeth, and H. Spurgeon Boyce. The committee was authorized to select its own chairman, and Dr. Boyce was elected. Dr. Ford served as vice-chairman and Dr. Cammack was secretary of the group.

At a meeting of the board of trustees on April 21, 1967, one year and six days later, Chairman Boyce announced that his committee was ready with its report. He said that through much prayer, and they believed the leading of the Holy Spirit, "We think we have found that individual who can best serve Campbell College as president." He then presented the name of Dr. Norman Adrian Wiggins of Wake Forest University's law faculty. The vote of the trustees was unanimous; Dr. Wiggins was elected.

President Campbell retired on June 1, 1967. One June 6, Dr. Wiggins assumed his duties as the new and third president of Campbell College.

The quick, smooth, and apparently easy transfer of presidential powers should not lead to the assumption that the change was without careful thought and serious evaluation, or that President Wiggins' election was a foregone conclusion from the beginning.

211

In his inaugural address President Wiggins quoted the late Nicholas Murray Butler, for many years a president of Columbia University, as saying that the passing of the position of power from one servant of a university to another was an incident, the university itself was lasting, and, it was hoped, eternal. Incidental? Hardly. Unimportant? Certainly not.

And the transition of the "position of power" at Campbell College was especially significant. For the entire life of the school, eighty years, it had been headed by Campbells, father and son. From the first day of the school's existence it had been uniquely a family undertaking. Since the citizens of the community were unable to pay J. A. Campbell to teach in their school, he operated it on his own, receiving his meager compensation from the tuition paid by the small band of students who attended. The plans, the philosophy, the promotion, the guidance, the financing was Campbell-based. It was more than a name that allied a family and a college. The very life and character of the institution had taken on the life and character of the Campbell family. For those who knew the family and the school, it was impossible to think of one without thinking of the other. In a very basic sense it would have been fitting to use an apostrophe in the spelling, "Campbell's College."

So it was no easy task that Chairman Boyce and his committee faced as they went forth to seek a new president. They were the recipients of many suggestions, much advice; some sought, much volunteered! A careful reading of minutes and an unhurried discussion with Dr. Boyce are enough to confirm that the committee took its work seriously. The members kept an open mind about their choice.

What type of individual did they go forth to find? What qualifications did they lay down? In connection with their task, one member said he remembered an incident when Yale University was seeking a new president in 1949. At a Yale Club dinner in New York City, Wilmarth Lewis, a member of the Yale Corporation, said to this group:

> Yale's next president must first of all be a Yale man and a great scholar—also a social philosopher who has at his fingertips a solution of all world problems. . . .
>
> He must be a good public relations man and an experienced fund raiser.

He must be a man of the world and yet he must possess great spiritual
qualities—

He must be a leader, not too far to the right, nor too far to the left,
and of course not too much in the middle—

As I have been talking, you have, I don't doubt, realized there is only
One who has most of thes qualities. But there is a question, even about
Him: Is God a Yale Man?

Dr. Boyce and his committee were advised to seek a man who
had executive ability, strong academic caliber, good public relations
"know-how," a great love for youth; a man who was aware of and
sympathetic to the school's direction and history; one who was able
to build on the past leadership without being limited by the same;
a leader who could and would relate to the local community and
the indigenous church; one who would socially identify but avoid
cliques; a president who was a committed Christian and a loyal
Baptist, having charisma, and between 40 and 50 years of age.

In making his report to the trustees on April 21, 1967, Dr. Boyce
said that his committee had met with thirty-one different individuals
from twelve different states in its attempt to find the right person
to fill the post. He did not add, though it was a fact, that Norman
Adrian Wiggins was the last person the committee approached.
The new president was only half tongue-in-cheek when he later
would say: "My name was the last in the barrel. When they came
to me, the members of the committee making the selection didn't
have anywhere else to go." It was the proverbial case of "acres
of diamonds," all over again.

However, before Dr. Wiggins allowed his name to go before
the trustees for a vote, the committee felt that it might be necessary
to add new names to that barrel. The young law professor was
not easily convinced. He enjoyed his teaching; he liked Wake Forest
University and he did not desire to become a college president.
From a financial point of view, as well as for prestige, being president of Campbell College was not the most desirable and glamorous
position to occupy. Dr. Wiggins had had, and would have, numerous
opportunities that seemed more colorful and attractive. These would
include no less than three different offers to head well-known law
schools. Yet, he finally agreed, if elected, to assume presidential
responsibilities at Campbell College.

He did meet many of the qualifications set forth by the committee. He was 43 years old, an alumnus of the school, a native of Burlington. His parents were solid citizens, hard-working and positively Christian. His father and mother were active in the First Baptist Church of Burlington, both teaching in the Bible school. Early in his life, at eleven years of age, Norman had accepted Christ and united with the church where his parents had taken him since infancy. His pastor was the beloved Reverend A. D. Kinnett, an alumnus of Campbell. Kinnett knew children and young people by name. He was comfortable in their presence; they were at ease with him. President Wiggins remembers that the pastor's study was the place where many frank, easy, confidential discussions took place. To A. D. Kinnett there was one school, above all others, where a young person from his church should study. That place was Campbell College.

The Wiggins home was not a place of wealth. The children worked, making their own financial contribution to the family larder. The president remembers working in a machine shop for twenty-five cents per hour, delivering newspapers on a route with 52 subscribers, mowing lawns, and running various errands. He had a brilliant career as a high school athlete, earning letters in football, basketball, and baseball. The fact that he was better at athletics in those days than he was at books is not surprising. But there was never any question about the wisdom of seeking a college education, not in the mind of his parents, in the wishes of his brothers and sister, in the prayers of Pastor Kinnett, or in his own desires.

It has been stated that nothing is more valuable in the life of an individual than a few happy memories from childhood. President Wiggins has more than a few. In speaking to a group of Campbell College alumni and friends in Burlington shortly after his election to the presidency of the college, President Wiggins recalled his early years in that city; he made a rather amazing statement. He said that he could not remember one unpleasant experience that he had known in that community. Everyone is selective in what he remembers from his childhood and youth. What he remembers may be as indicative of the character of the "rememberer" as the quality of what is available for recall. Still, to say that one does not remember a single unpleasant experience from his youth and childhood says something significant about the home, church, school,

President Norman Adrian Wiggins

and community. What it says is surely good.

In August of 1942 young Wiggins and a friend, Erwin Sykes, hitchhiked their way to Buies Creek and to Campbell College. Wiggins had never seen the college. His high school athletic coach, Walter Clayton, had recommended that young Wiggins be given an athletic scholarship. When he arrived at the school, there was no record of the recommendation. Besides, World War II was shifting into high-gear, and the athletic fields and courts were being depleted. But when he talked with President Leslie Campbell, he received the encouragement that students had been receiving from the beginning of the school. Leslie Campbell said: "Come on and enroll; we'll work it out someway,"—a sentence that Norman Wiggins has never forgotten. He was given an "athletic-work" scholarship. He was to play football, baseball, and basketball if the school had football, baseball, and basketball teams; that was doubtful. What was certain, and what young Wiggins would certainly participate in was the "work" part of the scholarship! He served as janitor of Layton Dormitory and kept the tennis courts. So, a touch of Horatio Alger is present; from janitor to president.

As stated, the war call was being heard on the campuses across the nation. Young Wiggins enlisted in the Marine Corps after he had been at Campbell for one semester. After the war he immediately returned to Campbell, a junior college then, for a year and a half. He collected his diploma and a wife. The wife, Mildred Harmon, was from nearby Coats. She, too, graduated from the college. The Wigginses proceeded to Wake Forest University where the husband-part of the team graduated magna cum laude. He then entered the law school at Wake Forest, graduating in 1952 with the LL.B. degree. As a student he was active in student government and the moot court arena. In August, 1952, following his graduation from law school in the spring, he studied for and passed the North Carolina Bar.

With an attractive young wife and three respected academic degrees to his credit, Wiggins was ready for gainful employment. He found it with the Planters National Bank and Trust Company in Rocky Mount. His title was trust officer. His ability was soon recognized, bringing promotions and additonal responsibility. He was active in the religious, social, civic, and legal life of the community, as well as in banking circles.

In December, 1954, he was invited to return to Wake Forest University Law School as professor. The offer was accepted with the understanding that he would remain with the bank for a period of time in order to discharge what the bank felt, and Wiggins agreed, was an obligation resulting from studies and training received while employed by the bank. There was an agreement with Wake Forest that he would seek additional academic training at Columbia University before joining the faculty at his alma mater. At Columbia Wiggins received the coveted Harlan Fiske Stone Fellow. While there he received two degrees, the LL.M. in 1956 and the J.S.D. in 1964. During this time Mrs. Wiggins continued her studies, also, receiving her master's degree in social studies from Columbia. In the fall of 1956 Dr. Wiggins began his teaching at Wake Forest Law School and, in 1964, along with his teaching responsibilities, was made general counsel for the University.

His special interests had been, and continued to be, in the area of wills and trusts. His reputation in the field extended far. At the time of his election to the presidency of Campbell College he was serving as chairman of the trust faculty of the Southwestern Graduate School of Banking at Southern Methodist University, College Park, Texas, and was a member of the faculty of Cannon Trust School of Brevard, North Carolina, and of the National Trust School of Northwestern University, Evanston, Illinois. He had published a highly respected work, consisting of two volumes, titled, *Wills and Administration in North Carolina.* He was also editor of the *North Carolina Will Manual.* As proof of his standing with and evaluation by his peers in the field of college attorneys, he was elected president of that national group.

Ed Wiggins was young, tall, handsome, winsome in personality, brilliant, ambitious, sincere, a deeply committed Christian, with a gifted, accomplished, and lovely wife to join him in the affairs of life. The two were ready; the "stars" were beckoning.

President Wiggins' inauguration took place on April 6, 1968. The event brought together the largest and most distinguished group of scholars and academic administrators ever to gather at "The Creek." More than 150 colleges and universities were officially represented. The schools were listed according to the date of their founding. Harvard University, like Abou Ben Adhem, "led all the rest," having been founded in the year 1636. Vardell Hall brought up the rear; its date was 1964. Learned societies, educational and professional organizations, were well represented. The legal educational forces were present. Greetings were brought by:

Dr. Charles F. Carroll
State Superintendent of Public Instruction
Dr. William H. Plemmons, President, Appalachian State University, for other Colleges and Universities
Mr. Carroll W. Weathers, Dean, Wake Forest University Law School, for Law Schools and Bar Association
Reverend Ben C. Fisher, Executive Director, Christian Higher Education, North Carolina Baptist State Convention
Dr. A. R. Burkot, Dean, Campbell College, for the Faculty of Campbell College
And the Presidents of the six other Baptist Colleges and Universities of the North Carolina Baptist State Convention

Additional greetings were brought by distinguished guests at the inaugural luncheon, including the new president's cherished friend and mentor, Gilbert T. Stephenson, of the Graduate Schools of Banking and Director of Trust Research Department, American Bankers' Association.

President Wiggins' inaugural address was quoted widely by news media and in the halls of academia. Early in his message he set forth the standard by which he would like his administration to be judged. The school should not be judged by the number of students admitted, by the number of students rejected, or by the number of students who failed to meet the school's standards; the school ought to be measured by the services and the contributions its graduates made to mankind.

He affirmed the school's relationship to past heritage and traditions, saying, "To the extent permitted by our resources, we are choosing as our goal distinctive Christian education of an optimum quality for all our students." He said the school would continue to keep the close ties with the Baptist denomination because the school was grateful for what the denomination stood for and was doing in the state, nation, and world. He wanted it firmly understood that his administration considered the place of the teacher as primary in the total mission of the college. To that end teachers would be sought who brought to the school more than catalogue knowledge. The school would continue to seek the kind of teachers who were capable of stimulating both intellectual and spiritual growth. He promised that the school would do all it could to secure adequate financial consideration for the faculty; effort would be put forth to give adequate sabbatical leaves for study and adequate financial resources for family care, but ". . . we will reserve membership on this faculty for those who find their greatest reward in seeing the student grow in wisdom and stature and in favor with God and man."

The new president voiced his interest in and his convictions about the student. He said in the future every effort would be made to attract the student of above-average scholarship, but, at the same time, the school would continue to seek the good average student. "Our program," he said, "will be designed to serve both the average and superior students who are willing to come and live by the simple rules of courtesy, decency and acceptable Christian principles." He closed his address by quoting the statement of Jesus, "Whoever would be first among you shall be servant of all."

The achievements of the administration of J. A. Campbell and Leslie H. Campbell have been noted. These two, father and son, served their own day and generation by the will of God and fell on sleep. The administration of Leslie Campbell was different from that of his father; had to be different. Yet, the ties with the past were kept and cherished. The administration of Norman A. Wiggins would be different from the administration of each of the Campbells. And, yet, his deep appreciation for what had been done under the leadership of each of the Campbells gave assurance that ties would be kept intact and that the enduring heritage and principles of the early days would be prized and embodied in all that he did.

As a senior college, Campbell was only five years old when President Wiggins was elected. The school received accreditation in December of 1966, just six months before he became president. In a real sense, he came to a new school. He came with a deep love for it. He was grateful for what the institution had meant to his own life and to the life of his wife. He had served on its boards, committees, and councils. He was aware of the educational vacuum created in eastern North Carolina by the removal of Wake Forest College to Winston-Salem.

As indicated earlier, President Wiggins had deep convictions about the Christian college. He began his tenure with a desire that amounted to a determination that Campbell should keep its strong allegiance to Jesus Christ and that it should have academic excellence—and in that order. Over and over he expressed to trustees, faculty, students, and friends that these two goals should have priority in his administration.

He frequently quotes the words of Charles Malik, United Nations delegate from Lebanon, later President of the UN General Assembly, who said that one day there would arise a college on whose campus Jesus Christ would feel at home. President Wiggins, without hesitation or embarrassment, affirms that he wants Campbell College to be that school. "The matchless teachings of Jesus Christ in an environment of academic excellence" is his goal. He says that there should be, there can be, no real conflict between moral excellence and the Christian imperative, nor does he believe it possible to have one without the other.

19.
NEW FIRING LINES

Biographers are well aware of the spiritual debt they owe their heroes. I believe they all share the feeling of responsibility expressed by Schorer. Would the subject approve this biography, would he feel it just and fair? If he should meet him in some future world, would he extend the hand of friendship? The biographer in truth lives surrounded by ghosts; the spirits of the dead and the truly great are near him as he writes.

Catherine Drinker Bowen[1]

I HAVE learned that when you have taken one trench, there is a new firing line beyond," said Justice Oliver Wendell Holmes. The new president of Campbell College understood. He was aware of traditions and achievements that sustained and made the school what it was. No one who knew him would doubt his appreciation for Campbell's heritage. Yet he knew that he would have to apply new remedies or expect new problems, that there was always a "new firing line beyond." He would retain and use the past, but he would not be afraid of the new; nor would he hesitate to expand and extend the old. He felt that a stubborn and obstinate retention of custom for custom's sake was as turbulent a thing as any innovation. A cursory view of the past seven years of his administration will leave no doubt as to his innovative approach. In so brief a period of time, with so many parts of President Wiggins' program just moving into gear, it would be exceedingly difficult if not hazardous to attempt an evaluation of his administration. Therefore, a more detailed listing of parts of his program seems in order.

Symbolic of his belief in and insistence upon in-service training, the new president enrolled during his first year as a member of the Executive Management Program conducted by the University of North Carolina Business School. He took as his principal project

221

for study the development of a five-year master plan for Campbell College. In 1971 he attended the IBM school in Poughkeepsie, New York, so that he would have a better understanding of how computer methodology could further the operations of the college. On coming to his new office he immediately identified himself with the forty other private colleges in the state. He served as president of the North Carolina Foundation for Church-Related Colleges and also as president of the North Carolina Association of Independent Colleges and Universities. Having served through the offices of two vice-presidencies, he was, as indicated, elevated to the presidency of the National Association of College and University Attorneys.

President Wiggins early revealed his interest in long-range planning for the campus. He let it be known that he thought beauty was important, important from the standpoint of what the college owed its students, important from the standpoint of securing interest and help from benefactors. Given two schools of equal need and promise, he believed the philanthropist would help the school that had beauty and attractiveness.

At his suggestion, the trustees employed the nationally known landscape architect, Robert H. Rooker of College Station, Texas, to give general guidance to campus development. As a first step toward making the central academic core of the campus pedestrian, Taylor Street, that bisected the campus, was closed. The sand and concrete walks would be replaced with brick and the wide space in front of the old Kivett and D. Rich buildings would become brick. The men's dormitories that ringed the campus circle would be moved to the perimeter of the main campus, leaving the inner space for academic pursuits. Thus, the inner campus would become completely pedestrian.

Other recommendations were placed in the hopper: a new religion building, student center, fine arts center, library expansion, extension of scientific facilities, a new physical education compound, construction of an 18-hole championship golf course, along with desirable acreage for new housing. A number of these projects have been completed or are under construction.

In February, 1969, the Chicago consultant firm of Gosner, Gerber, Tinker and Stuhr was retained by the college. The firm assigned Dr. Robert H. Stuhr, a Phi Beta Kappa graduate of Drake

University with a distinguished record of service to educational institutions to work with Campbell. Dr. Stuhr and the leadership of the college were able to communicate. Dr. Stuhr came to the position with the purpose of advising in the area of executive staff advancement, public relations, fund-raising, and related matters. He was to visit the campus eight times each year, usually for a period of two days per visit. During that time he would meet with professional and voluntary leadership groups of the college, putting the program of the institution under the microscope of the professional consultant.

The board of trustees of the college was enlarged from twenty-eight members to thirty-six. This made it possible to utilize the goodwill, interest, and professional experience of a larger number of influential men in North Carolina Baptist life. The board was organized within a stricter framework and additional duties were assigned. However, the school was allowed to use on the board of trustees only Baptists and these had to be residents of North Carolina. This was what President Leslie Campbell had seen as one handicap with which his successor would have to deal.

On November 7, 1968, "The Presidential Board of Advisors of Campbell College" came into existence. This board numbered thirty-six members, also. Its purpose was to "supplement the work of the Board of Trustees of Campbell College and to aid present and future programs of Campbell College by advising with the chairman of the Board, the president of the college, and other administrative officials." The work of the members of the group was to know the philosophy of the school, to understand and be able to explain the particular features of the college, to acquaint the people of North Carolina and other states, including the business community, with the values of Campbell College, and to make suggestions for the betterment of the school. This group would share "all prerogatives of the Trustees except final responsibility for policy-making." Once each year the board of presidential advisors and the board of trustees would meet together. Membership on the board of advisors would not be limited to residents of North Carolina, nor would its membership be restricted to Baptists. In this way President Wiggins hoped to extend the range and influence of the college and alleviate a difficulty pointed to by his predecessor.

On August 28, 1968, Campbell College made the headlines of the *American Banker,* daily newspaper of the United States banking business. The headline read, "TRUST PROGRAM HAILED AS MAJOR INNOVATION." In its September issue, both papers appearing about the same time, *The Tar Heel Banker,* paper for North Carolina's banking business, announced:

> "FIRST: Campbell College at Buies Creek announced August 23 that it will launch a major academic innovation. A trust major in business administration will be offered, beginning this month with fifteen students. In so far as is known, this is the first undergraduate course of its kind in the world."

The banking journal listed courses that would be offered: corporate finance, accounting procedures for estates: trusts, guardianships and agencies, fiduciary law, investments, taxations and estate planning. Another banking publication, the *Southern Banker,* featured the news giving a comprehensive report of the innovation, calling President Wiggins "one of the most talented individuals you will ever meet" and one well equipped "to launch a curriculum of this magnitude and need."

Gilbert T. Stephenson, the father, grandfather, and uncle of estates and trust business, a North Carolinian, took major time in his convocation address at Wake Forest University, his alma mater, to praise the program being instituted at Campbell. Dr. Herbert S. Croft, senior vice-president and senior trust consultant for First Union National Bank, was named director of trust education and professor of law.

Almost immediately, a complementary program, though not directly related, was established as the Southeastern Trust School at Campbell. This took place in 1969, just a year after the school instituted the trust studies program. The Southeastern Trust School is a project of the North Carolina Bankers Association, while the trust education program is, of course, a part of the program of the college. The two supplement each other. The facilities developed by one is available to the other, such as library holdings, space, and faculty. The banking group affirmed that the establishment of the trust school at Campbell owed much to President Wiggins personally. His wide and continuing interest in the field and his own professional publications and research in the area made him one of the most respected authorities in the field of trusts and estates. The first class graduated from the trust school in June, 1970. Forty-eight students received their diplomas.

From the beginning of his administration President Wiggins felt estate planning should be given major attention by the college, not just as an academic matter but for the welfare of the college itself. He knew the field personally; he believed it could become a major source of income for the college. A department was established and the office placed under the direction of a Campbell alumnus, one of the first to graduate with the new trust major in the area of business administration. To assist the director, a strong advisory estate-planning committee of twenty-eight off-campus specialists were appointed. Seminars were regularly held, an informational newsletter mailed out, and carefully planned contacts made.

In 1968 the college entered "the world of the computer." Until that time no courses in computer science were offered. Since that date its own computer equipment has been increasing, a qualified director placed in charge, and additional personnel added. Some courses are offered for credit in computer science. The business affairs of the college including current funds, plant funds, and endowment funds are handled by computer. The teaching staff in math, languages, and others are using the program. If the questions and problems become too complicated for the equipment stationed at the college, there is a tie-in by telephone sending-and-receiving, with the more sophisticated equipment at the Triangle Universities Computer Center at Research Triangle Park, twenty-five miles away.

In 1974 the college "took to the air" through owning and operating an FM radio station. Its call letters are WCCE, standing for "We Are Campbell for Christian Education." It is a 3000-watt station with a range of from 30 to 50 miles. The main purpose of the station is the same as the central purpose of the school, Christian education for life and living. The station expects to represent the college in concerts, dramatics, lectures, sports events, music, etc. The Sunday morning worship services from the two local churches will be broadcast. The station will also be an outlet for training campus talent and a facility for instruction for credit in radio communications.

One of the first official actions of President Wiggins was to request that the school apply for an Army Reserve Officers Training Corps, ROTC. He had seen such a program in operation at Wake Forest University and liked its work and influence on that campus. Too, he believed strongly that the country at large would benefit from having a sizable percentage of its military officers trained in civilian schools. In 1972 Campbell College welcomed its first ROTC unit. From the beginning of the program President Wiggins has been active in his support of the unit, has often spoken at its functions and for its promotion.

During the school year 1973-74, 150 full-time students at Campbell were members of the United States Army; close to half of these were special duty personnel. These men were members of "Operations Bootstrap." In this program the men, soldier-students, request permission from the army to complete their college degree; to be a member of the group a person must have had some college work. Six months are allowed for the completion of a two-year college degree, and up to eighteen months are allowed for the completion of a four-year degree. Students attend the school at their own expense, though they may use their GI Bill to cover tuition and fees. The student's military pay continues and the army bears transportation and moving costs if relocation becomes necessary. For every year of schooling permitted by the army, the student is obligated to give two years of active duty following graduation. The college has recognized that many of the persons applying for this program have had nontraditional backgrounds from the standpoint of academic requirements; so the institution works with the men to satisfy these requirements. Once the student has been accepted, however, he is on his own. Nothing special is done for the soldier-student that is not available to the traditional student. So when the bootstrapper completes the work required by the college for graduation, he has the knowledge that no favors have been granted.

As stated earlier, President Wiggins believes in cooperating with other schools and programs of mutual concern. Campbell became one of six private institutions in North Carolina to receive accreditation from the National Council for Accreditation of Teacher Education, NCATE. The school participated as one of the institutions in a pilot program for curricular study and possible revision instituted by the center for continuing Renewal of Higher Education of the North Carolina State Board of Higher Education. Campbell became one of the four schools in North Carolina cooperating with the public school system in the federally funded Career Opportunities Program, COP.

Through the years the college has ministered significantly to its own area, has been aware of and committed to giving major attention to students residing in Harnett and surrounding counties. In keeping with this concern, beginning in 1970, the school furnished the teaching staff for a full introductory liberal-arts program at the nearby technical institutes. Students enroll for this program and pay the rates set for those institutions by the North Carolina Community College System. The students are given dual enrollment, with the institute and with Campbell College. After satisfactorily completing the courses, up to 42 hours, in freshman and sophomore work, they are eligible for transfer to Campbell or to any other college or university. In 1972-73 there were 160 students enrolled in these programs. Twelve teachers from Campbell were giving a part of their teaching time to the program, and the college had forty students who had completed the work in the institutes and had come to Campbell for further study.

The financial status of the college has been enhanced through funds given to endow chairs in different fields. The Tyner Chair of Bible was created in 1964. Its financial structure has been enhanced in recent years. The chair is a memorial to Lewis and Martha Barnes Tyner, a distinguished Robeson County family noted for its leadership in Baptist life, educational affairs, and other constructive causes.

In 1969 the Campbell College Alumni Association began a movement to endow the Mabel Powell Chair of English. Miss Powell taught English and Latin at Campbell for 43 years: loved and respected, feared and dreaded, adored and abhorred more per pound-weight than any other teacher in the history of the school! Yet when old grads return to the school, they "beat a path" to the door of her small white cottage hard by the school.

The Graham A. Barden Chair of Government was activated in

1971, in honor of Congressman Barden who so effectively represented the Third Congressional District in the United States House of Representatives for many years. The Barden Chair has enlisted the interest of citizens far and wide who give special thought to good government. This Chair serves as the center of the department of government at the school.

In 1972 the Charles Barrett and Alma Dark Howard Chair of Religion was established by the Howard Christian Education Fund. The Chair honors the beloved Charles B. Howard and his gifted wife, Alma Dark Howard. Dr. Howard was college pastor and Bible teacher at the school for twenty-five years. As stated earlier, through the Christian Education Fund which he founded, promoted and shepherded, nearly 2,000 students have been aided and well over $2,000,000 placed in circulation. In addition to the endowed Chair of Religion, the fund is undergirding two scholarship funds of $30,000 each for students coming to Campbell College from specific areas.

The school year 1971-72 brought to the campus a new lecture series, "The Staley Distinguished Christian Lecture Program," which was originated by Thomas F. Staley "to bring to the college and university campuses of America, distinguished scholars who truly believe and who can clearly communicate to students." The program was initiated by Mr. Staley in 1969; therefore, Campbell was one of the schools to be chosen early for the series. At this time, 1974, there have been four runs of the lectures at Campbell. The lecturers were: Dr. Ernest Gordon, dean of the chapel at Princeton University; Dr. George E. Schweitzer, distinguished professor of the University of Tennessee; Dr. David H. C. Read, minister of the Madison Avenue Presbyterian Church, New York City; and Dr. Edward B. Lindaman, president of Whitworth College, Spokane, Washington. Dr. Lindaman was, previously, an executive with Rockwell International, making a vital contribution to the space program.

Dr. Wiggins is a strong believer in sports. As stated, his first contact as a student with the school was through a "sports-work scholarship." In 1970 Campbell placed its first golfers on All-American squads; the same year the school won a national championship. In 1969-70 Campbell had three coaches to win NAIA

District Coach of the Year Awards: Cole in soccer, Roberts in basketball, and Wood in cross country. In 1972 Coach Brown took three of his wrestlers who had won district championships to Oregon for national competition. Coach Cole's soccer teams were fifth nationally in 1969 and third nationally in 1970. President Wiggins sees that Campbell graduates who go on to professional sports are duly recognized. The two Perrys: Jim and Gaylord, baseball pitchers, both Cy Young Award winners, were given the college's "Distinguished Alumni Award." Cal Koonce, another major league pitcher, served as pitching coach at Campbell after retiring from professional sports. Since 1956 the school has had one of the best known, largest attended, and most successful basketball schools for young players. Repeatedly the instruction staff has been headed by "Coach" John Wooden of the famous UCLA Bruins. Other top national talent is brought to the college for the event.

One of the few undertakings on the campus expected to be self-liquidating is the Keith Hills Golf Club operation. The project, golf and family living, comprises 450 acres of land that was formerly used as the Campbell College farm. Ellis Maples of Atlanta was chosen to supervise the planning and development of the golf course. Maples has been rated as one of the two top designers of golf courses in America, having to his credit the three golf courses at Whispering Pines and three at Lake Surf. In May, 1973, the golf course at Linville, North Carolina, known as the Grandfather Mountain Course, which he supervised, was featured in *Golf Digest*. Maples believes the Keith Hills Course at Campbell has distinctive possibilities for championship golf.

The second part of the Keith Hills Country Club project deals with choice living areas. The promoters may have become a bit flowery but do keep to the facts in emphasizing the desirable nature of the area:

> Within commuting distance of two great metropolitan areas, Raleigh and Fayetteville, on the borderline between the Piedmont and the Central Plains, where the east meets the west in North Carolina lies beautiful Keith Hills, an ideal place for your primary or secondary home. A warmly agreeable community at its best within a great cultural area, Keith Hills offers a place where you can build your own home within whatever life style you choose. In the truest sense, Keith Hills has been planned from the ground up. It has been planned for a community of friendly people and families; yet, here you will find maximum privacy at all times whenever

you want it. The homesites are packed with magnificent trees; the water sites command unusual views, and the fairway frontal sites are equally as beautiful.

The promotional material goes on to emphasize that the community will have riding stables, with enchanting riding trails; there will be tennis, swimming, fishing, and, of course, the finest golf!

Since Dr. Wiggins came to the school the academic department of the college has been restructured in its governing procedures, a constitution drafted, and a faculty senate put into operation. The senate is, in effect, an executive committee of the faculty. It is composed of one elected representative of each department that grants a major and one member to represent together the departments that do not grant a major. A constitution has been drafted and put into operation. The office of two vice-presidents has been created—one for academic affairs and one for advancement, the vice-president for academic affairs serving as academic dean.

From the beginning of his administration President Wiggins has sought to give students increased responsibility in the work of the college. The new regime came on the scene in the 60's; because of the timing, disturbance from the students might have been expected. However, agitation was minimal. The president likes to say that while many students were parading, breaking, and burning, Campbell students were in the chapel praying. True, they may have had on black armbands but they were praying! From the first, President Wiggins has sought to communicate with the students. A regular student breakfast was inaugurated. Six students, appointed by the president of the Student Government Association, from groups wishing to talk with the president, individuals of the student body who desired contact with the president, or representatives or individuals with whom Dr. Wiggins desired contact, came. In an informal atmosphere, a give-and-take spirit, the concerns of the students as well as the position and intent of the school were discussed. The president has promoted better living conditions for the students along with increased student aid. Statistics will be given later.

In one of the few serious disciplinary problems involving a fairly large number of students, the president scheduled time for private, unhurried conferences with each student involved. While the difficulty resulted in a number of students being dismissed from the school, repeatedly parents of the disciplined students expressed gratitude to the president for the fair, creative, and personal way in which the matter was handled, especially his own involvement in the case.

Crucial to the welfare and progress of any college is the involvement of its alumni. Financial participation on the part of former students is important but not the only help that can be given. As a rule, potentially large givers, trusts, and foundations want to know how the alumni are involved in the promotion of a school. Again, a junior college is at a distinct disadvantage with its alumni. Those who are most able to give have usually gone on to four-year schools. These institutions are often first to claim the loyalty of these graduates. With Campbell becoming a four-year school, it had a much better chance of securing the commitment and the financial participation of its alumni. But such involvement on the part of alumni takes time. Campbell graduated its first four-year class in 1963. Those graduates have been out only eleven years, scarcely time for the average alumnus to become established so that major assistance could be given the college. Still, as later statistics will show, the increased participation is significant.

During the seven years of President Wiggins' tenure there have been individuals and families that could be placed in the large gift category. It was during this seven-year span that the college received its first million-dollar gift. The benefactor was E. P. Sauls of Garner, North Carolina, and Sarasota, Florida. Among other large givers the following names appear: Jack Kitchin, Norfolk, Virginia; Bobby Murray, Raleigh; Fred Taylor, Vass; Bobby Roberts, Durham; Charles B. Howard, Buies Creek; J. M. Shouse, Winston-Salem; Gale Johnson, Dunn; the B. Y. Tyners, Raleigh; and Fred R. Keith, Lumberton. Among other generous contributors the names of Ramsey E. Cammack, Robert A. Harris, Willis Kivett, Arial Creed, the Raymond Bryans, Mrs. J. Hunter Strickland, the Nelson Strawbridges, Miss Ora Cansler, Burrows T. Lundy, and Harry Carter stand out.

The following statistics tell an encouraging story. The seven-year story of President Wiggins' administration and the past fiscal year picture of his administration are given:

GIVING BY PUBLICS, 1973-74

Alumni	$ 129,405.89
Parents	17,628.00
Trustees	135,485.00
Presidential Board of Advisors	38,707.60
Faculty	8,646.31
Staff	11,054.23
Students	701.00
N. C. Baptist State Convention	383,001.88
N. C. Baptist Churches	7,726.67
Harnett County	13,785.27
Firms & Foundations Outside Harnett County	226,642.53
Individual Friends Outside Harnett County	181,730.74
Total giving by publics	1,061,428.05
Student Loans and Federal Grants	322,393.64
Total All Gifts	$1,766,823.57

GIFTS AND GRANTS, 1973-74

Fund	Source	Classification	Amount
Current Funds	N. C. Baptist State Convention	Unrestricted	$357,372.55
Current Funds	Foundations and Others	Unrestricted	290,414.90
Current Funds	Student Aid Grants Federal Gov.	Restricted	273,819.28
Current Funds	Student Aid Grants— N. C.	Restricted	310,347.36
Plant Funds	All Sources	Restricted	172,984.49
Endowment and Annuity Funds	All Sources	Restricted	194,555.99
National Defense Stu. Loan Fund	Federal Government	Restricted	167,329.00
		Total all Gifts	$1,766,823.57

PROGRESSION OF GROWTH, 1967-1974

Campbell's Combined Funds Comparative Balance Sheet, omitted here to conserve space, shows the following successive amount of increase in net worth of the college for each of the last seven fiscal years as follows:

1967-68, $459,821.72; 1968-69, $861,325.60; 1969-70, $1,035,960.94; 1970-71, $2,066,790.16; 1971-72, $1,568,686.93; 1972-73, $1,148,639.33; and 1973-74, $828,893.10.

The total increase in net worth of the college for the seven years has been $7,790,117.78. The percentage of increase for the seven-year period is 133.7%.

CAMPBELL NOW—GOAL $8.7 million

Last Five Years Gift Report by Publics

JUNE 1, 1969-MAY 31, 1974

Public	1969-70	1970-71	1971-72	1972-73	1973-74	Totals
Alumni	78,779.97	107,109.63	130,993.11	121,352.71	129,405.89	567,640.31
Parents	3,960.50	38,254.75	12,774.50	19,015.00	17,628.00	91,632.75
Trustees	89,873.00	81,910.56	73,412.50	82,020.00	135,485.00	462,701.06
Pres. Board of Advisors	24,375.00	74,535.44	306,532.07	74,577.65	38,707.60	518,727.76
Faculty	4,892.90	11,813.91	9,812.30	6,085.46	8,646.31	41,250.88
Staff	3,664.65	7,934.20	7,459.03	8,085.67	11,054.23	38,197.78
Students	300.00	3,715.92	46.70	811.66	701.00	5,575.28
Bapt. State Convention	313,321.41	286,552.57	318,819.46	353,145.97	383,001.88	1,654,841.29
Churches	15,811.42	6,937.58	28,963.46	6,212.08	7,726.67	65,651.21
Harnett County	15,408.99	74,773.21	21,162.77	15,451.53	13,785.27	140,581.77
Firms & Foundations Outside Harnett	124,448.99	247,909.47	194,614.40	218,393.87	226,642.53	1,012,009.26
Individual Friends Outside Harnett	83,224.20	1,097,083.04	278,937.31	283,838.85	181,730.74	1,924,814.14
Grants	245,205.07	1,250,998.88	404,342.30	146,866.83	320,000.00	2,367,413.08
Total	934,008.10	2,413,838.59	1,716,793.48	1,235,650.21	1,381,428.05	7,681,718.43

Five-Year Goal $8,700,000.00

Total Cash and Pledges $8,799,824.13

Oversubscription $99,824.13

Pledges $1,118,105.70

Note that for each of the seven years of Dr. Wiggins' administration the operating budget of the college was balanced. The net worth of the college increased during that time by 133.7%. During each of the seven years the college experienced an average net gain of $1,138,588.25. This took place during the time when many small independent colleges were being pushed to the wall of failure. The business manager of the college, Lonnie D. Small, who for twenty-five years has given wise, capable leadership to the business affairs of the college, called attention to a significant point that does not immediately make itself known from the statistics. The increase during the seven years was about equal to the funds received during that time through the "Campbell Now" program, showing that the money that came through that campaign went to the objects for which it was given rather than for organization and administration of a program to collect it. The national average cost of professional fund-raisers is 26.4%. The business manager has pointed out: "Had we gone that route [of the professional fund raisers] we would have been able to keep for the purposes given, only 75% of the total gifts. During the past seven years, our total promotional expenses have been budgeted for and borne by the current fund."

Another item that the statistics do not point up clearly is the morale of the college family. It is significant that during the year ending May 31, 1974, approximately 75% of all departments and functions operated for less than the approved appropriations.

The statistical chart speaks eloquently for student aid that the college furnishes. One item for which the president is especially grateful is the increased help that is being given to students from Baptist families. Free tuition is given to full-time students who are pastors or wives of pastors of Baptist churches participating in the program of the Baptist State Convention. Sons and daughters of ministers of Baptist churches which work through the program promoted by the Baptist State Convention, and children of associational missionaries and children of employees of the Baptist State Convention with headquarters in Raleigh are given an additional $200 each year. Scholarships are made available by Campbell to Royal Ambassadors and Acteens, missionary groups for young men and women within the churches. These scholarships range in value from $800 to $1,600 over a four-year period.

In 1972 the Snyder Memorial Baptist Church of Fayetteville bought and made available at the college a "missionary furlough home." The home is furnished, rent-free, to a missionary on furlough. The school offers free tuition to the children in the home who are of college age, enabling the missionaries to have their family together during furlough. The intent of the project is that by having the different missionary families on the campus, students will not only be introduced to "live missionaries" but also learn vital information on the countries where the missionaries serve. The college works with Snyder Memorial Church in selecting the missionary family that is to reside in the home. When this home was put into operation at Campbell, sixty other churches in the Southern Baptist Convention had furlough homes for missionaries. But to our knowledge, the one established by Snyder Memorial Church is the only one on a college campus.

Another indication of President Wiggins' interest in and his desire for relationship from the religious forces is shown by an organization of ministers known as "The Board of Ministers for Campbell College." It is a 160-member group. Its representation is drawn from three states: North and South Carolina and Virginia. Although made up of Baptist ministers primarily, other denominations may be and are represented. The board has a rotating membership: forty members come on and forty are rotated off each year. It nominates and recommends members, but the trustees of the college are required to elect. The purpose and work of the ministers is to inform, report on, and in all ways possible represent Campbell College.

The following letter is included because it evaluates the institution and thereby assesses the administration of President Wiggins. The report is from a source that can be counted on for objectivity:

Inner City Fund
300 M Street, Southwest
Suite N-600
Washington, D. C. 20024

August 18, 1971

Dr. Norman Wiggins, President
Campbell College
Buies Creek, North Carolina

Dear President Wiggins,

The preliminary Inner City Fund Report on higher education has been submitted to the Assistant Secretary for Planning and Evaluation of HEW. As soon as copies are available for distribution, you and Dean Burkot will each receive one. I am taking this opportunity to extend my personal thanks to you and the Dean for the wholehearted cooperation that you gave us. Because of that cooperation, and because Campbell College is so well managed, the quality of our program budget for Campbell exceeds that for any of the other schools that participated in the study.

As you know, we interviewed faculty, students and administrators and prepared program budgets for nine colleges and universities. These included Wesleyan, Berkeley, Drake, Chicago, N. C. State, Georgetown, George Washington, Laney State and Campbell. These schools were chosen to provide a partial cross-section of higher education in the United States.

Three things impressed us most about Campbell. First, we were very impressed with the detail, accuracy and retrievability of standard financial data. Second, we were pleased to discover how close to a program budget framework the operating control practices at Campbell already are. There was never any question about what inputs supported which outputs, and what the costs of the inputs and benefits of the outputs were. Of all the schools we studied, none were better prepared in a management sense to cope with the educational challenges of the 1970's. This may be making a virtue of necessity, but in these times sound management practices *are* a necessary virtue.

The last, but not the least, thing which especially impressed us was the consensus among students, administration and faculty on the mission of Campbell College. The students we talked with all agreed that failure to succeed and learn at Campbell could only be traced to a failure on the student's part to take advantage of the opportunities offered. The factors at work here are reflected in small classes, personal supervision, tutorials and regular, open student-faculty-administration discussion of issues of mutual concern. Campbell is an educational leader in this regard.

I hope that Campbell prospers and continues to provide a sound and rewarding educational experience for her students.

Sincerely yours,
Edward W. Erickson

Major programs, organizations, groups, projects, some new, some old, have been recorded. For most of these the administration of President Wiggins deserves credit, as it must assume accountability. Certainly seven years is too brief a period of time to tabulate results. But progress reports are encouraging.

In his dream Mr. D. Rich heard the Master Teacher, who is also the Lord of life, say: "Buies Creek Must Live." By the grace of God, through the loyalty of friends, plus the devotion and sacrifices of her servants, Campbell College does live and shall live!

Now, even the writer of the Fourth Gospel admits, when he comes to the close of his volume, that he has not given a full and

NEW FIRING LINES   **237**

complete account of all that his chief Character did and said. The author states that to do so would, he thinks, require more books than the world could contain! He affirms, however, that what his volume does contain has been written with a purpose: that his readers may believe certain Truth and know unfailing Life.

With what I trust is due reverence, with what I know to be honest humility, and with a consciousness of inadequacy amounting to distress, I bring this account of the founding and growth of Campbell College to an end.

The story has not been fully told; in many instances what has been told has the marks of incompetency. But all that has been written is to the end that those who read may know more fully and understand with greater appreciation that Campbell College made its way toward "the stars through difficulties." And, that there once was, is, and, within the continuing providence of God, ever shall be that "flaming wisp of glory" kindled on Harnett's gentle sands. So knowing and so appreciating, we may incarnate a little more fully the motives and goals that have always prompted the celestial journey.

Note

1. *Biography: The Craft and the Calling* (Little, Brown and Co., 1969), p. 151.

APPENDIXES

1.

FORTUNES OF THE FOUNDER

Heights of great men reached and kept
Were not attained by sudden flight,
But they, while their companions slept,
Were toiling upward in the night.

Longfellow

THE weather report for January 13, 1862, was as follows: "The weather is bright today, with a high wind prevailing that dries the road quickly." Good! For that morning little Jim Arch Campbell was born. And, as long as he lived, whenever he appeared, the sun came out. He brought the winds of encouragement, refreshment, and vigor. His life would be spent in drying the roads of life, giving a firmer foundation for the marching feet of the children of God. "The weather is bright today, with a high wind prevailing that dries the road quickly." YAH!!

James Archibald Campbell, the founding father of this school was born in a small clapboard house that still stands about ten miles from this spot. It is on the road between Angier and Fuquay-Varina.

His father was a farmer and blacksmith; later he would become a Baptist preacher. Neither he nor his wife had formal education. He and his son would study together, briefly, in a little one-room school near the home.

The Campbells were not newcomers to the area. The ancestor of the clan had been a member of what Malcom Fowler called the "Legion of Restless Men," who came over from Scotland in 1739, a boatload of them. They settled in this Cape Fear region, a region that the historian described as "a land of rolling hills and fertile bottoms covered with forests and longleaf pine, interspersed with mighty oaks, poplars, massive elms, beeches and walnut trees."

238

J. A. Campbell opened school here on a cold, misty, sleety morning. The date was January 5, 1887. Sixteen students answered to the roll call. Actually twenty-one had come, but five worked on the unfinished schoolhouse while sixteen, with the red-haired young teacher, met in the church building.

A total of 92 students enrolled for the spring term. The young teacher felt that it had been a good year. He invited young Josephus Daniels to be his commencement speaker. Daniels traveled the thirty miles from Raleigh by railroad; he came through Selma and to Dunn. He came by horse and buggy from Dunn. It took him a full day to get here from Raleigh. He could have come all the way by horse and buggy but it would have been hot, dusty, and bumpy. Besides, it would have taken a full day anyway.

Forty-eight years later, the spring of 1935, Josephus Daniels was again the commencement speaker. Now Daniels was a world figure: He was editor and publisher of the *Raleigh News and Observer*, former Secretary of the Navy under President Woodrow Wilson, former Ambassador to Mexico. I give you a quotation from his commencement address: "If you should ask me what the greatest revolution in North Carolina has been during the last half century and in what county, I should not hesitate to say it has been the building of this educational institution in Harnett County by Jim Arch Campbell. What he has done gives me faith in mankind.

How did James Archibald Campbell do it? By following the gleam; by favoring his bent; by watching for the open door.

He followed the gleam. The man had a dream, a purpose, a magnificent obsession.

He had a high and firm allegiance to Jesus Christ as the Lord and Master of his life. I do not state that as a matter of course or because it sounds good and you expect to hear it from me. I state it because it is true and because you cannot really understand J. A. Campbell or what he did apart from it. From the night in the little vertical clapboard house, resting on the gentle sands of Harnett County, when a man, who happened to have a black skin, turned the boy's life toward Jesus, to the day when he died with his face bathed in sunlight from the skies and from the heavens, he was a possessed man, possessed by Jesus Christ and his way of life. J. A. Campbell followed the gleam.

He publicly accepted Christ at the little church where his father preached; was baptized by his father, the first person his father ever baptized. Later he would feel led to become a minister of the gospel; he was ordained and began to pastor churches. He was a good pastor; he loved the people; he prayed for the sick; he buried the dead; he married the lovers; he counseled the confused; he built church houses. He followed the gleam.

He followed the gleam by dedicating his life to bringing light and learning to the people who walked in darkness. He would make them see the great Light! To this task he brought a rare native ability and a concentrated effort seldom seen by the sons and daughters of men. And, as rays of the sun focused on sheets of glass will burn through plates of steel as a needle will pierce tissue paper, so he cut through obstacles and difficulties that would have overwhelmed a less dedicated man. I quote: "I'm sure the bank wrote me off a hundred times; but help always came. Time and time again we were scraping bottom, but I knew I was doing something God wanted done; trying to make men out of boys. I put everything in his hands—and I worked my head off." Those are the words of Frank Borden, headmaster of the famous Deerfield School for Boys. It might have been said, and equally appropriately said, of J. A. Campbell.

From the beginning his passion was that his school prepare young men and young women for a living and for a life, not one but both. He was as concerned that Christ have his way in the classroom as that he have his way in the church house, no difference. Miss Mabel Powell remembers the first faculty meeting when she came on the faculty in 1925. Dr. Campbell began his words to them as follows: "You have not been asked to come on this faculty because of your degrees. Yes, we want capable teachers for we are concerned that the young people who come here secure a good education. But that is not why I have asked you to come to us. You have been invited to teach at Campbell because you know the Lord Jesus Christ as your personal Savior and because you love boys and girls." In the last conversation that Miss Powell had with J. A. Campbell during his last illness, he said: "I want you to promise me that, in as far as it is within your power, if the time ever comes when Christ is not honored in this school, the name

'Campbell' will come off these buildings." He followed the gleam.

He did not coddle his students. While he did everything for us, he expected everything from us. He taught us that what was within us was always greater than the circumstances outside us. Like God, he would not suffer us to be burdened beyond what we were able to bear, but there were times when we were sorry that he had so much confidence in our ability! I have been unable to find proof that Frank Leahy, the famous football coach at Notre Dame, was ever a student of J. A. Campbell's, but well he might have been; well he might have gotten his slogan from the red-haired Scotsman. Leahy put a poster on the gym door. On the poster in big letters were the words: "When the going gets tough, let the tough get going." Those were the last words his players saw before going on the field of combat. J. A. Campbell would have liked that! He followed the gleam.

Second, *he favored his bent.* There were areas of interest, disposition, temperament, abilities, and possibilities that were peculiarly his. He believed that these were gifts from God. He favored them.

See him. He was six feet tall. He had sandy-red hair and mustache; both were always carefully trimmed. His eyes were blue, sharp with the characteristic of quick change. They mirrored his emotions that could quickly change from smiles to tears, from deep conviction to light-hearted banter.

He blushed like a modest maiden. His coloring forecast his speech. We were able to anticipate his humor before it was put in words; the very anticipation of some choice bit of wit would bring a glow to his appearance. The blush would begin at his collar band, move up across his cheeks, emphasize the crowfeet at the corners of his eyes, mount in temples and forehead and climb into his tawny hair. By this time he was speaking the words, the anticipation of which had brought the glow to his countenance. He reminded us of the freshman who wrote to her parents: "I love college," she said. "I feel good! I have made a lot of friends; I have put on weight. In fact," she wrote, "I weigh 118 lbs. stripped for gym." Her father wrote back, "I am glad you are enjoying college. But I am concerned. Who is this Jim you are stripping for?" From his shirt collar to the top of his head there was a ruddy glow as he anticipated telling that story. I remember it as if it had been yesterday!

He walked with a firm and steady stride. His gait and carriage announced that he knew where he was going, why, and what he intended doing when he got there. He had rich emotions. His red hair announced that he was not afraid of a fight. He never sought one, never ran away from one, and seldom lost one that was forced on him. I once heard him say: "There' are those of you who talk about controlling temper; some of us control more temper in an hour than others of you know in a year."

His promotional skill was legendary. He never gave himself to a project or person that he did not believe in strongly; he did not give his support lightly. But once he gave it, every stubborn ounce of his energy went to that cause or person. A citizen of this community who knew him well and had often crossed swords with him said: "J. A. Campbell is the greatest promoter I have ever seen. Had he been a patent medicine salesman, he would have become a millionaire."

He was a born and matured leader. Charisma exuded from his quiet demeanor. Dr. Charles B. Howard brought a friend, Charlie Moore, to visit with Dr. Campbell. On the way back to Franklin County, Mr. Moore was strangely quiet. Finally Dr. Howard said to him: "Well, what do you think of Dr. Campbell?" Mr. Moore replied: "Whatever group he is in, he will be the tallest man present." It was close to the truth. Wherever J. A. Campbell sat, that was the head of the table. Coming into any group, you would see heads turn toward him, eyes focus upon him; the group would become quiet and attentive, waiting for J. A. Campbell's comments, observations, or questions. This was without effort or pushiness; it was not what the man said, not what the man did; it was the man himself.

He had a special gift for hard work, tight discipline, sane frugality, and disturbing sacrifices. His days were long, often sixteen hours.

For years he carried a full load of teaching;
He administered the school;
At times he was Superintendent of County Schools;
At times he sold insurance;
At times he was bank president;
Always he was pastor of churches;
Always he was a farmer;

In the evenings at home, by the fire, he graded papers;
     he wrote and edited a paper; he prepared sermons and chapel talks; he answered letters, always by hand, sometimes fifteen to twenty in an evening. Letters were answered the day of arrival.
He read papers, magazines, and books;
     Clippers and a paper-knife were always handy; he ran an extensive clipping service: jokes, folk sayings, proverbs, poems. These would find their way into his paper and into his chapel talks and sermons.

He believed firmly along with Lincoln in what is sometimes referred to, and not always kindly, as the Protestant ethic:

He did not believe you could bring prosperity by discouraging thrift;
That you could strengthen the weak by weakening the strong;
That you could help the wage earner by pulling down the wage payer;
That you could help the poor by destroying the rich;
That you could build character and courage by taking away initiative and independence.
Or that you could help persons permanently by doing for them what they could and should do for themselves.

He believed that one reason so many people did not recognize opportunity when they met it was that opportunity frequently went around in overalls and looked like hard work!

He believed the undisciplined life was not worth living; that the difference in a powerful, life-giving river and a useless, disease-infested swamp was the banks that disciplined the waters.

The work, the discipline, the sacrifice that he asked of us, he exemplified and demonstrated in his own life. There was never any question about his willingness to give his best, his all, and then just a little more. "Like a bridge over troubled water, He laid him down." Over his great heart, his sympathetic mind, his courageous will, we, his students, crossed over to a better and a more useful life.

Whatever else may be said about increased cost of fees, tuition, room and board, and other expenses here at Campbell College, no student can pay for his education. The hard discipline, the sacrificial work, the lonely vigils, the agonizing prayer, and all but actual blood that was mixed with the brick and mortar of the early buildings on this campus make us, the students, forever indebted to the founder and those noble souls who stood by his side and laid themselves down over troubled waters no less than their captain that those who would come after, might cross over to a day and a life that was beyond them.

He watched for the open door. He followed the gleam; he favored his bent; he watched for the open door. And he was never averse to giving that door a gentle but firm shove.

Once Stuart Kinzie interviewed Charles Coburn the great actor. Kinzie began in the usual way by asking Coburn what a person needed to do in order to get ahead in life. Did he need brains? did he need energy? did he need education? Coburn shook his head. "Those things help, of course," he said, "but there is something I consider even more important: *knowing the moment.*"

What moment? Coburn continued: "The moment to act—or not to act. The moment to speak—or keep silent. On the stage, as every actor knows, timing is the all-important factor. I believe it is the key in life, too. If you master the art of knowing the moment, in your marriage, in your work, your relationships with others, you won't have to pursue happiness and success. They'll walk right in your front door."

J. A. Campbell knew the moment. He watched for the open door. This was true in the beginning of the school here. Paul Green said: "Campbell College came into existence because the soul of a community needed it and because there was a man who had the vision of how to fill that soul's need."

For the life of me, I cannot see how J. A. Campbell could have done what he did at another time in history! With all due reverence, "In the fullness of time God sent forth his son," James Archibald Campbell.

Consider that time. By the calendar, J. A. Campbell was born only 112 years ago. There are people living today who are that old. So, by the calendar his birth was only a short time ago. But the calendar is not always the best instrument for measuring time; events may be better. And, by events, J. A. Campbell was born a thousand years ago.

When he started his school here, one out of every three persons in North Carolina could neither read nor write.

Three years after he started his school, every school building in the state combined was worth less than one million dollars. Our new religion building cost 1¼ million. The average teacher's salary was $25 per month.

When J. A. Campbell was born, every third person in North Carolina was a slave. The day after the birth of J. A. Campbell the *Fayetteville Observer* carried the following announcement:

> Sale of Negroes—The following sale of Negroes took place in this city yesterday. The sale was conducted by J. J. Moore, auctioneer, and considering the times, the prices realized were very good:
>
> | | |
> |---|---|
> | Betty, 65 years old | $800.00 |
> | Ida, 60 years old | 400.00 |
> | Caroline, 32 years old | 475.00 |
> | Lemuel, 32 years old | 550.00 |
> | Louisa, 17 years old | 660.00 |
> | Lizzie, 17 years old | 535.00 |
> | Wiley, 80 years old | 1.00 |

You see, J. A. Campbell was not born 112 years ago; only the calendar says that. By events, he was born a thousand years ago. And the soul of the community needed what he could give it.

And the yeast of enlightenment was at work. It was the chosen moment. The door was opening and J. A. Campbell was ready.

The morning of the birth of J. A. Campbell, James M. Barrie was two years old, George Bernard Shaw was six, Robert Louis Stevenson was twelve, Thomas Edison was fifteen, and Alexander Graham Bell was fifteen. On the day that he was born there appeared in the *Register*, forerunner of the *News and Observer*, an announcement of the publication of a book by George Eliot called *The Mill on the Floss* and one by Nathaniel Hawthorne called *The Marble Fawn*. If time allowed, I think I could prove to you that J. A. Campbell was able to perceive the tidal quality of time; he was able to project plans, to float ideas, to undertake movements on the crest of time's tide. And, therefore, many of these led on to fortune when at another time the countryside would have been strewn with their wreckage. He was a man, take him for all in all; we shall not see his like again.

2.

ACCESSION OF THE SON

AND James Archibald Campbell died in a good old age, full of riches and honor; and Leslie, his son, reigned in his stead."

The date of J. A. Campbell's death was March 18, 1934. Eight days later, on March 26, Leslie succeeded him as president of Campbell College.

In his inaugural address the new president said: "This is not a coronation day. Rather it witnesses the solemn dedication and surrender of all there is in our life to a holy cause."

When he took office his salary was less than $1,000 per year. The enrollment of the school was 312 students. The total assets of the institution were less than one-half million dollars. Of the twelve buildings on the campus, several had been dwelling units. The total faculty numbered twenty-two.

Let me structure this address in threes: Leslie Campbell had three superior assets; he faced three overshadowing obstacles; he made three magnificent contributions.

First, *the assets*. One, he was a Christian by choice and conviction and practice. Speaking to the congregation of his church in 1969, he said:

> Sixty-five years ago this spring, at eleven years of age, I was attending school in the old tabernacle, the only building on the school campus at that time. One morning that spring, during a revival meeting, I walked down the isle and confessed Christ and a few days later they took me down to Kivett's pond and baptized me into the membership of the church. . . . From the standpoint of membership I am probably the oldest living member. My grandfather Pearson, then its oldest member, threw the first shovel of dirt in the excavation for erecting this building and I was chosen to throw the second.

He had deep Christian convictions and rich emotions but he seldom traded on sentiment. To him religion was a way of life growing out of deep and abiding principles that were anchored in a personal relationship to Jesus Christ.

There was never any question in his mind as to the position of Campbell College in its relationship to the Christian gospel. Speaking to the trustees, at their request, in 1966, he said:

> In some way the ideals, the affections, resolves and will power of coming generations of youth must be lifted. I know of no such regenerating dynamic to be found outside the Christian concept. If Campbell College and other church-related colleges fail in their Christian witness, the future of the church and our whole society may well be in jeopardy.

President Campbell harnessed that Pegasus of high principle. During my own student days here I saw and felt his plow as it turned the fallow soil of human hearts. One instance. A series of revival services was being held on our campus. The school was in an ugly and rebellious mood over an incident that had arisen. The gospel of good news and good will was being preached, but the students were not buying it. No life was being touched. We came to the last day of the special services, to the last service. Leslie Campbell asked a group of students and members of the faculty to meet him during the hour of worship. I was in that group; we met in the old Phi Society Hall, third floor back. It was an hour that I shall never forget. There I saw, heard, felt, experienced Leslie Campbell tearing his heart from the deep canyons of reticence where it preferred to dwell and laying it on the altar of agony; there he invited us to behold it. He did not know, he said, who or what was to blame for the condition that had arisen. He could almost say that he did not care who or what was to blame. "Blame me," he said, "blame me totally and completely; I gladly assume full responsibility. But in the name of the Christ of love and goodwill let us go from this room as one."

The miracle of healing took place; hearts were melted and merged. When we left the room I walked down the hall and looked out on the service in the chapel below. The invitation was being given and persons were filling the isles, coming to make their confession, to grant and to accept forgiveness. I felt a presence by my side and turned. There was Leslie Campbell with an expression on his face that few students were ever permitted to see. He was a Christian.

And, he was a dreamer. A teacher who was on the faculty when the new president took office and remained on the faculty throughout his administration says that the quality that characterized his life above all others was just this: *He was a dreamer.*

His trustees and business associates did not always appreciate that quality in Leslie Campbell. For the dreamer is not invariably practical; at least it does not seem so to those whose responsibility it is to translate those dreams into brick and mortar and buildings. Yet, without the dreamer there would have been no brick and mortar and buildings. He once said, "To plan too small for the future of the college may be as reprehensible as to plan too optimistically."

The lines of O'Shaughnessy are appropriate:

> We are dreamers of dreams,
> World-loosers and world-shakers . . .
> Yet, we are the movers and the shakers
> Of the world forever, it seems.

Leslie Campbell was a dreamer.

And, he was human; he was humane. He was more than a dreamer who dreamed buildings in the sky and insisted that they be built on his campus. His friends and neighbors and those of the college family who allowed themselves to really know him, remember Leslie Campbell for his humility, neighborliness, and his utter lack of pretense.

A member of the faculty remembers when her mother died. Soon the president was at her door asking, "Can I help?" "No, Dr. Campbell, I do not know of anything that you can do. Thank you for coming." "Well," said the president, "these may help." And he handed to her plane, train, and bus schedules that he had checked, verified, and marked. She never forgot.

A student from the Far West received news of his father's death. Soon the president was at the door of the student's mobile home, asking: "Is there anything I can do? Do you have money to go?" The student remembers.

One recalls that when she and her husband came to Buies Creek, they moved into a house with weeds covering the yard and crowding the door. President Campbell assured the new faculty members that the maintenance people would come to cut the lawn. Several days passed; grass and weeds were still growing in the yard. Each day President Campbell, not his secretary, called to ask about those weeds. On Saturday morning the new teacher heard a lawn mower and said to her husband, "Well, finally, they have come to cut our lawn." A little later she looked out her window and was amazed and embarrassed to see the president of the college, coatless, shirt open, sleeves rolled-up, mowing her lawn.

Out of considerable knowledge, I put Kipling's words in Leslie Campbell's mouth, though he would never have spoken them:

> I have eaten your bread and salt.
> I have drunk your water and wine.
> The deaths you died I have watched beside
> And the lives you lived were mine.

Three assets: He was a Christian, a dreamer and a great human.

Now, *the overshadowing obstacles.* Of course it is nothing new for a college president to face obstacles. President Clark Kerr of the University of California at Berkeley, my neighbor for a half dozen years, said he had learned that the three major administrative problems on a campus were: "sex for the students, athletics for the alumni, and parking for the faculty." At Campbell the problems were somewhat different. The faculty did not have automobiles, the alumni had forgotten about athletics, and the students. . . .

President Campbell had other problems. The first was a great depression. He came to office in 1934, the trough of that awful economic debacle. Writing of the experience, he said:

> It was all that we could do to hold things together. . . . We even used the barter system and many students helped pay for their tuition by bringing us potatoes, corn and other foods. We had to tell our teachers that if they would stay, we would have to pay them on the basis of them sharing their salaries in proportion to what we could collect. Enrollment dropped to less than 300, and most of the students were working their way through school.

I have in my files the record of produce brought by a student to be applied on his board bill; it is typical of what was taking place:

> 12 pounds of flour
> 5 pounds of Irish potatoes
> 4 pounds of butter beans
> 3 pounds of string beans
> 3 pounds of shelled butter beans
> 14½ pounds of shelled string beans
> 2½ pounds of corn meal
> 5 biddies weighing eight pounds.

One who was on the faculty at the time remembers an evening when President Campbell called the little faculty together, nineteen in number, faced them with choking voice, and said, "It looks as if we shall not be able to make it." There was silence for a time and then one of the nineteen stood and said, "Well, Campbell may not make it but let us die first." It was the needed word. She had articulated the spirit of the little group. And because of that spirit and by the grace of holy God, the college did "make it."

That is the heritage of all who benefit from Campbell College today. I walk these grounds early in the morning, late at night, when the sun is high overhead, when the moon and all the "hosts of heaven" ride in majesty across the sky. Accompanying me are the spirits of those indomitable men and women who held this institution together in those dark days. And I tell you, these are the just men and women made perfect. They are "those who came out of great tribulation and have washed their robes in the blood of the Lamb." This I do verily believe. And I believe they stand, and shall stand, "before the throne of God and he who sitteth on the throne shall dwell among them. They shall hunger no more nor thirst any more. For the Lamb who is in the midst of the throne shall feed them, and lead them unto fountains of living water."

There was a second overshadowing obstacle that President Campbell faced. It was World War II. Toward the close of the 30's the country, and Campbell College as a part of it, began to climb out of the cellar of that depression. Then in 1941 America was hurled into the blood bath of war. Campbell took the brunt. Men and materials were thrown into the war effort. Male students were gone. Buildings ran down, roofs leaked, plumbing rusted, floors sagged, paint pealed, rain blew in through the windows, and the grounds were weed-grown.

Finally came the armistice. Then Japan signed the formal surrender on the battleship *Missouri*, September 2, 1945. The war was over. Then came the veterans. They crowded about the doors of learning and were ready to remove the roofs if it took that to get in. Campbell College, along with other schools, somehow made room. It looked as if the institution was finally getting the green light. But just as President Campbell was ready to floorboard the pedal, another problem loomed on the path ahead.

That obstacle came in the form of the removal of Wake Forest College to Winston-Salem. On July 30, 1946, the Baptist State Convention voted to accept the Z. Smith Reynolds offer and move the college to the city of "weed and smoke." In the same Convention a motion was made to offer the old Wake Forest campus for a strong junior college. That motion passed; the Baptist State Convention was on record as favoring the establishment of a junior college at Wake Forest.

On November 13 of that same year, Dr. M. A. Huggins, General Secretary of the Baptist State Convention, published a major article in the *Biblical Recorder* strongly recommending that Campbell, Chowan, and Wingate abandon their present locations and merge to form one strong junior college to be located on the campus of old Wake Forest.

Faced with such proposals, with such action by the Convention, all building and advancement at Campbell came to a standstill. Who would be so bold as to plan a future for Campbell College at its present site? If any were so bold, or foolhardy, as to plan, who would be so unrealistic as to give the necessary funds for building when it looked as if the school would have to close its doors and move seventy-five miles? If there is any question about the devastating effect that these conditions had on the college, consider this: from the beginning of the war in 1941 to the final decision on the disposition of the old Wake Forest property in 1950, only one building was constructed on Campbell's campus, a period of nine long and depleting years.

The president faced three overshadowing obstacles: the depression, World War II, and the threat of removing his school from its ancient landmarks.

But he made *three magnificent contributions.* First, under his leadership the school became a four-year institution. The year that Wake Forest College moved to Winston-Salem the Baptist State Convention went on record as favoring the establishment of a four-year Baptist college in eastern North Carolina. Another tizzy!

A strong Committee of 25 was appointed to study the matter. In due time the committee made its report and recommended that Campbell College consider becoming a four-year institution "as soon as they think desirable and possible." The alumni of the college were busy. A letter was sent out to all Campbell College alumni living in North Carolina asking their reaction to Campbell's becoming a four-year college. Incidentally, that letter went out over the signature of a young law professor by the name of Norman Adrian Wiggins. The poll was taken; the votes were counted. Result? Twenty to one in favor of the four-year proposal. The trustees of the college went into session. After careful deliberation, they voted unanimously to move toward a four-year school.

In the fall of 1961 the first junior class enrolled. In due time that class advanced to senior standing and on May 31, 1963, 132 of them were "ready, able and willing" for graduation. It was an accomplished fact, Campbell College had become a four-year institution.

Second, Leslie Campbell brought that four-year institution to full accreditation in the shortest possible length of time. From the beginning the president made it clear that his goal was not just a four-year college, but a four-year, degree-granting college with full accreditation. He said, said repeatedly: "We are not interested in changing from a first-class junior college to a second-rate senior institution. We shall go first-class all the way or we shall not go at all."

The president and Dean Burkot—whose mammoth contribution at every juncture of this achievement and especially at this point cannot be overemphasized—conferred with officials of the Southern Association of Colleges and with the North Carolina College Conference, asking for their guidance and cooperation in attaining accreditation. The school went by the book, page by difficult page. Often the school was ahead of the book. Therefore, in the minimum length of time, three years after the school became a four-year college, full accreditation was granted. The action was taken in Miami, Florida. President Campbell and Dean Burkot were, of course, there to receive the accolade.

Returning home, their train was delayed. It arrived in Dunn at 2:30 on the morning of December 2, 1966. The president, Mrs. Campbell and the dean were exhausted, tired, sleepy. But when they stepped from the train on that cold December morning, the sight that met their eyes and the sounds that greeted their ears went far to wipe out all semblance of fatigue. For there at the station, shivering in the cold, were 500 (one reporter said a 1,000) students, faculty, neighbors, and friends, shouting their words of thanks and congratulations! Jimmie Jordan, student government president, speaking for the group, said that they had come to the station and braved the December's chill to show their gratitude to the two men who had been chiefly responsible for the achievement in which all present and future students would participate. It was done! They had gone first class all the way.

Third, Leslie Campbell led in the building of physical facilities that were adequate for that four-year accredited college. When the decision was made to upgrade the school, plans for developing and enlarging the institution's facilities moved into overdrive. Blueprints covered drawing boards, financial drives were projected, campaigns were launched.

Representative A. Hartwell Campbell, son of the president and chairman of a campaign to raise $2,000,000, recalling another dramatic moment in the life of the school, placed his arm about his father's shoulder and said, "Don't worry, Daddy: we are going to build you a four-year college and it will be a good one, too!"

There was a breathless quality about those days. You had a feeling that time was being measured not so much by breaths taken as in heartbeats missed! Writing in the *Durham Morning Herald*, Allan Whiteleather, said: "Buildings are going up faster than weeds at Campbell College. One dormitory was completed in 90 days flat!"

He did not exaggerate, consider the record:

1934—Leslie Hartwell Campbell elected president; Paul Green Outdoor Theatre dedicated
1937—Fred N. Day Dormitory, central section, opened
1940—Second D. Rich bequest received
1941—Campbell Junior College accredited by Southern Association
1946—B. Herbert Taylor Athletic Field opened
1948—Britt Dormitory completed
1951—Laundry and dry cleaning plant constructed
1952—Carter Gymnasium completed
1953—New Dormitory for Men completed
1954—Jones Dormitory opened
1955—Hatcher-Blackmon Carillon dedicated
1956—Kitchin Dormitory for Men opened;
       campaign to raise $325,000 completed;
       Carrie Rich Memorial Library enlarged and dedicated

1957—Marshbanks Dining Hall renovated and enlarged
1958—Baldwin Dormitory for Men opened
1959—New Dormitory for Men completed;
      Campbelltown Apartments erected
1960—Powell Dormitory opened;
      John S. Pearson Infirmary opened;
      Erwin Forest donated
1961—James E. and Mary Z. Bryan Dormitory opened;
      James A. Campbell Administration Building opened
1962—North Dormitory for Women opened;
      South Dormitory for Men opened;
      Science Building opened;
      D. Rich Auditorium renovated to become Turner Chapel
1963—Northeast Hall for Men opened;
1964—Baggett Acres given;
      Tyner Chair of Religion launched
1965—Godwin Maintenance Building opened
1967—New Hall for Women opened;
      Full accreditation of the college achieved;
      Leslie Hartwell Campbell retired
1970—"He was not for God took him"
1971—Leslie Hartwell Campbell included in the distinguished list,
      100 Years 100 Men

Under his administration the institution rose from a small junior college with an enrollment of 312 students to a four-year, degree-granting, fully-accredited, senior institution with an enrollment of 2,200 students, facilities valued at $7,000,000, and an operating budget of $2,700,000.

Leslie Hartwell Campbell retired in June, 1967. He had been president of the school since 1934, a period of 33 years, the longest tenure of office for any college president in North Carolina. He was 75 years old. The school had been in existence only five years when he was born. At the time of his retirement he had witnessed the erection of every building on the campus. As teacher, dean, and president he had served the school for more than half a century.

And Leslie Hartwell Campbell died in a good old age, full of riches and honor; and his student, Norman Adrian Wiggins, reigned in his stead.

3. The "Original 16" Plus Five

January 5, 1887

J. M. Byrd
Flossie A. Byrd
Mamie A. Byrd
Frank W. Ennis
J. A. Hamilton
J. H. Hamilton
Harvey M. Holleman
E. B. Johnson

Willis R. Johnson
W. M. McNeill
E. F. McNeill
Clarence McNeill
U. H. Parker
Cornelia F. Pearson
John S. Pearson
Jimmie Patterson

H. S. Byrd
D. M. Hamilton
J. F. Hamilton
J. H. McNeill
Lonnie Stewart

The second list of five students had come for the first morning of school but agreed to work on the school building since it was not ready for occupancy.

4. ALUMNI ASSOCIATION EXECUTIVE COMMITTEE

1974

Bruce Beasley, President
Bill Bethune
Joe Edwards
Bill Julian
Calvin Knight
W. H. Ledbetter
Carroll Leggett

Mrs. M. B. Matthews
William McIver
Gilmer Parrish
Charlie Robertson
Stewart B. Warren
Mrs. Marietta G. Watson

5. DISTINGUISHED ALUMNI

1965-1974

1965   Rev. Eugene Olive
1965   Wesley Watts
1965   Dr. Norman A. Wiggins
1968   Franklin Douglas Byrd, Jr.
1968   Albert E. Clark
1968   Romulus A. Hedgpeth
1968   William Grey Humphrey
1968   Dr. Malcolm C. McIver, Jr.
1969   Dr. Carlyle Campbell
1969   Frederick Ralph Keith
1969   Frank Spurgeon Masten
1969   Dr. Elmer L. Puryear
1969   Dr. Herman T. Stevens
1969   Dorsey Battle Teague
1969   John Allen Wilkins
1970   Millard F. Booe
1970   W. Carroll Bryan
1970   B. B. Creech
1970   Dr. James L. Johnson
1970   Mrs. Gladys S. Satterwhite
1970   S. F. Teague
1970   Dr. J. B. Willis
1971   Brantley C. Booe
1971   Robert A. Harris
1971   Dr. Ralph A. Herring
1971   William B. McIver
1971   Milford Quinn
1971   Claude E. Teague
1971   Stewart B. Warren
1972   Lewis Edward Boroughs
1972   H. Spurgeon Boyce
1972   Gaylord Jackson Perry
1972   James Evan Perry, Jr.
1972   Marjorie Spence
1973   W. A. Johnson
1973   Irene Mooney
1973   Dr. D. Russell Perry
1973   Dr. Kyle M. Yates
1974   Dr. J. Winston Pearce
1974   Mrs. Sarah E. Spivey
1974   Rev. J. Boyce Brooks
1974   Dr. William Robert Proffit

6. Board of Trustees

1975

Terms Expiring 1978

Lacy Collier	Fayetteville, North Carolina
Dr. Ramsey Cammack	Burlington, North Carolina
Rev. Tom Freeman	Dunn, North Carolina
Dr. Will H. Lassiter, M.D.	Smithfield, North Carolina
Carroll Leggett	Washington, D. C.
Clyde J. Rhyne	Sanford, North Carolina
Lamar Simmons	Lillington, North Carolina
Edgar A. Thomas	Lexington, North Carolina
Charles Whitley	Washington, D. C.

7. TRUSTEES LISTED ALPHABETICALLY

1912-1974

Emmett C. Aldredge	Dunn, North Carolina
Charles Andrews	Chalybeate Springs, North Carolina
Mrs. G. B. Andrews	Fuquay Springs, North Carolina
James Austin	Clinton, North Carolina
Dr. James S. Ayers	Clinton, North Carolina
J. W. Baggett	Fayetteville, North Carolina
Allen Bailey	Charlotte, North Carolina
Miss Mattie Bain	Coats, North Carolina
J. E. Baker	Burlington, North Carolina
E. H. Ballentine	Varina, North Carolina
W. D. Barbee	Seaboard, North Carolina
W. C. Barrett	Laurinburg, North Carolina
Mrs. W. C. Barrett	Laurinburg, North Carolina
Henry Barringer	Hendersonville, North Carolina
Woodrow P. Bass	Fayetteville, North Carolina
Herbert W. Baucom, Jr.	Oxford, North Carolina
R. W. Boling	Fayetteville, North Carolina
Brantley C. Booe	Winston-Salem, North Carolina
Lewis Boroughs	Greensboro, North Carolina
H. Spurgeon Boyce	Durham, North Carolina
Dr. Claud Bowen	Greensboro, North Carolina
Bruce Boyers	Goldsboro, North Carolina
O. G. Bradley	Chalybeate Springs, North Carolina
Dr. Street Brewer	Roseboro, North Carolina
R. C. Bridger	Bladenboro, North Carolina
J. Melville Broughton	Raleigh, North Carolina
Victor E. Brown	Williamston, North Carolina
Raymond A. Bryan, Jr.	Goldsboro, North Carolina
W. Carroll Bryan	Goldsboro, North Carolina

R. D. Buie	Fayetteville, North Carolina
M. E. Bullard	Wilmington, North Carolina
James F. Bullock	Varina, North Carolina
J. M. Byrd	Coats, North Carolina
J. W. Byrd	Duke, North Carolina
James C. Cammack	Smithfield, North Carolina
James A. Campbell	Buies Creek, North Carolina
A. Hartwell Campbell	Wilson, North Carolina
Harry C. Carter	Greensboro, North Carolina
A. H. Carter	Wallace, North Carolina
Don Clayton	Fayetteville, North Carolina
J. C. Clifford	Dunn, North Carolina
R. J. Clifford	Lexington, North Carolina
John T. Coley	Rocky Mount, North Carolina
Lacy Collier	Fayetteville, North Carolina
A. B. Conrad	High Point, North Carolina
Ben Cox	Burlington, North Carolina
Ariail B. Creel	Greensboro, North Carolina
Gilmer Cross	Goldsboro, North Carolina
A. G. Crumpler	Fuquay Springs, North Carolina
Robert Culler	High Point, North Carolina
George W. Davis	Farmville, North Carolina
Howard G. Dawkins	Kinston, North Carolina
Fred N. Day	Winston-Salem, North Carolina
Henry B. Day	Raleigh, North Carolina
Ira W. Day	Raleigh, North Carolina
D. T. Dickie	Henderson, North Carolina
W. C. Downing	Fayetteville, North Carolina
Marion L. Eakes	Greensboro, North Carolina
Mrs. L. L. Edgerton	Goldsboro, North Carolina
Yancey Elliott	Salemburg, North Carolina
Jack M. Euliss	Burlington, North Carolina
Merrill Evans	Ahoskie, North Carolina
Ben C. Fisher	Wake Forest, North Carolina
John C. Fletcher, Jr.	Charlotte, North Carolina
Dr. William Folds	Walkertown, North Carolina
Howard Ford	Wilmington, North Carolina
Jere D. Freeman	Wilmington, North Carolina
Tom Freeman	Dunn, North Carolina
Clayton Fulcher, Jr.	Atlantic, North Carolina
Mrs. Clayton Fulcher, Jr.	Atlantic, North Carolina
A. Lincoln Fulk	Spring Hope, North Carolina
B. P. Gentry	Lillington, North Carolina
Albert C. Greene, Sr.	Fayetteville, North Carolina
Roscoe Griffin	Rocky Mount, North Carolina
Maurice Grissom	Elizabeth City, North Carolina
Worth P. Gurley	Raleigh, North Carolina

Mrs. Robert Hall	Mocksville, North Carolina
H. G. Hancock	Bonlee, North Carolina
Frank Hare	Angier, North Carolina
Robert A. Harris	Spray, North Carolina
Blanton Hartness	Sanford, North Carolina
A. Paul Hatley	Whiteville, North Carolina
M. S. Hayworth	Rocky Mount, North Carolina
Elmer Hedgepeth	Fairmont, North Carolina
R. A. Hedgepeth	Lumberton, North Carolina
Mrs. R. A. Hedgepeth	Lumberton, North Carolina
Jesse A. Helms	Raleigh, North Carolina
Cecil W. Henderson	Wilmington, North Carolina
H. C. Herring	Fairmont, North Carolina
Dr. R. A. Herring	Winston-Salem, North Carolina
Addison Hewlett	Wilmington, North Carolina
Dr. J. Henry Highsmith	Raleigh, North Carolina
Addison Hill	Burlington, North Carolina
Dennis Hockaday	Durham, North Carolina
Sam Hocutt	Goldsboro, North Carolina
Ed F. Hodges	Fairmont, North Carolina
R. P. Holding	Smithfield, North Carolina
H. M. Holleman	Asheville, North Carolina
Howard Holly	Burgaw, North Carolina
John W. Holmes	Farmville, North Carolina
Dr. John H. Horne	Greenville, North Carolina
Dr. Charles B. Howard	Buies Creek, North Carolina
George Howard	Fayetteville, North Carolina
W. W. Hutchins	High Point, North Carolina
Colon Jackson	Fayetteville, North Carolina
P. S. Jones	Kinston, North Carolina
Walter B. Jones	Fairmont, North Carolina
W. H. Jones	Kinston, North Carolina
Mrs. W. H. Jones	Kinston, North Carolina
Miss Margaret L. Johnson	Raleigh, North Carolina
W. S. Johnson	Lillington, North Carolina
J. B. Julian	Fayetteville, North Carolina
Fred R. Keith	Lumberton, North Carolina
A. Paul Kitchin	Wadesboro, North Carolina
Willis E. Kivett	Southern Pines, North Carolina
Z. T. Kivett	Buies Creek, North Carolina
Ralph E. Langdon	Fayetteville, North Carolina
J. E. Lanier	Calypso, North Carolina
Dr. Will H. Lassiter, M.D.	Smithfield, North Carolina
J. G. Layton	Lillington, North Carolina
Mrs. J. G. Layton	Lillington, North Carolina
Carroll Leggett	Washington, D. C.
Roy Lewis	Charlotte, North Carolina
Dr. Randall Lolley	Winston-Salem, North Carolina
W. C. Lucas	Asheboro, North Carolina

Raymond B. Mallard — Tabor City, North Carolina
B. P. Marshbanks — Buies Creek, North Carolina
Dr. B. P. Marshbanks — Lillington, North Carolina
Miss Flossie Marshbanks — Raleigh, North Carolina
LeRoy Martin — Raleigh, North Carolina
Santford Martin — Winston-Salem, North Carolina
William Foy Martin — Winston-Salem, North Carolina
Dr. Hugh Archie Matthews — Buies Creek, North Carolina
Charles McEnally — New Bern, North Carolina
B. F. McLeod — Buies Creek, North Carolina
W. L. McLeod — Norwood, North Carolina
Dr. J. F. McKay — Buies Creek, North Carolina
Wiley W. Mears — Rocky Mount, North Carolina
James I. Miller — Wilson, North Carolina
J. T. Mills — Buies Creek, North Carolina
Dr. W. Donald Moore — Coats, North Carolina
William M. Morgan — Angier, North Carolina
Mrs. William M. Morgan — Angier, North Carolina
Bobby Murray — Raleigh, North Carolina

James Nance — Fayetteville, North Carolina
W. E. Nichols — Coats, North Carolina
Mrs. W. E. Nichols — Coats, North Carolina
C. H. Norris — Cary, North Carolina
Charles S. Norwood — Goldsboro, North Carolina

J. A. Oates — Fayetteville, North Carolina
Mrs. Eugene Olive — Wake Forest, North Carolina
R. M. Olive — Fayetteville, North Carolina
Claude O'Shields — Wilmington, North Carolina
J. R. Overby — Smithfield, North Carolina

W. M. Page — Fuquay Springs, North Carolina
D. Earle Pardue — Burlington, North Carolina
Yates Parker — Raleigh, North Carolina
Alonzo Parrish — Benson, North Carolina
N. T. Patterson — Coats, North Carolina
O. F. Patterson — Sanford, North Carolina
Tommy J. Payne — Robersonville, North Carolina
J. Winston Pearce — Durham, North Carolina
Dr. D. R. Perry — Durham, North Carolina
Robert E. Pomeranz — Sanford, North Carolina
Mrs. Robert E. Pomeranz — Sanford, North Carolina
J. F. Pope — Dunn, North Carolina
P. F. Pope — Coats, North Carolina
T. H. S. Pope — Buies Creek, North Carolina
Gerald Primm — Greensboro, North Carolina
Roy M. Purser — Raleigh, North Carolina

Milford Quinn — Warsaw, North Carolina

W. K. Rand — Durham, North Carolina
Mrs. W. K. Rand — Durham, North Carolina

T. L. Reardon	Buies Creek, North Carolina
Clyde J. Rhyne	Sanford, North Carolina
T. L. Rich	Fairmont, North Carolina
J. T. Riddick	Durham, North Carolina
Dr. H. C. Roberts	Coats, North Carolina
W. Earl Robinson	St. Pauls, North Carolina
A. Paul Rogers	Tabor City, North Carolina
Ernest P. Russell	Dunn, North Carolina
Granville Ryals	Wilmington, North Carolina
John Scalf, Jr.	Caroleen, North Carolina
George Bruce Schell	Red Springs, North Carolina
J. Brian Scott	Rocky Mount, North Carolina
D. H. Senter	Chalybeate Springs, North Carolina
George Simmons	Wadesboro, North Carolina
Lamar Simmons	Lillington, North Carolina
Mrs. Charles Lee Smith	Raleigh, North Carolina
G. Dewey Smith	High Point, North Carolina
A. P. Stephens	Morehead City, North Carolina
D. E. Stewart	Raleigh, North Carolina
H. C. Stewart	Lillington, North Carolina
Hunter Strickland	Four Oaks, North Carolina
Mrs. Hunter Strickland	Four Oaks, North Carolina
W. S. Strickland	Dunn, North Carolina
Fred Taylor	Pinehurst, North Carolina
H. B. Taylor	Dunn, North Carolina
R. G. Taylor	Dunn, North Carolina
D. B. Teague	Sanford, North Carolina
S. T. Teague	Goldsboro, North Carolina
Edgar A. Thomas	Lexington, North Carolina
B. Townsend	Murfreesboro, North Carolina
LeRoy Townsend	Lumberton, North Carolina
Charles R. Tucker	Parkton, North Carolina
B. Y. Tyner	Raleigh, North Carolina
W. H. Upchurch	Oxford, North Carolina
Mrs. I. M. Wallace	Buies Creek, North Carolina
Dr. D. E. Ward, Jr.	Lumberton, North Carolina
George W. Warren	Wilson, North Carolina
George W. Warren, Jr.	Kinston, North Carolina
Wesley Watts	Lumberton, North Carolina
Earl McD. Westbrook	Dunn, North Carolina
Charles O. Whitley	Mt. Olive, North Carolina
C. V. Whitley	Zebulon, North Carolina
Jack B. Wilder	Greensboro, North Carolina
Dr. R. B. Wilkins	Raleigh, North Carolina
F. Carter Williams	Raleigh, North Carolina
Percy H. Wilson	Raleigh, North Carolina
Mrs. Robert W. Winston	Lillington, North Carolina
W. M. Womble	Sanford, North Carolina

Harry D. Wood	Leaksville, North Carolina
Carl Worley, Sr.	Selma, North Carolina
Edgar M. Wyatt	Raleigh, North Carolina

8. Presidential Board of Advisors

1974

James R. Nisbet, Chairman

Terms Expiring 1975

Harry Stroman Bagnal	Winston-Salem, North Carolina
James Norment Britt, Jr.	Lumberton, North Carolina
James Richard Coates	Norfolk, Virginia
Rev. David Hoke Coon, Jr.	Lexington, North Carolina
Thomas Harry Gatton	Raleigh, North Carolina
Andy Bryant Hardee	Whispering Pines, North Carolina
Robert Cannon Hayes	Charlotte, North Carolina
The Honorable David Henderson	Washington, D. C.
J. Addison Hill	Burlington, North Carolina
Gilliam King Horton	Wilmington, North Carolina
John Stewart Howard	Salemburg, North Carolina
Allan Covert Mims	Rocky Mount, North Carolina
John W. Pope	Fuquay-Varina, North Carolina
Frederick H. Taylor	Troy, North Carolina

Terms Expiring 1976

Claude Shuford Abernathy, Jr.	Newton, North Carolina
J. J. (Jack) Barnes	Fayetteville, North Carolina
Irwin Belk	Charlotte, North Carolina
Harry C. Carter	Greensboro, North Carolina
John H. High	Rocky Mount, North Carolina
Frank B. Holding	Smithfield, North Carolina
Dr. Gale Denning Johnson	Dunn, North Carolina
Tom Keith	St. Pauls, North Carolina
Jack F. Kitchin	Chesapeake, Virginia
Dr. Robert P. Morehead, Sr.	Winston-Salem, North Carolina
C. James Nelson	Charlotte, North Carolina
James Robinson Nisbet	Charlotte, North Carolina
Roger Page, Jr.	Winston-Salem, North Carolina
John Robert (Jack) Riley	Raleigh, North Carolina
John W. Stackhouse	Goldsboro, North Carolina

Terms Expiring 1977

Dr. Ned B. Ball	Blowing Rock, North Carolina
William Loomis Burns, Jr.	Durham, North Carolina
Albert Clark	Falls Church, Virginia
William L. Corbin	Swansboro, North Carolina
Mrs. Lucille L. Ellis	Kenly, North Carolina
Charles W. Gibbes	New York, New York
O. W. (Bill) Godwin, Jr.	Dunn, North Carolina
Dr. Charles Barrett Howard	Buies Creek, North Carolina
Richard Howard	Denver, North Carolina
Burrows T. Lundy	Clinton, North Carolina
Miss Irene Mooney	Madison, North Carolina
Dr. David Russell Perry	Durham, North Carolina
Mrs. Crawford S. Rogers	Norfolk, Virginia
Robert P. (Bob) Rupert	Dunn, North Carolina
Ernest Paskel Sauls	Garner, North Carolina
Robert P. Taylor	Norfolk, Virginia
Wade H. Webb	Erwin, North Carolina
Whitley Hood	Benson, North Carolina
George Sloan, Jr.	Wilmington, North Carolina

9. Faculty Listed Alphabetically

1887-1974

(Giving Year the Teaching Began)

Mrs. Lucy Adcock	1930	Erskine B. Bailey	1923
Howard E. Allen	1959	Ruby M. Bailey	1962
Miss Jessie Allen	1926	Mrs. J. A. Bain	1913
Sarah Lorraine Allen	1952	Harold C. Bain	1958
Ernestine F. Allred	1967	Clifford Edwin Bair	1948
Mrs. Ollie Anderson	1919	Doris Baker	1967
Victor L. Andrews	1912	Herbert Marshall Baker	1945
J. William Angell	1950	Julia Ellen Baker	1943
J. Delmer Ashworth	1963	Mrs. Margaret Davidson Baker	1945
Sanford Emmett Ayers	1928	Miss Verner Haskin Baker	1924
Mrs. Sanford Emmett Ayers	1928	Mrs. E. P. Barbee	1922
Elizabeth Ayscue	1934	Barbara Dell Barbee	1958
John Edward Ayscue	1927	Nathan Carl Barefoot	1924
Mrs. John Edward Ayscue	1927	Douglas L. Barger	1968
A. Paul Bagby	1946	Effie Barker	1907
Muriel Martin Bagby	1954	William Allen Barnett	1948
John Robert Bagget	1898	W. C. Barrett	1900
Joseph Abram Bagget	1905	Wallace Bartosz	1967

R. Robert Basham, Jr.	1968	Millard R. Brown	1963
Donald George Bassett	1966	James Walter Bryan	1946
Charles T. Battin	1962	Mary Bryan	1912
L. Stanford Beard	1961	Pauline Bryan	1914
Christine Hudson Beasley	1973	Lena Bullard	1919
Mrs. J. S. Beatty	1921	John T. Bunn	1962
Neill McLaurin Beatty	1960	A. R. Burkot	1935
George M. Beavirs	1901	Dale F. Burnside	1970
Lycurgus V. Belcher	1909	Ada Burt	1919
Judith Ann Bell	1963	Estelle Burt	1925
James E. Bengil	1961	Nolie Burt	1916
Miss Nolia Benson	1893	Jarris B. Byrd	1898
Charles Bickley	1966	John M. Byrd	1889
Rachel Bickley	1966	Walter P. Byrd	1906
T. H. Biles	1921		
Charles M. Billings, III	1955	Marguerite Cain	1931
Thomas Harper Binford	1901	Gaston Evon Calvert	1970
Courtney R. Bixby	1952	Arthur Carlyle Campbell	1910
Elma Black	1937	Bessie Campbell	1915
Ernest G. Black	1963	Catherine McLean Campbell	1953
Willie Ruby Blackburn	1941	James Archibald Campbell	1888
J. F. Blackmon	1926	Mrs. James Archibald	
J. C. Blanchard	1900	Campbell	1890
Mrs. Ana Bland	1926	Leslie Hartwell Campbell	1910
Judith Ellen Bledsoe	1962	Mrs. Ora Green Campbell	1926
Grace Bazemore Bond	1956	Silas F. Campbell	1900
J. Nurney Bond	1956	Joyce M. Canfield	1973
Mrs. Abbie Benton Bonsteel	1926	Belle Cannady	1916
Millard Franklin Booe	1914	Ernest Franklin Cannady	1966
William Bryan Booe	1917	Flora Cannady	1919
A. E. Booth	1888	Ora Carr Cansler	1947
Joseph Bouchard	1949	Lillian Etheleen Carr	1946
Mrs. Littlie H. Bouldin	1931	Otis Ward Carroll	1964
Miss Thelis Bowden	1935	Marion F. Cathey	1968
Audrey Hagan Bradley	1969	Mrs. Virginia Kivett Chanault	1931
Mrs. Josephine Harmon Bradley	1926	Tennyson Po-Hsun Chang	1961
Lillie Bradley	1951	Franklin D. Cheatham	1973
Sidney Ora Brandon	1926	Nelle Rives Cheek	1927
Maude Britt	1914	Mabel Virginia Cheek	1928
Sarah Lorraine Britt	1951	Alta Chitty	1928
Elizabeth Britton	1962	Doris Mary Christian	1963
Grace Britton	1956	Harold D. Christian	1963
Mrs. Ethel Upchurch		Karin Nordenhaug Ciholas	1973
Broadhurst	1923	Paul Ciholas	1968
Mrs. J. A. Broadhurst	1921	James Archibald Clark	1901
Harriette Brogdon	1948	H. Jo Ann Jones Claus	1966
F. Floyd Brookens	1964	Malcolm Clifton	1957
Jennie B. Brooks	1970	Miss Lela Cobb	1924
Lula Frances Brooks	1925	Samuel Herbert Cockburn	1964
Shelby M. Broughton	1968	James Cole	1960
Constance Brown	1939	Roy Lloyd Coleman	1968
Gerald Y. Brown	1966	Mayme Collier	1909

Willie Mae Fletcher Collier	1946
Joseph S. Collins	1967
Elsie M. Colvin	1966
Herman D. Colvin	1966
Benjamin Richard Compton	1967
Mrs. Ruby Griffin Conlin	1944
Owen Sergeson Connelly, Jr.	1950
Ruth Burnley Cook	1911
Tommie Lou Corbitt	1943
Clay Costner	1965
Theodore J. Connas	1955
Bessie Mae Cowan	1949
Nathan Emory Cox	1904
Junius Troy Creech	1919
James A. Crisp, Jr.	1960
Herbert S. Croft	1970
Ronald C. Crossley	1966
Johnny L. Crow	1965
Kelly R. Crump	1961
H. Caleb Cushing	1947
Betsy Campbell Dail	1964
Stanley Dail	1964
Joseph Leroy Dare	1958
Mrs. Della Poole Daughtry	1919
Hargrove Bellamy Davis	1948
Russell Duke DeMent	1962
Miss Annie Denmark	1907
J. V. DeVenny	1897
Edward Homer Dew	1907
J. H. Dickerson	1899
Mary Jane Dickerson	1962
Clinton F. Dodson	1931
Leonore D. Doromal	1956
Leonora A. Dorsey	1941
James A. Doubles	1941
Pattie Simmons Dowell	1962
Mrs. J. L. Downing	1943
William Carlyle Downing	1911
Mrs. N. G. Duncan	1927
R. E. Duncan	1926
Stacy Allen Duncan, M.D.	1926
Edward Duvall	1964
James Edward Easley, Jr.	1969
Leflett Teed Easley, Jr.	1960
Cronje B. Earp	1971
Horace B. Eason	1915
Miss Lucy B. Eaton	1907
Mrs. Virginia Kivett Edgerton	1924
Clarence H. Edwards	1941
Clifford E. Edwards	1896

Mrs. Ethel Thomas Edwards	1925
George Leron Edwards	1925
Hazel Edwards	1925
Martha Elizabeth Edwards	1947
Mary H. Eliason	1937
Nancy Blair Eliason	1960
Cenieth Catherine Elmore	1965
Fred Emmerson	1939
Cora Ervin	1907
James LeRoy Faison	1952
Janell Farris	1941
David R. Fisher	1965
Charles Johnson Fleetwood	1910
F. H. Fleming, M.D.	1931
A. Gene Floyd	1952
John Dawson Follett	1950
T. Harold Folwell	1965
Mary Judith Fortenbacher	1952
Cordia Franklin	1923
Ruth Franklin	1947
John Albert Freeman	1966
John F. Freeman	1967
Mrs. Susanne H. Freund	1947
Edith T. Frey	1968
Mrs. Sudie Rhodes Frink	1947
Bruce C. Fryer	1965
Eugene Norfleet Gardner	1930
Mark Lawrence Gardner	1972
F. R. Garrett	1946
Nelson Garrison	1963
Albert Clark Gaskill	1966
W. Conrad Gass	1955
Charles Edward Gatch, Jr.	1965
Raymond Walter Gau	1969
William Teague Gay	1962
Joel S. Georges	1968
Stephen R. Gerlach	1971
Leland J. Gier	1935
Mrs. Ella Lord Gilbert	1931
Joseph A. Glover	1965
Lewis William Godlove	1963
Patrick Forest Goolsby	1963
George S. Graham	1957
Virginia B. Graham	1960
Marie Whitford Gray	1965
Ora Green	1923
Lewis C. Greene	1907
Ray Lee Greene	1946
John William Grice	1973
Jessie Clegg Griffin	1953
John D. Griffin	1965

Mabel Griffin	1935	Mrs. John E. Hollis	1945
Nedra Groupe	1948	A. C. Holloway	1893
Gerald Giles Grubb	1941	Carolyn Coggins Holmes	1968
Helen Guion	1940	W. P. Holt, Jr.	1929
Allen Guy	1950	Mary L. Holtzclaw	1935
Mrs. Allen Guy	1950	Miss Donnie Honeycutt	1919
Edith M. Guy	1961	Arthur Clifton Hood, Jr.	1962
T. Sloane Guy	1906	Edgar W. Hooks, Jr.	1962
		Robert C. Hope	1964
Neil D. Haldeman	1970	Rose L. Horn	1944
Elizabeth A. Hall	1965	Charles A. Horton	1956
J. H. Hall	1897	Jeanette Horton	1967
Wilbur G. Hall	1895	Mrs. Stella Horton	1919
Samuel C. Halstead	1970	Mrs. Susan Horton	1956
Elizabeth Hamilton	1967	William Stewart Horton	1966
Mary Jane Greene Hamilton	1963	Louis S. Hovis	1968
Marjorie Hannah	1923	Mrs. Alma Dark Howard	1947
Howard G. Hanson	1963	Charles Barrett Howard	1934
Josephine Harmon	1919	C. Edward Howard	1963
C. L. Harris	1930	Charles Jack Howard	1954
Miss Jodie Harris	1916	Christine D. Hudson	1969
Mrs. Mary E. Harris	1927	Isham B. Hudson	1916
Mrs. Minnie W. Caldwell		Q. G. Hudson	1899
Harris	1941	Robert G. Hudson	1968
Oscar N. Harris	1972	Irma Huff	1949
Harry Hartsell	1927	Kay Haire Huggins	1968
Marina Hawkins	1944	Mary Louise Hunt	1950
George A. Hawks	1967	Mrs. Minnie M. Hussey	1929
W. M. Hawley	1896	Ronald W. Hyatt	1963
Arthur W. Hayes	1971		
Nelson Appleton Hayes	1925	Herbert F. Ingle	1965
Julietta Haynes	1963	E. R. Ivey	1963
Laurine Haynes	1930	Miss Carra Jackson	1922
Mrs. Lillie Page Haynes	1919	Carolyn L. Jackson	1966
Robert S. Hays	1928	Jerry Francis Jackson	1965
Harlow Z. Head	1971	Walter S. Jacobi	1965
Cherrill Paul Heaton	1972	B. W. Jenkins	1944
Carimae Hedgpeth	1933	Miss Marion Palmer Jervis	1924
John R. Hemphill (Captain)	1971	Ruth Jinks	1925
Raymond LeRoy Henry	1929	Bessie F. Johnson	1924
Mary Eloise Herbert	1952	E. Weldon Johnson	1953
Charles Herring, Jr.	1960	Falk Johnson	1937
Gordon Rea Herring	1914	Frank Dudley Johnson	1966
Joseph P. Hester	1972	Grace Johnson	1961
Miss Malva Hight	1926	Lena Johnson	1904
Rilda Mae Hill	1936	W. Lee Johnston	1972
Mary Ruth Clark Hilliard	1968	Mrs. Alberto Jonas	1947
Ella W. Hinchman	1967	Mrs. A. N. Jones	1928
W. Kenneth Hinton	1970	Annie M. Jones	1907
Olivia Blanche Hocutt	1930	Henry Broadus Jones	1964
Robert Alan Hogg	1956	Henry M. Jones	1968
Effie Holland	1910	John Lewis Jones (Captain)	1905

Robert Allan McIntyre, Jr.	1962
Joseph F. McKoy, M.D.	1910
Anna Jean McLamb	1948
Mrs. Grayce Holland McLamb	1950
Bernard Franklin McLeod	1908
N. H. McLeod (Captain)	1899
Alexander D. McNeill	1904
T. J. Melvin	1898
Lelia McNeill Memory	1908
Richard M. Meyer	1971
Clifford R. Miller	1971
Martha Mitchell	1948
Charlotte Mix	1957
Sah Kuhn Moak	1966
Soon Wha Moak	1967
John J. Monoski, III	1969
Ralph W. Montgomery	1972
W. M. Montgomery	1893
Nettie Moon	1919
Tee DeWitt Moor	1924
Mrs. Mollie Partlow Moor	1925
Anne T. Moore	1963
Gerald Bruce Moore	1971
Mary Rica Moore	1969
Mildred Moore	1936
Mrs. A. Duke Morgan, Jr.	1948
Betsy Ann Morgan	1953
Miss Mary Morris	1922
Wilma Morrow	1935
Dale C. Morter	1966
Evelyn Moss	1906
Joseph F. Moss	1967
Jerry E. L. Moye	1970
Edith C. Mulkey	1963
Nannie May Murchison	1911
Vann M. Murrell	1963
Richard M. Myer	1971
John V. Myers	1954
Joseph Hugh Nanney	1960
William C. Naylor	1971
Elijah L. Nelson	1957
Mrs. I. T. Nelson	1929
Lucile Nelson	1945
Dorothy Newcomer	1965
Richard S. Newcomer	1965
Stewart A. Newman	1967
Mattie Newton	1921
Robert Lee Newton	1958
Lawrence R. Nicholson	1969
H. Monty Nock	1970
Billy R. Norman	1966

Hugh Jones Norris, Jr.	1970
Ethel Clare Norton	1935
Dwight Lamar Norwood	1973
Phares S. Nye	1964
Owen Odum	1919
L. C. Ogburn	1898
Alexander M. Okimoto (Captain)	1973
Anderson Moore Oldham	1948
Etta Oldham	1921
Linda Jean Oliphant	1969
Miss Iula Olive	1904
Earl N. Olmstead	1950
Thomas Gregg O'Neal	1962
Mrs. Ollie Gertrude Young Osburn	1938
Mrs. Cecile Osment	1949
Ada Overby	1927
Virginia D. Overman	1944
Lula Little Overton	1962
Hubbard Fulton Page	1902
Lillie Page	1914
Walton McArthur Page	1924
Harold D. Parcell	1970
Mrs. Jessie Allen Parker	1924
Lorena Parker	1948
Marceline L. Parker	1963
P. G. Parker	1929
Thelma Parker	1927
O. F. Patterson	1921
Grace Payne	1943
Sandra Peabody	1970
J. Winston Pearce	1971
Cornelia F. Pearson	1888
J. S. Pearson	1894
Maryly Van Leer Peck	1965
Judson Peele	1895
Louise Pender	1943
John Jacob Penick	1969
Alice Geraldine Perkins	1959
Robert L. Perkins	1965
Hubert Amos Perry	1910
Otis Person	1922
Max R. Peterson, Jr.	1970
Richard Campbell Pettigrew	1926
Robert R. Phebus	1953
Donald E. Phelps	1958
Herman D. Phelps	1954
William Roy Phelps	1969
Mary Jane Phillips	1961
Mrs. W. H. Phillips	1916

Carl T. Pickett	1961
David H. Pierce	1961
Robert Neil Piper	1969
Thelma Stewart Pippin	1960
Mary Josephine Pitcock	1943
Stephen S. Van Der Ploeg	1973
Louise Beasley Pollans	1973
Jessie I. Pollard	1962
S. Gordon Ponder	1966
Della V. Poole	1897
R. Lester Poplin	1930
Annie Portis	1900
John Wiley Portis	1899
Claud F. Powell	1966
Douglas F. Powell	1968
Mabel Powell	1924
Mary Craig Powell	1966
Nell Powell	1954
L. Wolcoot Prior	1938
Mrs. Edna Queener Proffit	1945
Annie B. Pruitt	1952
Elmer L. Puryear	1971
Mrs. Lois Bradley Puryear	1946
Gene H. Rafanelli	1971
Dorothy Coleman Ramos	1963
Frank Ramos	1967
Kenneth T. Raynor	1962
James M. Reeves	1965
Douglas E. Reinhardt	1972
Mrs. Mary Frances Remsburg	1949
Thomas H. Reynolds	1965
Lela Faye Rich	1965
George Greer Richards	1926
Mrs. George Greer Richards	1925
Erika Richey	1969
Benjamin Franklin Ricks	1930
Charles B. Riddick	1909
Edith Imogene Riddick	1947
Margaret C. Riddle	1966
Danny Lee Roberts	1964
Cowin C. Robinson	1968
Zon Robinson	1935
Otho J. Rock	1900
P. H. Rogers	1893
Lucile Rorex	1940
Mrs. Anna Rosamon	1913
J. H. Ruebush	1906
Thomas Croft Rutherford	1959
Inez Gehring Sadler	1956
R. H. Satterfield	1948

Gladys Strickland Satterwhite	1953
Mrs. Grover Saunders	1929
Emmett F. Sawyer	1948
Iris Gray Scarborough	1969
Robert V. Scholz	1964
Hannah P. Scoggin	1967
Mitchel W. Sellers (Major)	1972
Theophilus Yates Seymour	1928
Mrs. Theophilus Yates Seymour	1928
B. M. Shacklette	1919
Mrs. Florence Shaw	1895
Phillip Carl Shaw	1969
Ronald H. Sherron	1965
Mary Bates Sherwood	1968
Mary James Shutt	1938
Ellen Sikes	1967
Margaret R. Simmons	1968
Martha Simons	1944
Reid B. Sinclair	1971
James Dudley Sistrunk	1965
Marvin Lucian Skaggs	1934
Rodnal H. Skaggs	1967
Alice Louise Smith	1948
Beulah Smith	1935
Donna Wilke Smith	1968
H. H. Smith	1935
Herbert Young Smith	1903
Lonnie Smith	1900
Norman Earl Smith	1947
Robert E. Smith	1938
S. David Smith	1951
Troy Faith Smith	1969
Cora Smithwick	1894
Evelyn Snider	1929
Dorothy Snipes	1954
William Franklin Snoddy	1908
Robert F. Soots, Jr.	1965
Frances Ethel Sorgee	1950
Malcom South	1962
Texie Sowers	1950
Esther Ward Spillman	1952
Jack S. Spratt	1969
Ivy Kenyon Stafford	1943
W. Richard Stallings	1961
Linda Jean Oliphant Stanford	1970
C. P. Stasovich	1936
Mrs. Phyllis Mason Stephenson	1948
Dorothea L. Stewart	1961

Maude Stewart	1895	Mrs. Bradeene Blackmon Vail	1951
Elizabeth Stillwell	1949	Bruce Hamilton Vanderhoof	1969
James W. Stines	1968	William J. Vanderwall	1967
Joyce Peterson Stines	1968	J. Daniel Vann, III	1962
Edward Hoyle Stinson	1966	Sallie Vaughan	1946
John L. Stokes, III	1970	Bayred O. Vermillion	1967
W. C. Stone	1962	Jean M. Vickery	1970
William C. Strange	1971	George A. von Glahn	1968
Gladys Strickland	1925		
Vernon Stumpf	1967	Louise A. Wade	1969
Frank Summerfield	1973	Edyth Walker	1934
Mrs. Ruth Franklin Sutton	1949	Ernest Marshall Walker	1947
George R. Swann	1954	I. M. Wallace	1914
Mrs. Virginia Truitt Swann	1948	Jerry McLean Wallace	1970
Lois Sweaney	1912	Mary Jane Walters	1905
Willard S. Swiers	1968	Troy F. Smith Ward	1969
Robert M. Swinson	1963	C. C. Warren, Jr.	1950
Bessie Tally	1917	Mrs. Josephine Lasater Warren	1951
Cleo Baucom Tarlton	1957	Lela Warren	1936
Clara Eulalia Taylor	1936	Miss Mary Warren	1914
Gary A. Taylor	1969	Robert J. Washer	
Jerry Duncan Taylor	1961	(Lieutenant Colonel)	1973
Mrs. Louise Randall Taylor	1943	Thomas B. Waters	1968
Louise Todd Taylor	1964	Wendell William Weaver	1962
Ruby Faye Taylor	1964	Benjamin Davis Webb	1962
Samuel Farris Teague		Charles Wellborn	1965
(Captain)	1904	Charles H. Wellons	
Sanfjord B. Teu, II	1966	(Captain)	1896
Wayne Wesley Thomas	1960	Frances Greene Wells	1960
John G. Thompson	1959	Elonza McKinley West, Jr.	1961
Phyllis J. Thompson	1948	Frank E. Weyer	1962
Thomas R. Thornley, Jr.	1970	Robert Lee Whipple	1945
Myrtle Fuller Tillman	1954	Claude Williams White	1947
Cary C. Todd	1966	Ernest A. White	1972
Zula Tomlinson	1897	James Daniel White, Jr.	1969
Mrs. Minnie D. Townsend	1945	Mary Jane White	1958
G. A. Tripp	1945	Jonathan H. Whitehurst	1969
Leonore Doromal Tuck	1959	Miss Annie Whitty	1912
William P. Tuck	1958	Frederick William Wiegmann	1944
J. B. Tugwell	1899	Norman Adrian Wiggins	1968
Amanda Martin Turlington	1945	Cameron Willcox	1949
Miss Maggie Turner	1900	Miss Georgia Williford	1904
Rufus Benton Turner	1967	Kathryn Willis	1946
Walter Alan Tuttle	1959	D. G. Wilson	1893
Wayne C. Tyner	1963	William Jackson Wilson	1961
Cecil H. Unthank	1964	Edmund W. Winston	1969
Benjamin B. Upchurch	1926	Peter A. Wish	1969
R. T. Upchurch (Captain)	1900	George K. Wood	1969
W. H. Upchurch (Captain)	1898	Harry D. Wood, Jr.	1948
J. B. Usry	1947		

Marshall Woodall	1966	Charles G. Yarbrough	1965
P. D. Woodall	1896	Mrs. Harriet Yearby	1912
Carolyn Lamar Wray	1943	Gail Yoder	1972
Joe Willie Wray	1945	Paul M. Yoder	1962
William W. Wright	1946	Frederick Zomzely	1940
Roy Blanton Wyatt, Jr.	1973		

10. Honorary Degrees

1968-1974

Ned B. Ball
Carl E. Bates
Olin T. Binkley
Dr. Landrum R. Bolling
H. Spurgeon Boyce
Rev. James C. Cammack
Ramsey Eugene Cammack
Dr. T. L. Cashwell, Jr.
Dr. W. Perry Crouch
James Earl Danieley
Ben C. Fisher
Thomas M. Freeman
Claude F. Gaddy
Edwin Maurice Gill
Paul Eliot Green
John Hancock Hay
Earl Bruce Heilman

Dr. Charles B. Howard
John E. Lawrence
Graham A. Martin
Charles Wiley Phillips
William H. Ruffin
Robert Walter Scott
Mrs. Mary Duke Biddle Semans
Budd Elmon Smith
Fred Leslie Taylor
Col. William S. Terrell
Bunyan Yates Tyner
Carroll Wayland Weathers
Cameron West
Archibald Lee Manning Wiggins
Tony Derrell Wilson
John Wooden

11. Baptist Student Union Presidents

1927-1975

1927: B. C. Lamb
1928: Flora Lee Holloway
1929: John Edwards
1930: J. Boyce Brooks
1931: Ruth Snipes
1932: Ed Chamblee
1933: Tyler Dunn
1934: Gerald Motley

1935: Cornelia Forest
1936: Edith Williams
1937: Mildred Marshbanks
1938: Jack Gross
1939: Jack Gross
1940: Carlton Mitchell
1941: Fannie Terrell
1942: Calvin Knight

1943: Calvin Knight
1944: Clarence Mangum
1945: Emma McPherson
1946: Mary Baity
1947: Warren Turner
1948: Annie Stuart
1949: Norman Harris
1950: Emogene Douglas
1951: Roy Thornberry
      Joe Lavett
1952: Lawrence Oliver
      Harvey Williams
1953: Mary Jane Whitlaw
1954: Elba Rouse
1955: George Hodges
1956: George Peacock
1957: Emmanuel Pegram
1958: Robert Adams

1959: Rubylene Waters
1960: James Clifton
1961: James Clifton
1962: Russell Morris
1963: Russell Morris
1964: Willard Brown
1965: Jackie Evers
1966: Bill Hall
1967: ⎫
1968: ⎪   Leadership by the
1969: ⎬   Council as a whole
1970: ⎪   for these years
1971: ⎭
1972: Winslow Carter
1973: Gary Hudson
1974: Kate Lee
1975: Tommie Speight

12. Epsilon Pi Eta

Charter Members—1930

Clyde Glosson
Ruby Griffin
Linwood C. Murphy
Gaynelle Green
Margaret Satterwhite
Marguerite Cain
Herbert Hood
J. Winston Pearce
T. G. Chaney
Queenie Richardson
C. E. Privott
Vera Eugenia Lee
Annie Laurie Vestal
Edith Stephenson
Dolly Aycock
Ralph Arnold

Honor Society—1929

Paul Harrel Cale
T. G. "Thad" Chaney
Rosa Maye Edwards
Clyde Glosson
Annie Laurie Harrelson
Flora Lee Holloway
Thomas Early Jordan
Milton "Theodore" Lee
Constance Medkiff
Esther Moon
Audrey O'Brian
Timothy Francis Savage
Annie Carolyn Warren

The first list gives the original charter members of Epsilon Pi Eta. The Honor Society that was organized in 1929 did not take the name of "Epsilon Pi Eta" until a year later. The first members of the Honor Society in 1929 are included in the second list. (In 1975 Campbell College was approved for membership in Phi Kappa Phi, national academic honor society. Members enrolled at Campbell in Epsilon Pi Eta at the time became charter members.)

13. Epsilon Pi Eta

Presidents

1929: Paul Cale
1930: Clyde Glosson
1931: J. Winston Pearce
1932: Mack Wallace
1933: Evelyn Shoe
1934: May Marshbanks
1935: Jeff Beale
1936: Cullen Hall
1937: William Ballentine
1938: Joe Talley
1939: Wilbur Lamm
1940: Edwin Andrews
1941: Elmer Puryear
1942: Clarence Bowen
1943: Donald Keyser
1944: Jimmie Cheek
1945: Aaron Phipps
1946: Mary Baity
1947: Anne Green
1948: Charles Campbell
1949: James Faison
1950: Nancy Marshbanks
1951: Dewey Yarley

1952: Yvonne Stafford
1953: Dot Howard
1954: Billy Mobley
1955: Frank Campbell
1956: Ruth Bordeaux
1957: Billy Wilson
1958: George Hill
1959: Raleigh Castello
1960: Sandy Bryan
1961: Howard Marshall Hamilton
1962: Robin Hudgins
1963: Cary Todd
1964: Margaret Carolyn Reaves
1965: Felton Ray Godwin
1966: Warren Lee Gay
1967: Tony Mabry
1968: Mary Ann Fryer
1969: Janie Strickland
1970:
1971: Sally Simmons
1972: Charles Sikes
1973: Elton Caviness
1974: Vickie Wynn

14. First Graduating Class of Junior College

May 17, 1928

Mary Elizabeth Adams
Katherine Frances Bland
George Dewey Danner
Benjamin Andrew Darden
Mary Lillie Dewar
James Bernice Hardy

Sophronia Vandelia Harrell
Henry Dowell Jones
Florence Isabel McDonald
Thelma Fay Morgan
Annie Worth Odum
Zula Ellen Rogers

15. First Graduating Class of Senior College

1963

Bachelor of Arts

Betsy Jo Armstrong
Nancy Elizabeth Armstrong
Stephen Haywood Averitt
Richard Dale Beck
Ronald Charles Clapp
James Arnold Clifton
Grace Suzanne Cox
Thomas Clair Edwards
Sandra Fay Greenhill
George William Harding, Jr.
Donald Lee Harrington
William Kinzy Hobbs, Jr.
Robert Alton Hudgins
Roger Leon Jackson
Celia Jo Jernigan

Stanley Hughes Johnson
William Hersten Ledbetter, Jr.
Carroll Harden Leggett
Patricia Ann Martin
Kathryn Emilie Martus
Howard Blount Mathews, Jr.
Jerry William Morris
Richard Jerome Pope
Robert Chase Raiford
Edna Faye Russell
Timmie Allen Sellers
Blackwell Stith
Jerry Eugene Surratt
Marion Parker Sykes, Jr.
Benny Burton Wood
William Thomas Wood

Bachelor of Science

Walter Glenn Andrews, Jr.
Alfred Slade Ballou, Jr.
Joseph William Barber, III
Jerry Bradley Biggs
John H. Bland, Jr.
Charlotte Marie Bobbitt
Louie Elario Bonardi, Jr.
William Keith Bond
John Mark Boone, III
James Edward Brinson
Leila Grey Britt
Joseph Edwin Brooks
Reginald Steven Brown
Jerry Alexander Burkot
William Holmes Burnette
Jane Timberlake Burton
Richard Morgan Byrd, Sr.
R. Wade Caskey
Georgia Kincaid Cates
Martha Lee Clardy
Anna Jane Clark

Rebecca Williams Coleman
Thomas Jack Colley, Jr.
David Oliver Conrad, Jr.
Julius David Corbett, Jr.
Judith Lynn Currin
Nancy Stocks Curtis
Albert Daughtry
Guy Elliott Duncan
Brenda Stewart Edwards
Charles W. Eichhorn
Shadye Magdalene Ennis
Floyd Iredell Enzor
Robert Lee Ezzell
Alma Katherine Flake
Larry Claude Floyd
Thomas W. Garrard
Rufus Duke Garrell
Cornelia Wilson Garrison
LaVerne Nunnery Gillis
Carlisle Wingage Harrell, Jr.
William Carey Hedgpeth

George Robert Hicks, Jr.
Betsy Rose Hood
Cleo Veal Hood
William Theodore Hood
Gloria Faye Hopkins
Leslie Ralph Howell
William Stonecypher Hudgins
Luther Simpson Jackson
Mary Mitchell Jackson
Jewel Pruitt Johnson
Harry B. Johnstone
Leo Curtis Kelly, Jr.
Thomas Lantz Lackey
Haywood Arthur Lane, Jr.
Jan Harlee McDonald
William E. McDonald
Mary Joe Gardner McLamb
Janice Pearl McQueen
Joseph Perkins Marley, Jr.
Nancy Sue Maynard
James Franklin Meade
Charles Ellis Morrison, Jr.
Kathryn Thomas Oakley
Seavey Manford Page
Mildred Edith Pahl
Roby N. Parker
Donald Haynes Parrish, Jr.
Rose Ellen Parrish
Thomas Lloyd Pendergraft
Harriet Wells Phillips
Foster F. Prevatt, III
Charles Scott Pritchard

Charles William Pritchard
William Miles Pritchard
Doris Elizabeth Randolph
Larry E. Reid
Jerry T. Salmon
Kursat Sarigol
Robert William Sawyer, IV
Robert Sawyer, IV
Margaret Ann Scott
Murray Hobart Scripture
Jo Anne Selby
Bernard Robert Smith
Nixon Pearce Smith
Paul Elwood Smith
Judy Spence
Allie Nathaniel Stegall, Jr.
Winifred Upchurch Stewart
Jack Lewis Stone
Deloit Strickland
Warren Trent Strickland
Cecil Earl Stroud
Joe Warren Sullivan
Vernon Ray Sullivan
Charles Thomas Trent
Gwendolyn Clemmons Tutor
Francis Dale Twombley
Mary Margaret Tyson
Jean Shepherd Vaughan
Thomas Dorsey Ward
Madeleine Marie Watkins
Koa Egeta Williams

16. BOARD OF MINISTERS

1974

Executive Committee

Chairman—Ray K. Hodge
Vice-Chairman—Ray W. Benfield
Secretary—Emmanuel Pegram
Committee Chairmen—Henry B. Stokes   Ronda E. Robbins
                   William T. Mills   Bob D. Shepherd

Terms Expiring 1975

Bill R. Almond, Jr.
J. Garland Bordeaux
Fred J. Braswell
Vernon Braswell
William R. Bussey
Ben W. Cox
H. Buel Creason
Robert D. Davis
James B. Gibson
Gerald C. Goodwin
E. W. Greene
John Frank Hendley
Joseph P. Hester
Alden Lee Hicks
E. W. Howard
Charles H. Howell
Donald O. Kimrey
H. Phillip King
Hoyt Lock
C. Aubrey McLellan

D. Wayne Martin
William F. Martin
Charles F. Middleton
Phillip Ray Morrow
Horace V. Murray
Donald G. Myers
William E. Nelson
M. A. Pegram
Rudolph R. Pulley
James R. Rowles, Jr.
James C. Shelley, Jr.
Casper R. Smith, Jr.
Herman L. Smith
John Spencer
Alfred E. Staley
Elliott B. Stewart
Charles L. Tanner
Jerry Wallace
Vernon Williams
Diffie O. Wright

Terms Expiring 1976

A. T. Ayscue
G. Milton Bettini
Jack W. Byrd
Robert A. Cantwell
Ed C. Chamblee
Charles G. Coffey
E. Gordon Conklin
William Henry Crouch
Charles T. Dorman
Clarence E. Godwin
Norman B. Harris
James F. Heaton
L. D. Holt
Stanley K. Howard
Crate H. Jones
John W. Lambert
John E. Lawrence
W. W. Leathers, Jr.
Gaylord Lehman
John R. Link

J. C. McQueen, Jr.
Maynard H. Mangum
H. Everette Marion
William T. Mills
Harold Mitchell
Billy T. Mobley
Henry A. Morgan
Julian Motley
M. O. Owens, Jr.
Roger L. Patterson
Baxter Prevatte, Jr.
Horace W. Ricks
Gerald K. Riggs
Ernest P. Russell
John Ryberg
Charles E. Stevens
Tobie P. Stone, Jr.
G. Scott Turner
Robert L. Weatherspoon
L. M. Woolweaver

Terms Expiring 1977

Neil J. Armstrong
A. Howard Beard
Dearl Bunce
Dennis L. Burton
Alvin F. Butters
James C. Cammack
Frank R. Campbell
Russell T. Cherry
Edward H. Daniel
Dean Dillard
Victor S. Dowd
C. W. Driver
Floyd Enzor
Earl D. Farthing
Garland L. Fouchee
Thomas M. Freeman
William J. Furr
Earl L. Harden
Cecil Harkey, Jr.
J. Dewey Hobbs, Jr.

Charles F. Hodges
Horace L. Jackson
E. Weldon Johnson
J. H. Knight
Charles L. McMillan
A. Leroy Parker
James S. Potter
Donald M. Price
Coy C. Privette
Max G. Reece
Ronda E. Robbins
Woodrow W. Robbins
Charles Stafford
Henry B. Stokes
Donald Swinney
Carey C. Todd
Jack B. Wilder
C. Paul Willis
Thomas C. Womble
Joe Zimmerman

Terms Expiring 1978

Morris H. Andrews
B. C. Beal, Jr.
Ray W. Benfield
Hugh L. Borders
J. Boyce Brooks
Charles Bullock
T. L. Cashwell, Jr.
Robert L. Clegg
Robert L. Costner
Daniel M. Deaton, Jr.
C. Douglas Farmer
Jim Harmon
Henry B. Herring
Jack Hinton
Ray K. Hodge
Julius Holloway
Roger Jackson
Walter S. Jones
Howard C. Knight
H. E. Langford

W. Randall Lolley
J. Richard McDuffie
James B. McQuere
F. Jimmie Mize
Raymond E. Moore
J. Marshall Neathery
Robert L. Newton
Emmanuel Pegram
J. Stephen Perrou, Jr.
Bennie E. Pledger
Michael T. Ray
Ronald L. Richardson
Leonard Rollins
Gene Russell
Shannon A. Scott
Tim A. Sellers
Bob D. Shepherd
Horace G. Thompson
Gene T. Tuten
William T. Webb

17. Alma Mater

Hubbard F. Page

Honor to thee, dear old Campbell College,
For the help thou givest in the hour of need;
When we fare forth in the quest of knowledge,
Thou dost safely lead.

Chorus

Long life, Campbell College,
Dear old Campbell College,
Radiant with the light Divine.
Loyal we will be to thee forever—
Guard thy sacred shrine.

Bright the days we've spent within thy portals,
Fitting hand and heart for deeds of high renown;
Hence we'll go to win the fairest laurels
For thy regal crown.

We will hold thy name and honor stainless
In the van of battle, through the fiery fray;
Wrong shall not besmirch thy banner waneless
Till Time's latest day.

For many years the "Alma Mater" by Professor Hubbard F. Page was the college song. Since the early 70s, the Jimmie Tutor song has been in use.

18. Student Enrollment of Academy and College by Years

1887-1974

1887—	91	1896-1897	212	1906-1907	580
1887-1888	135	1897-1898	257	1907-1908	514
1888-1889	128	1898-1899	235	1908-1909	462
1889-1890	suspended	1899-1900	310	1909-1910	495
1890-1891	130	1900-1901	397	1910-1911	505
1891-1892	139	1901-1902	410	1911-1912	506
1892-1893	154	1902-1903	429	1912-1913	550
1893-1894	175	1903-1904	469	1913-1914	546
1894-1895	201	1904-1905	504	1914-1915	463
1895-1896	226	1905-1906	574	1915-1916	544

1916-1917	579	1936-1937	745	1955-1956	782
1917-1918	450	1937-1938	784	1956-1957	929
1918-1919		1938-1939	732	1957-1958	1023
1919-1920	694	1939-1940	713	1958-1959	1101
1920-1921		1940-1941	486	1959-1960	1182
1921-1922	666	1941-1942	433	1960-1961	1333
1922-1923	565	1942-1943	430	1961-1962	1447
1923-1924	620	1943-1944	410	1962-1963	1593
1924-1925	612	1944-1945	316	1963-1964	1884
1925-1926	740	1945-1946	368	1964-1965	2060
1926-1927	767	1946-1947	456	1965-1966	2256
1927-1928	738	1947-1948	658	1966-1967	2474
1928-1929	840	1948-1949	755	1967-1968	2500
1929-1930	836	1949-1950	564	1968-1969	2600
1930-1931	800	1950-1951	453	1969-1970	2402
1931-1932	698	1951-1952	433	1970-1971	2306
1932-1933	684	1952-1953	468	1971-1972	2207
1933-1934	751	1953-1954	591	1972-1973	2401
1934-1935	847	1954-1955	649	1973-1974	2341
1935-1936	789				

INDEX